Mysticance

a guide to

Secrets, Mysteries, Sacred Sites

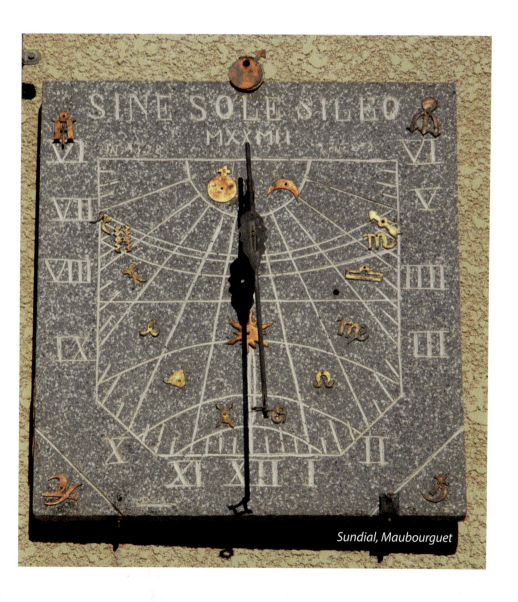

Sundial, Maubourguet

Caunes-Minervois

a guide to
Mystical France
Secrets, Mysteries, Sacred Sites

Nick Inman

FINDHORN PRESS

© Nick Inman 2016

The right of Nick Inman to be identified
as the author of this work has been asserted by him in accordance
with the Copyright, Designs and Patents Act 1998.

First published by Findhorn Press in 2016

ISBN 978-1-84409-685-5

All rights reserved. The contents of this book may not be reproduced in any form,
except for short extracts for quotation or review,
without the written permission of the publisher.

British Library Cataloguing-in-Publication Data.
A catalogue record for this book is available from the British Library.

Photographs – see credits on page 256
Edited/proofread by Allan G. Hunter
Cover and interior design by Thierry Bogliolo
Printed and bound in the EU

Published by
Findhorn Press
117-121 High Street
Forres IV36 1AB
Scotland, UK

t +44(0)1309 690582
f +44(0)131 777 2711
e info@findhornpress.com
www.findhornpress.com

In July 1985, I set off for France with my bicycle, certain that I was going to find something, even if I didn't know what. This book is dedicated to all those who shared that summer in Le Cèdre — a place and experience that exists now only in memory — and to the friends who are part of my present-day life in France; and, above all, to Clara, who connects the two.

Pont-Neuf, Toulouse

Contents

Introduction: How Not to Get There	**9**
The Value of Legends	12
The Language of Symbolism	20
Sacred Geometry & The Meaning of Numbers	22
I. Following the stars: The Great Routes of Pilgrimage Through France	**25**
The Symbol of the Scallop	30
Destinations of Pilgrimage	38
II. Raw Landscapes: The Transcendental Power of Nature	**41**
Sacred Springs and Wells	43
The Sacred Heights	52
III. Artists of the Underworld: Visions in the Darkness of the Painted Caves	**55**
Cave Paintings in France	57
Natural Caves	62
Subterranean Spaces	68
IV. Silent Stones : The Riddle of the Megaliths	**71**
Menhir-Statues	76
Lands of the Dead	82
V. Idols Unknown: The Evolution of the Gods of Old	**85**
Druids Ancient and Modern	88
The Gods Become Decoration	92
From the Goddess to the Black Virgin	96
VI. Awake in Dreams: An Initiation to the Temples of the Romanesque	**101**
Chi Ro	108
Romanesque Sculpture	112
Christian Iconography	114
VII. Babel Revisited: The Grounding of the Gothic Enlightenment	**117**
Labyrinths	120
Stained Glass	123
Mythical Monsters	126
Monasteries	130
VIII. Heresy of Perfection: The Doomed and Enduring Belief of the Cathars	**133**
Cathar Locations	137
Angels and Fairies	144
The Devil	146
IX. Custodians of Ancient Knowledge: The Knights Templar and their Heirs	**149**
The Hospitallers	152
Compagnons du Tour de France	154
Templar Sites	156
Mystics of France	160
X. The Legendary Laboratory: Alchemists of the Past and Present	**163**
Châteaux of the Alchemists	169
Magic and Witchcraft	172
The Tarot	176
XII. Spirit in our Times: Finding Meaning in Modern France	**179**
Latter-Day Churches	182
The Dechristianization of France	184
Faiths of France	188

Table of Contents 7

Riquewihr, Alsace

Travel Guide — **191**
- **1. Brittany** — **192**
  - King Arthur of France — 194
  - Carnac, Locmariaquer & Gavrinis — 196
  - Mont Saint-Michel — 198
- **2. Normandy** — **200**
  - Wayside Crosses and Shrines — 201
- **3. The North** — **201**
  - The Wheel of Fortune at Beauvais — 202
- **4a. Paris** — **203**
  - Notre-Dame de Paris Cathedral — 205
- **4b. Ile de France** — **205**
- **5. Champagne, Lorraine and Alsace** — **206**
  - Joan of Arc — 206
  - Alsace's Half-Timbered Houses — 207
- **6. Burgundy** — **208**
  - Ley Lines of France — 210
- **7. Loire Valley** — **211**
  - Spiralling Spires — 212
  - Chartres Cathedral — 214
- **8. Massif Central** — **216**
  - Astrology — 217
- **9. The Rhône and the Alps** — **218**
- **10. Provence** — **219**
  - Mary Magdalene in France — 221
- **11. Languedoc** — **222**
  - UFOs in France — 223
  - Round Churches — 225
  - Rennes-le-Château — 226
- **12. Dordogne, Lot, Tarn & Aveyron** — **228**
- **13. Western France** — **230**
  - Two and Three Faces — 232
- **14. The Pyrenees** — **233**
  - The Fall of Montségur — 234
  - Lourdes — 236
  - The Mystery of the Cagots — 239
  - The Cyclic Cross of Hendaye — 240

End Notes — **243**
- General Information — 244
- Walking the Pilgrimage Routes — 246
- Notes on Sources — 248
- Bibliography — 250
- Index — 252
- Acknowledgements, Picture Credits — 256

Church ceiling in Cheylade, Auvergne

Introduction

How Not to Get There

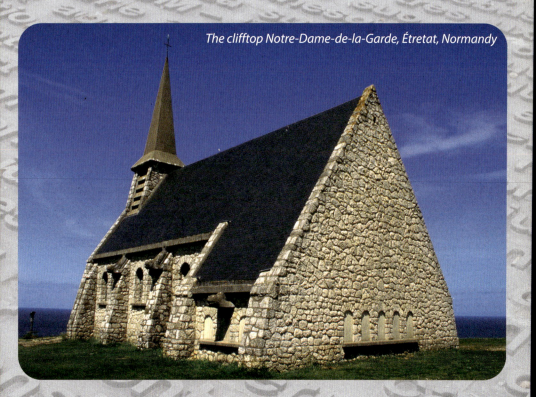

The clifftop Notre-Dame-de-la-Garde, Étretat, Normandy

Why visit the same old sights of France in the same routine way when you can make your trip an altogether more enriching experience? With only a slight shift in vision, you can go beyond the ordinary and familiar to explore unseen dimensions.

My brother-in-law, Angel, runs a shop close to the centre of a large city. Every day tourists come in and ask for directions to the cathedral and he patiently explains the way to get there. Most of these enquirers listen, nod, leave the shop and head off in the opposite direction to the one indicated.

Why this should be, neither Angel nor I knows. We have discussed the possible answers. It would be easy to dismiss these disobedient travellers as deaf, absent-minded or stupid. Could it be that they dislike the authority in his voice, or that they are too proud to take his advice and don't want to be told what to do? Then why ask? Do they just like making conversation so that they feel they have made contact with a native – the information being of no importance?

If these people are not stupid or devious, then it is possible that they are wise. It is almost as if the words that are exchanged are a code with a hidden meaning, nothing to do with orientation; a meaning which is understood by the receiver but not by the giver.

I like to think these tourists are errant sages. Their request is sincere but they are disappointed to hear that they are so close to their goal. They want an idea of where they are going but not an exact idea. To be given precise directions is like being handed a plan of a maze with the route to the exit marked. If they obey the instructions, they will be tempted to hurry on and deny themselves any sense of adventure. Instead, they want to spin out the search a little longer, to continue in the excitement of movement before they come to rest.

In their wisdom they have realized that there are two aspects to any journey. There is the destination, but there is also the experience of getting there – and the latter holds an enchantment of its own. It is all the stuff that happens around the core ac-

Stained glass in the Église de Saint-Jean-de-Montmartre, Paris

tivity of sightseeing that makes a holiday come alive.

Experience is often treated as the side-effect of travel: it is that which we can't help having in the process of going where we are going. We are wary of it because it is unpredictable and leaves no record. It may vary between the ecstatic and the painful but it always remains in the realm of feelings and is therefore intangible. The best you can do with it is turn it into an anecdote and try to recreate the emotions of it each time you tell the story.

Professionally, I can't afford to indulge such thoughts. As a travel guide writer, it is my job to stick to the facts and eliminate the airy-fairy variables. I need to get my readers where they are going, tell them what they are looking at, and move them on to the next location.

To write a guidebook, I have to pretend that travel and life can be reduced to the permanent, visible, solid, describable and predictable. The idea behind modern travel is that you have the experiences you want to have and minimize or ignore the rest.

I know that this is not always possible. The point was brought home to me one day while researching a guide to Istanbul. I was being paid to walk the streets with a sketchpad, camera and clipboard, recording details that would be rendered into pithy text and lavish illustrations. As I was making my way around the old city, I crossed a junction and happened to glance down a side street. It was deserted and there was nothing of interest for any tourist, but there was one object that caught my eye. Beside an open workshop door, a plain wooden coffin leaned against the wall at an angle of 45°. Where I live you don't see coffins displayed like everyday items of hardware. You only see them occupied at funerals and they are always made of varnished hardwood and polished brass to soften the reality of death. This one was crudely made as if it were a carpentry project. It stood on an alien street and had nothing to do with me and I only glimpsed it for a second, but it invaded my thoughts without my wanting it to.

I wondered who that coffin was for. Was he or she alive still or dead? Did that person and I have anything in common except our mortality? I was suddenly transported elsewhere and found myself plunged into a spontaneous stream of consciousness about the nature of death.

The sight of the coffin changed my experience of the city. I had been given a necessary reminder that I couldn't hope to understand the *Hagia Sophia* and the *Blue Mosque* in terms of their architecture and history alone. Both were conceived as expressions of belief in the innate meaning of life – life now and *post mortem*. A religious building is almost meaningless, I realized, if I could not empathize with the supernatural feelings of the people who built and used it. My intellect was of only limited use.

I had gained a personal insight that I couldn't put in the guidebook I was compiling. I couldn't send the reader to an obscure backstreet to see a coffin merely for the sake of hearing my metaphysical speculations. That made me wonder whether I should be changing the way I wrote about travel.

When we travel, we are always exploring two realities simultaneously: the one that you see before you and that we commonly agree on – countries, cities, monuments, food, festivals, etc. – and the one inside you, which, of course, interacts in some mysteri-

The Value of Legends

Mystical France is a country of many reliable facts – places, dates, people, recorded events – but it also embraces less literal forms of knowledge which need to be approached with the imagination.

The difference between truth and fiction is an important one to uphold but it is not always as clear as we would like it to be. If we dismiss everything that is not verifiable out of hand, we stay on safe ground but we miss so much of interest.

There isn't always solid evidence on which to base a judgement, and what do you do when it is lacking or questionable? To go back in history, we are forced to pay attention to orally transmitted stories, that is, legends. The stories of Mary Magdalene living in Provence (see p221) and King Arthur in Brittany (see p194), or of the Holy Grail being buried near Rennes-le-Château, could be dismissed out of hand as dubious, improbable or even ridiculous, but a far better approach would be to look at them with an open, enquiring mind and treat them as a different category of knowledge, somewhere between the certain and the fanciful.

A legend is not as neatly dealt with as a myth or a made-up story. Unlike a myth, a legend may or may not begin with a basis of truth. To begin with, it is passed on orally and adapted and embroidered with each telling, to suit the audience and the times. At some point, it is picked up by writers and artists, and given more concrete forms. Images, in particular, give the mind something more convincing to engage with.

Listening to – or reading about – a legend centuries after its inception, it is impossible to know what to believe or not; what can or cannot be proved or disproved. Many books seek to bridge the gap between the sure and the vague, spinning hypotheses using the words "if" and "could". Such books may be entertaining and thought-provoking but they can never be sound scholarship. We must not confuse "a mystery" in the sense of evidence that anyone can examine but which has not or cannot be explained, and "a mystery" in the sense that somewhere some thing seems mysterious to us. This latter, personal kind of mystery may not be communicable to other people but this doesn't make it any less real to the experiencer of it. We should be wary of accepting what we are told at face value.

It doesn't matter what the truth of a legend is as long as we don't lose our bearings and confuse what is entirely made up and what is entirely true.

Whether they are true in essence or in every detail, legends are important. They take us to places where we might otherwise not go. They inspire the imagination. They suggest alternative interpretations of history and of beliefs that have become so deep-rooted that we are not even aware they are beliefs.

Beyond simple gullibility or scepticism, they prompt us to think metaphorically and symbolically. This reminds us that the numinous cannot be reduced to data and that sometimes we have to look at reality from a different angle if we are see beneath its surface.

Carved face on organ, Saint-Savin

ous way with the outer reality.

We are most familiar and comfortable with the first kind of reality. We know it and trust it. We can easily talk about it and compare notes with each other. Materialists say that it is all there is. Everything else is a product of biology, of brain architecture and chemistry.

I find this an unsatisfactory explanation for the rich experience of being a sentient creature. My thoughts, dreams, ideas, emotions and altered states of awareness seem to have a reality beyond material definitions. To account for human kindness and love, for the mystery of another conscious being, and for the religious impulse behind the *Hagia Sophia* solely in terms of the interaction of genes and environment seems inadequate in two senses. It is dull and it makes us miss something.

To travel, to go away from home, is an opportunity to ask what we may be missing by sinking into routine ways of thinking. We may go travelling in search of pleasure, sensation, stimulation, memories or many other reasons, but we get most out of it when we are aware of both realities and give them equal importance. This is the only way to see beyond the surface of things and find the deeper quality, the essence, of wherever we are.

Mystical travel is simply a door left open to the possibility that there are other dimensions of experience that we can access if we either allow ourselves to go there, or at least do not stop ourselves with our minds. These other dimensions may not be translatable into maths and science, rationality and logic, but that doesn't mean we should dismiss them as hallucinations.

Mysticism for Beginners

The word, "mystical", comes loaded with connotations and is frequently misunderstood. Although it is associated with religion and unreality, it doesn't require of you any faith or suspension of disbelief.

You don't have to be a special person with transcendental gifts in order to think mystically, or be a member of a sect initiated into bizarre convictions. Nor do you have to be unhinged, poetical and floating above the earth. You don't have to be contemptuous of evidence and facts.

Mysticism, it is true, often goes with religion, but the two are not synonymous. It is important to make a distinction between the outward trappings of religion – its structures, personnel, rituals, texts and rules – and the urge to find out more about the numinous. Indeed, religion and mysticism can come into conflict. Institutionalized religion often involves the assertion of power over the adherent, and mystics within theistic traditions have frequently been forced into the position of rebels and troublemakers.

Religion, therefore, is not a prerequisite of mysticism and there is no reason why a staunch materialist-atheist shouldn't go in search of mystical experience. All you have to do to explore mysticism is release your mind from its preconceptions and accept there may be experiences that that are not subject to everyday human comprehension. Anyone who thinks that there is nothing that the human mind cannot comprehend as objective fact is forgetting that we are born mysteriously and we disappear into the mystery of death. Why should we regard the space between these two events – a space in which we make temporary sense of what happens to us – as any less mysterious?

Mysticism and mystery are closely related but they are not quite the same thing. They both concern the unknown (and perhaps the unknowable) but not everything mysterious is mystical. Mysticism is not a playful delight in puzzles; it looks through each puzzle for the meaning it contains. It looks beyond the appearance of things to that which is fundamental and perennial.

Mystical knowledge is not of the same nature as ordinary knowledge. It is often "hidden but not hidden". It is there in front of you if you look at it from a particular angle but easy to walk past if your mind is on mundane things. Access to it demands attention and dedication. It has to be approached in the right manner: sensitively, obliquely and in a suitably receptive state of consciousness.

A mystical truth is wrapped in enigma – as is often the case in alchemy – but not out of prohibition, ownership or exclusivity. It is to ensure that the seeker only accesses it deliberately, and with due intention and care. If, on the other hand, someone else comes upon it by chance – in a frivolous, critical or closed state of mind – it will not appear the same.

The language of this cryptic knowledge is allegory and symbolism. Where a concept is difficult or impossible to put into words, it can only be alluded to as a symbol.

A mystical approach to reality has certain qualities:

- It involves entering into altered states of consciousness and awareness. It engages the mind but is not a process of mind; that is, it does not come out of the everyday, practical part of the mind.
- It is about the amplification of awareness. To be mystical is not necessarily to see something "else", something that is not there for other people, but to seeing more of everything. The phenomena of existence function on many different levels at the same time: the microcosm and macrocosm are always related. The plain, demonstrable fact co-exists with the complex ungraspable truth.
- It is transcendent. It creates a metaphorical bridge from here to there, except that there aren't any "heres" or "theres" in mysticism.
- It is often paradoxical or nonsensical when viewed from the perspective of the everyday mind. One tool of mysticism is the open question for which there may be no answer.
- It is unlimited and available all the time, everywhere. It can even occur spontaneously, in flashes of inspiration, or at times of ecstasy or personal crisis.
- It is a process, not an end in itself. There are no ends, only new beginnings or new directions.
- It sees the subjective and objective as working definitions only. Really, they are entwined. The viewer is inextricably involved in any observation of the world. The self and everything that comes with it (especially the emotions) cannot be separated from the phenomenon in view.

How to Travel

Travel is the act of moving away from home, and mystical travel is doing this in a way that goes beyond curiosity, amusement or utilitarianism. It is driven by the urge to see more, to look deeply into the place where you find yourself in order to understand more about both it and yourself.

If mysticism is available all the time everywhere, it could be argued that there is no point in going anywhere. Why budge? We could answer this by saying that we move because life is movement and we are restless creatures, but that would not be

Window, Albi

Mosaic wall, Lourdes

the whole truth. This is because there is a good spiritual reason to travel. You are not quite yourself when placed in a new and unfamiliar context and this can awaken parts of us that otherwise lie dormant. Certain places have an effect on us at crucial times of our lives. They can, if we let them, wake us up.

The conventional purpose of travel is to see a different place to the one you are used to. If we change one word in this formula, we get an altogether more interesting mission statement: the deeper purpose of travel is to see a different you to the one you are used to. To travel mystically does not mean to go and see a place and have an experience as a by-product, but rather to deliberately seek experiences triggered by a place.

The ordinary, tangible reality of France is well covered by travel guides. I have written plenty of them, giving detailed descriptions of history, architecture, tradition and local lifestyle. This information, important and interesting to know, is presented as if it means the same to every traveller whoever he or she may be. This book is intended to complement existing guides, taking up where they leave off. I am not going to tell you about the achievements of kings and aristocrats, or where to stay or eat or shop. Instead, I am going to invite you into unexplored territory – the invisible, mystical France that overlaps the material.

What is a Mystical Place?

An obvious question at the outset is: what is mystical place? Everywhere can be mystical but some places are undoubtedly more mystical than others.

A mystical place is one that is potentially conducive to a mystical experience: it stimulates, induces or facilitates a sensation of being in contact with the intangible, invisible "otherness". It could be thought of as a launch pad, or a transporter from somewhere to an elsewhere.

There is nothing precise about this. Some places are accepted by collective agreement to be intrinsically mystical. Mostly, however, mysticism is an individual experience and the judgement of which place does and does not serve as a gateway to it is a personal one. Visiting a particular place that is supposed to be mystical will not automatically lead to having a transcendental experience; conversely, you may find yourself transported by some location that doesn't seem to have anything conventionally mystical about it.

Time is also an important variable. A place may not seem mystical at all one day, but the next seem entirely different. Whether or not a place speaks to you also depends on the conditions under which you visit it. Mont Saint-Michel endures crowds at the height of summer but becomes a very different place midweek, off-season, in the discouraging weather of winter. Some lonely, unheard of chapel in the Auvergne, or undistinguished dolmen in the Aveyron, may prove to be a more potent place to sit and meditate than a Gothic cathedral built with the express purpose of connecting the faithful with the divine but busy with a daily traffic of tourists.

Over a lifetime, it is possible for a relationship with a place that we repeatedly visit to change radically. The geography remains the same but we change inside ourselves and see the world with an evolving vision.

This book cannot possibly be an exhaustive list of mystical sites in France and inevitably it is a personal selection. Some of the places mentioned here are well known, others are mostly unheard of. Some are worth crossing an ocean to visit, others are more modest locations that may only be worth visiting if they lie close to your planned itinerary or if they mean something special to you.

In order to decide which places to include, I have followed three broad criteria. I think of a mystical place as having certain feelings attached to it. A mystical place potentially does several things:

1) It enables me to get out of myself, out

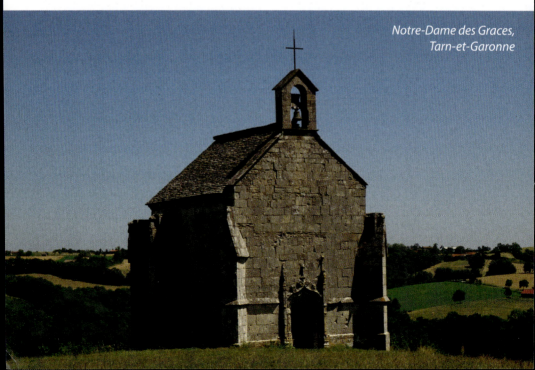

Notre-Dame des Graces, Tarn-et-Garonne

of time and away from "here". It puts me in the presence of the sacred, wondrous, and unintelligible. It encourages me to disengage my rational, logical mind and inhabit the expansive, higher me, which has access to other dimensions and sees other views of reality. It is conducive to altered states of consciousness. It allows me to get safely lost, to be constructively disorientated, to shake things up inside me and see where they land, which I need to do from time to time so as to know where I am.

2) It also allows me to feel more myself, more awake, aware and alive than normally. Paradoxically, this is entirely compatible with getting out of myself. Such a place can still the restless, doubting everyday self. It encourages me to accept who I am and how things are for me. I am able to look inward and outward at the same time, and be aware of what is going on in both directions simultaneously. It engages all my senses. It empowers me. It inspires me either to creativity or strong feelings of empathy or love. It generates "good" emotions; it encourages virtue and healing.

3) It allows me to feel connected to everyone and everything else, and to see myself in context. It lets me feel that I am part of something much bigger, and not an insignificant part. It gives me an inkling of the workings of the universe. It offers me the opportunity to explore esoteric information or wisdom. In this way it can facilitate co-operation, goodwill, integration and peace.

These criteria are not quantifiable; they are often vague and subjective. A mystical place cannot be identified by ticking a certain number of boxes on an inspector's checklist. It will have something intrinsic which you, as a visiting individual consciousness, either respond to in the moment of your visit, or don't.

Saint-Émilion, Gironde

Many different kinds of places are mentioned in the chapters that follow, and listed in the gazetteer (travel guide) at the end. Among them, some stand out:
- All religious sites must at least be considered potentially mystical. There are far too many of them to fit into a single book and many of them are obvious and easy to find. Here I discuss the most interesting of them, especially places of pilgrimage. France is predominantly Catholic but other Christian denominations and other religions are covered.
- Prehistoric monuments. While we don't know what these were used for, it is obvious they were carefully sited for particular reasons, perhaps to do with currents of earth energy, and that they served some purpose not to do with everyday living.
- Wild places, particular sacred rocks, mountains, trees, springs and so on.
- Sites associated with alchemy and magic.
- Sites associated with mysteries that hint at lost or secret wisdom, such as those to do with the Cathars and the Templars. Although several mysteries are explored here, this is not a book about mysteries. Not every mystery has a mystical connotation.

This list is not restrictive or exclusive: you can have a mystical experience anywhere, even in the lifts of the Eiffel Tower, in the chambers of Versailles or on the beach at Saint-Tropez.

This list is not exhaustive. It is not the strict definition but the quality of a particular place that counts. A mystical location has a unique combination of qualities, of subtle distinguishing characteristics, that may not even be expressible in words.

Such places are sometimes overtly spectacular and well-known but often they are the opposite. Rather than being brash or branded, they might be subtle and suggestive. A mystical place may not be identifiable as such at first sight. It may take a moment to adjust your mood, to shift from functional to receptive to interactive in your response. It is surprising how many worthwhile places are found by chance or by changes forced upon a well-laid travel plan. Any wise traveller knows that he will get to where he needs to go, no matter how much preparation he makes and whether or not he stops to ask for directions on the way.

Revealing the Other France

The first part of this book looks at Mystical France thematically through chapters on pilgrimage routes, wildlife, cave painting, megalithic monuments, gods and goddesses throughout history, Romanesque and Gothic churches, the Cathars, the Knights Templar, alchemy and finally the survival of mysticism in the modern world. Interspersed with these chapters are a number of shorter and longer features, each examining a specific topic that relates to the main subject. The chapters and features can be read in any order.

After the chapters comes a travel guide detailing a selection of interesting sights to visit in each region of the country. These pages are punctuated by features explaining the significance of key locations in detail. At the end of the book, I give some practical guidance for getting the best out of a trip to the mystical sites of France.

A great many fascinating themes are crammed into Mystical France – the identification of angels, devils' bridges, labyrinths, indecipherable writing, ley lines, magic, the sacred lore of plants – and all of them perhaps deserve much more coverage than I can give them here.

Like my brother-in-law, Angel, all I can do is point out which direction you may want to go in. The rest is up to you.

Seeing Beyond   19

Musée de Cluny, Paris
(Musée du Moyen Age)

Worlds beyond Words:
The Language of Symbolism

Mysticism has its own language: that of esoteric symbolism. To learn to recognize these symbols, ponder on them and interpret them as far as possible is to gain access to an expansive other, semi-secret world.

Symbols are everywhere in France. Some are conspicuous, while it is easy to mistake others for meaningless decoration. The tarot (see p176), alchemy and astrology (see p217) are symbolic languages in themselves. Prehistoric people made their own enigmatic marks on cave walls (see p55) and stone tablets that may or may not be symbols.

Churches are based on sacred geometry (see p22) and numerology, and full of Christian iconography including angels (see p144), the devil (see p146) and innumerable variations of the cross (see p201). Renaissance châteaux and palaces make prolific use of symbols, often pagan in origin, and meant to enhance the status of their owners through allegory.

Symbols are also frequently seen on old rural houses, barns, and even pigsties. It is easy to ignore the popular, informal use of symbols and to forget that in superstitious ages in the past, everyone had a working knowledge of symbolism out of necessity. The power of priests to counteract malevolent forces was known to be limited and the right symbol in the right place on a façade, door, keystone or weathervane could attract good luck, prosperity and fertility to a household and its livestock. Conversely, talismans could be used to ward off the many dangers that could visit at any moment: pests, storms, drought, illness, nightmares, sterility, the evil-eye curses of witches (see p172) and the cunning, predatory schemes of evil spirits. Some symbolic domestic accoutrements are even sold by chain DIY stores. Shutters all over France are still held open by a little iron catch called a *tête de bergère*, a shepherdess' head. This little person, wearing a flat hat and scarf, is turned upright when the shutters are folded back and remains in this position during sunny daylight hours, ever vigilant for the coming of bad weather.

Not all of this is primitive nonsense, however charming: there is good psychology behind it. Symbolism in every day life reminds us not to be gullible and complacent. Folklore is riddled with symbolic language meant to teach valuable lessons of caution and self-sufficiency. Fairy tales reveal themselves to have an altogether different sense if they are taken at more than face value.

In contrast to this, the modern age makes great use of symbols, particularly in brand logos. These are consciously designed rather than inherited and while they often draw on esoteric geometry or imagery, they are intended to promote the interests of particular groups of people (for example to generate profits for shareholders and management) rather than speak altruistically to our higher selves. They always refer to a shared, concrete reality, suggesting desirable qualities that a consumer would want to be associated with, rather than nebulous concepts difficult to put into words.

An esoteric symbol is different. It conveys or evokes sense rather than communicating a precise message and the meaning varies according to who is receiving it and how old or spiritually developed he or she is.

An esoteric symbol cannot have a precise definition. It deals with matters that are beyond words, that cannot be reduced to language. It focuses on particular things to do with spirituality and the divine. It speaks to us directly, to the subconscious brain without passing through the judgemental intellect. It suggests rather than specifies and is always interpreted personally by the receiver in his own unique frame of reference.

To get the most out of mystical France it is, then, necessary to be alert to the presence of symbols and to allow that these symbols may have no literal, fixed meaning. The important thing is to ask such questions as: what might the maker of this symbol have intended to say to his contemporaries and his successors? And, what has this symbol meant to other people? Finally we must ask, what does this symbol mean to me? Any meanings may take time to come as you concentrate your attention and try to perceive ever deeper layers of meaning.

In this fashion, a symbol forces us to stretch our minds and to use them in different ways. This is particularly true when there is no commonly agreed interpretation, when the code book that created the symbol has been lost. When a civilization fades or dies, its symbols fall into disuse and they become no more than pictures, patterns or curiosities. Good examples of this are the intriguing "alphabet" used on the tablets at **Glozel**, near Vichy (see p216); the rock engravings in the remote **Vallée des Merveilles** in the Alps (see p220); the masons' marks that dot the stonework of medieval churches; and the paintings, hand prints and hundred of unexplained signs that seem to be spread at random through the caves of the Dordogne and the Pyrenees.

All of these – indeed all symbols – present a challenge to us. But they also offer the potential for deep insights into other ways of experiencing the world. We may never know the right answer but we can still explore symbols if we don't get trapped in just one way of framing the world. There are only so many ways for another human being to think and we are all connected to the same universe, with the same sense-making brains and the same senses. This means that symbols can provide meanings that are available to any one of us – if we wish to stay open to them.

Post Office, Louviers, Normandy

Sacred Geometry

For the ancient Greeks, all geometry was sacred since it expressed unchanging relationships in which the whole and parts were considered simultaneously. "Geometry is the queen of meaning," writes John James, "because properly used, it combines form, number and symbol."

In the Middle Ages, geometry was one of the seven liberal arts, considered to be essential to a rounded intelligence that could perceive the world on many simultaneous levels. Without the emphasis given to the subject, we would not have the great Gothic cathedrals or other religious buildings of France we see today.

A building which "works" is one in which the invisible geometry "works". A purely functional modern building is based on an assortment of rectangles that suit industrial building needs and budget rather than any sense of harmony. It is an efficient structure whose aim is to make those who use it efficient. A sacred building is also meant to be efficient but in an entirely different sense: it aims to put anyone who enters it with the right frame of mind and in the right state of mind to commune with the numinous.

The geometry of the building is at once apparent but hidden – it is there if you look for it but we are not usually aware of it. It is also highly symbolic with each line, shape and proportion chosen deliberately within the whole.

Geometry begins with the siting and orientation of the building, and the plan is based on it. The medieval architect began by drawing a template that would not be on obvious view but from which all forms derived.

Fundamental to the form of the building are its three main axes: the vertical (the view towards heaven), the horizontal longitudinal (west to east, from door to altar: the journey that the worshipper makes) and horizontal transverse (north to south, representing the feminine and wisdom).

Sacred geometry makes conscious use of number and shape as well as certain mathematical relationships, notably the golden ratio, the square root of two (an irrational number) and the Fibonacci sequence (in which the next number is the sum of the previous two).

In the Middle Ages, precise geometry was achieved with what we think of as rudimentary instruments, and sometimes an imperfection can be detected in a cathedral. This is not due to faulty measurement but is a deliberate declaration by the architect that anything made my man cannot be as good as anything made by God.

Mosaic floor, Morlaàs

The Meaning of Numbers

Until the Renaissance, numbers were thought of as qualities rather than a means to do sums. Each had its own mystical properties. In esoteric systems, including the design and decoration of religious buildings, number is never random and always symbolic. Number is a means by which to express rhythm, proportion and harmony.

Odd numbers are considered more sacred than even numbers because they are indivisible by two and therefore incorruptible. Even numbers, in contrast, refer to the created world and humanity. They are of course complementary.

- **One** (the point, dot or circle) represents indivisible unity, the universe, the individual and God.
- **Two** (the line) enables comparison and thus evokes dualism and the world of opposites, and particularly the eternal duel between good and evil. It also represents equality and symmetry.
- **Three** (the triangle) was the most spiritual of numbers to the medieval mind. It is the number of generation, since it results from 1 plus 2. It is the number of the Trinity in Christianity and of all triads such as past, present and future. See p232.
- **Four** (the square or rectangle) is the number of matter and of the earth. In geometry it produces the square, a stable shape. There are four seasons, four elements and four compass points. The cross has four limbs. "On earth we live by the number four; in heaven, by three," write Gaston Duchet-Suchaux and Michel Pastoureau in *The Bible and the Saints*.
- **Five** (the pentagon) is the number of a human being who has four limbs plus a head and five senses. More than that, it is the number of integration, being the feminine two added to the masculine three. It is also the number of the occult, of the five-pointed star or pentagram, and of the rose, which has five petals.
- **Six** (the hexagon) denotes harmony, a pleasing combination of 2x3, 3+3, 2+2+2, and 1+2+3. Creation took God 6 days to complete. A combination of upward and downward pointing triangles superimposed results in the 6 pointed star or *Star of David* that to the alchemists means, "as above, so below". It is the number of human sexuality. France itself is familiarly known as "the hexagon" because of the shape of the country.
- **Seven** (the heptagon) is a holy and magical number, a signifier of religion, harmony and the completed cycle. There are 7 days of the week (God rested on the 7th day of Creation); 7 colours of the rainbow; 7 pillars of wisdom; 7 wonders of the world; 7 planets in pre-modern astronomy; 7 deadly sins and theological virtues. The *Book of Revelation* – the strange, esoteric book of the Bible that is referred to frequently in church art and in the *Apocalyse* in Anger – uses the number seven throughout.
- **Eight** (the octagon) speaks of resurrection, of birth, life, death and rebirth, and is therefore much prized by Christianity. Several French churches have eight heads placed over the doorway indicating the way to eternal life. On its side, the number becomes the *lemniscate*, the sign for infinity.
- Nine (the nonagon or enneagon) is the highest single digit and signifies achievement. It also refers to heaven and the hierarchy of the angels. A pregnancy comes to fruition in nine months. It is also the number of initiation.
- **Ten** (the decagon) is, of course, the sum of our fingers and thumbs, and the Ten Commandments.
- **Eleven** (the hendecagon) is the nearing of completion, the arrival of the penultimate hour.
- **Twelve** (dodecagon) is an exception of the odd-sacred, even-profane rule being the number of fulfillment and completion. There are 12 months in a year, 12 signs of the zodiac, 12 apostles, 12 tribes of Israel. It is divisible by many of the significant numbers that precede it: 1, 2, 3, 4 and 6.

Najac

Following the Stars
The Great Routes of Pilgrimage Through France

Pilgrims' boots hanging on a house, Saint-Jean-Pied-de-Port

Since medieval times, pilgrims have been making their way along the various paths across France that converge on two crossing points in the western Pyrenees. Are these simply the well-trodden routes of the pious or does the pilgrimage to Santiago de Compostela have more ancient, esoteric significance?

Mystical France

Where do you begin to explore mystical France? The answer could be: anywhere. Wherever in France you happen to find yourself. Simply set off from the house or hotel where you are staying, or from the port or airport you have arrived at, and follow your instincts.

A better alternative, if you want some guidance, is to look for the nearest scallop shell. This is the symbol of one of the great pilgrimage routes of Christendom, to the shrine city of *Santiago de Compostela* in Spain. The *Chemin de Saint Jacques* (Way of St James) crosses France obliquely in four variations converging on the western Pyrenees. Each year, tens of thousands of people make all or part of the journey on foot, by bicycle or by some other means of transport.

The end point may be in Spain, but a pilgrimage is a route as well as a destination. France is co-custodian of the St James phenomenon. Most of the rallying points are in France and there are more kilometres of footpath in France than Spain – almost 3500 km (2200 mi.) of principal routes and many more kilometres of subsidiary routes. Many travellers choose to travel through the lush countryside of France, visiting the shrines along the way, without continuing into Spain.

Some travel for fun; others have more earnest reasons to make the journey. All are taking part in an ancient tradition of mysterious origins.

From East to West

In the first millennium, Santiago de Compostela was virtually unheard of outside Spain and no one would have thought to go there from France. Early pilgrims didn't travel far. Most of them made only short trips to shrines within easy reach of their homes – a two or three days' return journey was a sufficient test of faith. Anyone who wanted the challenge of a longer pilgrimage went east to Rome or Jerusalem. The earliest record of such a journey we have is from a man we know only as the "Bordeaux Pilgrim" who travelled to Jerusalem via Constantinople in the year 333. He crossed southern France via Auch, Toulouse, Narbonne, and Arles, visiting shrines on the way, before crossing into Italy.

Around the turn of the first millennium, however, the direction of pilgrimage unexpectedly switched the other way. Christianity had no need for another place of long-distance pilgrimage and yet Santiago rose to eclipse its more famous rivals. The usual reason given for this is that the road to Rome was infested with bandits and Jerusalem had been lost to the Muslims – but this only happened towards the end of the 13th century, well after the Santiago pilgrimage had become established.

Neither is distance the reason for the change in direction because the road to Santiago is no shorter than that to Rome. Santiago and Rome are almost equidistant from Paris (just short of 1700 km/1056 mi.), and from the closest point of French territory (670 km/415 mi.).

Why then did the faithful turn away from Rome, one of the great stages in the drama of Christianity, a city charged with historical and religious importance, and choose instead to make for an obscure place with no great pedigree? The road there was arduous and there were many more famous shrines in Europe that would have better served as an object of pilgrimage.

Pilgrim statue, Hôpital des Pélerins, Pons

The Power of a Legend

The ostensible lure to Santiago was a legend. As early as the 9th century, a story began to spread through Europe that the body of St James the Greater had been discovered at Santiago de Compostela. There are many variations of this apocryphal tradition but its essence is as follows. After the crucifixion, St James travelled to Iberia to convert the heathen natives. On his return to the Holy Land, he was beheaded by Herod Agrippa, becoming the first apostle to be martyred. His disciples placed his body in a boat without oars or sails and set it adrift in the Mediterranean. Miraculously, it reached the Atlantic coast of Galicia at the port of *Iria Flavia*. The body was buried a short way inland, on the site now occupied by Santiago cathedral.

Why should such a tenuous story, that has nothing to do with the Bible, be enough to convince thousands of people to make the trek through unfamiliar places and across often drab and inhospitable landscapes to a distant city of no other significance? Faith does not require proof but there must have been some more compelling reason to travel to Galicia than to venerate dubious relics.

There are several possible explanations, including the prosaic and the political. Santiago, unlike its rival cities, was fresh and untainted in reputation. It had no heavy history of conflict and martyrdom attached to it. It was not, like Jerusalem, contested between religions and did not have Rome's whiff of paganism lingering over it. It was entirely Christian. When the pilgrimage took off, Spain was already in the late stages of the Reconquest. Muslim armies had tried and failed to invade France in the 8th century. For a while, they had conquered and held large parts of the Iberian peninsula but now they were on the run as the Christian princelings of the north pushed them ever further south. Santiago was the bastion of Christian resurgence.

Why St James?

Why, of all Biblical personalities, should James the Greater have become the patron saint of the most important pilgrimage in Western Europe?

James is one of three fishermen on the Sea of Galilee who are chosen as disciples by Jesus. The other two are James's brother John and Simon (Peter). Together they form an inner core of devotees close to Jesus. James is the second apostle to die, after Judas, and the first to be martyred, beheaded by Herod Agrippa in AD44. John, meanwhile, is charged with taking care of the Virgin Mary after Jesus's death and Peter goes on to found the Church in Rome.

This, in the hindsight of the Middle Ages, left James as the only member of the triumvirate without a posthumous function. He was chosen by the Christians of Spain, who were fighting to recover their lands from Islamic invaders, as a suitable figure to rally round. The choice of James was backed by the powerful monastery of Cluny because he was an authority powerful enough to rival Rome.

In his book, *The Jacques and the Mystery of Compostela*, the writer Louis Charpentier suggests an altogether different explanation. St James of the Bible has nothing to do with it. The route, he says, is one of initiation and is named after Maître Jacques, the legendary founder of the Compagnons (see p154).

"…above all, you may meet your Self and find that you are never alone – that is surely the primary purpose of pilgrimage, perhaps life itself."
—John Brierley, *A Pilgrim's Guide to the Camino de Santiago.*

A long-distance pilgrimage, from the Pyrenees to the Atlantic, was a good way for Christendom to prove whose land this now was and would be forever more. St James was nominated as the patron saint of the Reconquest and his shrine represented the triumph of the true faith over the infidel.

The pilgrimage was given a boost by the ambitions of the monastery of **Cluny**, in Burgundy, a rival political power to the papacy. Cluny was in its ascendancy at the same time as the pilgrimage was developing (the late 10th to the early 12th centuries) and it invested time, money and monk-power in building hospices and monasteries along the route. It became good business, temporal and spiritual, to send the faithful westwards away from Rome.

All of this, however, only explains the macro-trends of medieval history. To understand why the Santiago route became such a spectacular success, we have to know what drove so many individual pilgrims to undertake it. Why would they be persuaded to go the "wrong way" – not towards the source of their faith but away from it? Could there be some psychic current here that ran deeper than Christianity?

By the High Middle Ages, there was a desire for an arduous pilgrimage route as a test of spiritual stamina and a means of repenting of a lifetime's burden of sin. The destination had to be somewhere else, not in the heart of Europe but far away from the homes of the travellers; and it had to have an element of adventure attached to it.

Spain was the great unknown. It was foreign and recently reconquered, although still harbouring a legacy of orientalism. Above all, it was hidden behind mountains and therefore mysterious. Walk towards the Pyrenees from anywhere west of Toulouse and you are struck by the appearance of this serrated line of peaks rising abruptly out of the plain, blocking the horizon and with the midday sun hanging directly over them. They look as mountains should: a tall, spiky and impassable chain giving no clue as to what is behind. Even today, they can only be crossed at a few

The doorway of Basilique Sainte Marie-Madeleine in Vézelay

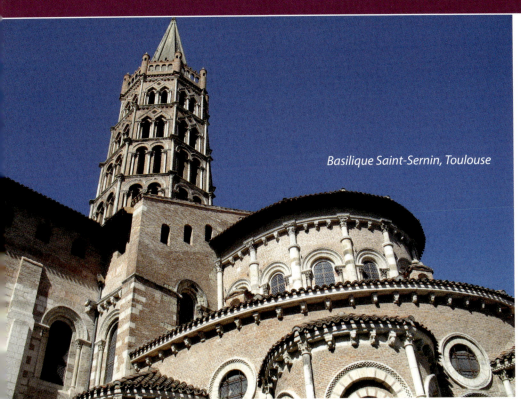
Basilique Saint-Sernin, Toulouse

points at the head of long, deep valleys.

For the medieval traveller to cross the mountains after weeks of travel was to leave familiarity behind and strike out on a no-nonsense test of faith which would provide a stock of good stories to tell on his return.

The Dying Sun

Once across the mountains, the French routes turn sharply right, towards the west, and this direction was not insignificant to the medieval mind.

To go westwards was to walk deliberately away from the "home sea" of the Mediterranean, central to the cult of Christianity.

Far ahead was the Atlantic and one of the most westerly points on the European mainland. Santiago de Compostela stands back from the sea and three or four days' extra hiking beyond it is one of the three ends of the earth: Fisterra (the others being Finisterre in Brittany and Land's End in Cornwall).

Santiago was at the opposite end of the medieval world to Jerusalem and it represented the opposite forces of nature. If Jesus was the light, the known, the reliable, Santiago represented the darkness and the unknown. The Romans knew the Mediterranean as *Mare Nostrum* (Our Sea) and the Atlantic as the *Mare Tenebrosum* (the Sea of Shadows). The coast of Fisterra is also

> "The deeper significance of the pilgrimage…is that it symbolizes the inner pilgrimage we make to the centre of our Being. The inner Being is separate from the body and the soul, through which we feel; separate also from the mind with which we reason. It is here that resides our human essence…Those of us who, through the grace of God, are aware of this inner Being, are conscious of, and able to see, as with the eye of God, both the world within us and the world outside us."
> —Jean Hani, *Symbolism of a Christian Temple*, translated by Malcolm Miller

The Symbol of the Scallop

The shell of the scallop, *Pecten maximus*, a seawater bivalve mollusc, has been used as an emblem of St James and the pilgrimage since around the turn of the millennium. One reason given for this is that the resurrected St James (or, in some stories, a drowning mariner that he saved through miraculous intervention) emerged from the sea covered in scallops.

A half scallop shell has its uses. It was an easy souvenir to pick up on the seashore near Santiago, or to buy from a vendor in the city. It became an essential accessory for the pilgrim as a signifier of his calling. In a practical sense, it could be used to scoop up water from a stream or as a collecting bowl: it is said that when a pilgrim begged alms he would be given as much grain as would fit in his shell.

One reason for the scallop to be adopted as a universal symbol for the pilgrimage is that it is distinctive and easy to draw. It can be represented in a number of ways, even with only four lines: the outline and three rays in the middle.

It is more than a graphic device, however, and much significance can be read

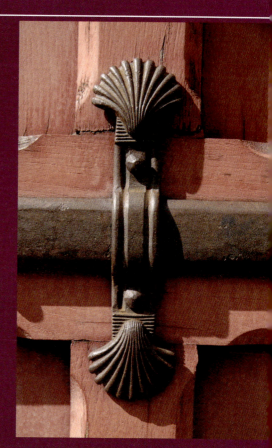

into it. If it has endured as a symbol for a thousand years it must speak subliminally to the human psyche.

The concave face of the shell is associated with femininity and fertility – as in Botticelli's *The Birth of Venus*. It represents nurturing, concealment and inner action. The outer convex face that can be seen all along the pilgrimage route stands for the opposite of inner nurturing: actively going out into the exterior world and taking physical action. The shape suggests the letter Omega (Ω); a horseshoe (for good luck); an outspread hand (the ribs representing the fingers); a head and shoulders; a halo; and the sun setting over the horizon. This last image may be closest to the truth if the pilgrimage is read as an initiation trek westward towards a symbolic death and resurrection.

Musée de Cluny, Paris

known as the *Costa da Morte*, or the Coast of Death.

The significance of all this may seem of mild curiosity to the modern mind but before the Enlightenment and modernity, symbolism was an exact and fluent language understood by anyone religious and that, in the Middle Ages, meant everyone. On the route to Santiago, layers of meaning are piled upon one another; some are obvious; some take a lifetime to untangle.

Day after day, the medieval pilgrim making his way across northern Spain walked with the passage of the day into the setting sun. The west was where the sun died in order to be reborn from the darkness – if God so wills.

Setting out each day just before dawn, the pilgrim would look up at the sky and see the Milky Way tracing the path ahead of him across the black sky as if it were his astrological destiny, leading him onward to the unpassable ocean. There, if he was able to reach his destination in the right frame of mind – humble, penitent, of good faith – he could die to the world, turn round and return home a different person more in tune with the cosmic forces that governed his world.

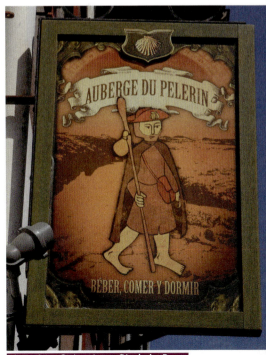

Inn sign, Saint-Jean-Pied-de-Port

> "It has been a characteristic of pilgrimages and of the tourist industry that both have attached themselves to surviving remnants of an earlier era. The Middle Ages had a passion for religious relics; we have a passion for historical relics – ruined temples, preserved cities, objects laid out in museums, bits of yesterday to be collected. The Middle Ages themselves have become a part of our own store of relics."
> —Edwin Mullins, *The Pilgrimage to Santiago*

The Highway of the Middle Ages

All these factors – exoteric and esoteric – brought life to the route and it became immensely popular. The first recorded pilgrim was Gotescale, bishop of Le-Puy-en-Velay, in the Massif Central, who made the trip in 951. The great river of the pious flowing across Europe reached its height in the 11th and 12th centuries.

The more people travelled to Santiago, the more facilities sprang up to serve them. Churches, monasteries and hospices were built to cater to pilgrim traffic. Religious houses, especially those run by the Benedictines, had a duty of care to all travellers, but especially pilgrims.

We know a great deal about the buildings along the route because we can still visit them today, but we know surprisingly little about the medieval pilgrims themselves.

There is only one direct, if unreliable source about their habits, a manuscript held in Santiago cathedral library called the *Codex Calixtinus* or *Liber Sancti Jacobi*. This was written in the 12th century, and dedicated to Pope Calixtus II who died in 1124. It is anonymous and usually credited to Aimery (or Aymeric) Picaud, a monk and sometime pilgrim from Parthenay-le-Vieux (west of Poitiers). The fifth and last part of the manuscript is often described as the world's first travel guide but is too sketchy, colourful and prejudiced to give us much information.

With care, knowledge and imagination, however, we can infer a great deal about medieval pilgrims. In many ways they were very similar to us although we too often regard the Middle Ages through the filter of our own prejudices and sense of superiority.

Most of the many pilgrims who took the Way of St James were driven by earnest belief. They made the pilgrimage to atone for sins, show their repentance and seek forgiveness.

Medieval Europe was overtly religious. There was only one permitted mainstream religion and one version of it (that we now call Catholicism). Religious thinking permeated life and was used to differentiate between beneficial and harmful knowledge.

The existence and omniscience of God, the truth of the Bible, and the teachings of the Church were all unassailable. Hell was a real prospect and one day it would be too late to negotiate your way out of it. Damnation was uppermost in their minds, as we are reminded by the great *tympanum* at Conques.

It would be a mistake, however, to think that all medieval travellers were in a pious trance, their gaze fixed on the next world, slavishly obedient to a religion that allowed no freedom of thought.

Medieval pilgrims travelled for a mixture of motives, as we do, including the search for sensation and experience. Some of them simply wanted to get away from home. Pilgrimage offered one of the few legitimate reasons to travel and see new and marvellous things of the world.

For all the infrastructure provided on the route, pilgrimage in the Middle Ages was still a difficult undertaking. To set

Gibraltar stela, where the Via Podiensis, Via Turonensis and Via Lemovicencis meet.

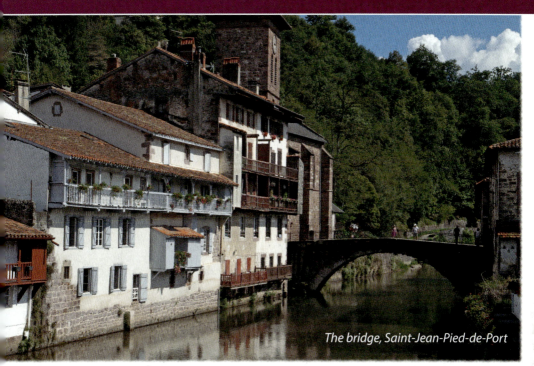
The bridge, Saint-Jean-Pied-de-Port

out on one was to commit to a long journey of unpredictable conditions, little comfort and utter self-reliance. An unexpected crisis could be dangerous or even fatal. There was no guaranteed sick care and there was no way to take a short cut, or, for almost all pilgrims, to travel faster in an emergency than on foot.

There were no stable national borders, and no signposts – the traveller set out in what he hoped was the right direction and asked along the way without the benefit of a universal *lingua franca*. Roads were of variable quality and the people who lived along them equally variable: they could be helpful or hostile. The welfare of the pilgrim relied on the honesty and goodwill of those who could help him.

Safety and success depended on shrewdness, the goodwill of strangers and on sticking together with other pilgrims wherever possible.

For this reason, the pilgrim made sure to identify himself in the way he dressed so that he would be known by those who had a common interest with him or who were willing to help supply his needs. He wore a broad brimmed felt hat, the brim turned up at front, and a heavy cape. He carried an 8-foot stave on which hung a gourd for carrying water. He had with him a scrip or pouch and a bowl for meals. He also wore somewhere on his person a scallop shell, real or depicted, the badge of the pilgrim.

The pilgrimage was an earthly as well as a spiritual affair. There was good business to be made by enterprising or unscrupulous individuals working the routes. True-hearted pilgrims were accompanied on the roads by false pilgrims who preferred to travel and collect alms rather than to stay in one place and work, and by storytellers who span yarns about their travels in village squares in return for board and lodging. There were also professional beggars and thieves, adding to the heterogeneous mobile community as if a counterbalance were needed to the piety and solemnity. The pilgrimage was thus a cocktail of devotion and chicanery, piety and materialism, as can be seen in any shrine city today.

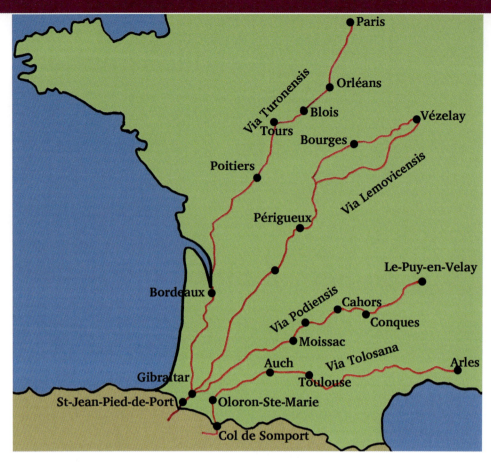

The Modern Pilgrimage

Today's pilgrimage is often talked about as if it was a direct continuation of an unbroken heritage, but it is not. The pilgrimage declined as the modern world came into being. It fell out of fashion when the Wars of Religion made Catholic piety a contemptible commodity in some parts of France and, above all, when the Renaissance and Enlightenment caused people to question faith, superstition, the obedience to ecclesiastical authorities and the ways to remedy sin.

What we see today is a recreation of the medieval pilgrimage for modern tastes. The obvious difference between the pilgrim of old and his modern counterpart is that, for the latter, it is mainly or exclusively a leisure activity. There is no longer a close link between religion and pilgrimage. Anyone can set off for Santiago as long as he can pay his way, agnostic and atheist included. No philosophy or justification is needed.

The modern traveller often undertakes the route as a personal challenge, getting an "official" passport stamped at each of the nominated overnight stops to prove that he has really done what he set out to do.

The scallop shell, meanwhile, has become an identifying trademark of the pilgrimage, a multilingual, cultural brand. You see it everywhere in a myriad of forms: on ceramics, on walls, underfoot on pavements, and over arches.

The modern pilgrimage across France consists of four great routes that cross the country more or less northeast to southwest. Each begins from a designated city (based on the medieval assembly points).

Via Turonensis

The longest and most northern route sets out from **Paris** and runs for 970 km (600 mi.) into the foothills of the Pyrenees. The medieval rallying point is marked by the lonely **Tour Saint-Jacques**, which is all that is left of a medieval church. From here, pilgrims cross over the **Ile de la Cité** with **Notre-Dame** on their left and make their way up the rue Saint Jacques through the Latin Quarter towards the Porte d'Orléans. The route leads from Paris to Orléans and then down the Loire river to **Blois** and **Tours** (from which this branch of the pilgrimage gets its name). **Chartres** is to the north of the route but a stream of pilgrims from there would have met the main thoroughfare. The *Via Turonensis* continues south through **Poitiers**, **Melle**, **Aulnay** and **Saint-Jean-d'Angély**, through the Saintonge to **Bordeaux**. Beyond the Landes, it reaches the Basque Country and continues to **Saint-Jean-Pied-de-Port** which, as its name says, stands at the bottom of a mountain pass. Across this pass is Roncesvalles in Spanish Navarra.

Via Lemovicencis

Pilgrims in the northeast of France converged on the great Romanesque basilica dedicated to Mary Magdalene at **Vézelay** in Burgundy. From here, there was a choice of two routes via either **Bourges** or **Nevers** to reach **Limoges**. The route continues through **Périgueux** and the Dordogne and after crossing Gascony meets the *Via Turonensis* at **Gibraltar**, a modest crossroads a short way from **Saint-Jean-Pied-de-Port**.

Via Podiensis

It's uncertain whether this route was used as heavily in medieval times as the previous two routes but it is certainly popular with modern hikers. It is classified as one of France's long distance footpaths, *grandes randonnées*, GR65. It begins at the cathedral of **Le Puy-en-Velay** in the southern Massif Central, where a black virgin is venerated. It passes through **Conques**, **Figeac**, **Cahors**, **Moissac** and then diagonally traverses Gascony to meet the other two routes at **Gibraltar**.

Hount de Bach, thought to be an old well, in the Adour valley

Via Tolosana or Chemin d'Arles

The southern route makes its way independently across the Midi from **Arles** in Provence (the church of **Saint-Trophime**) through **Toulouse** (after which the route is named) and **Auch**, and then turns sharply south at **Oloron-Sainte-Marie** to travel down one of the deep valleys perpendicular to the highest parts of the Pyrenees. It crosses into Spain at the Col de Somport and turns west to eventually meet up with the route coming from **Saint-Jean-Pied-de-Port** to form the *Camino Francés*, the French Way

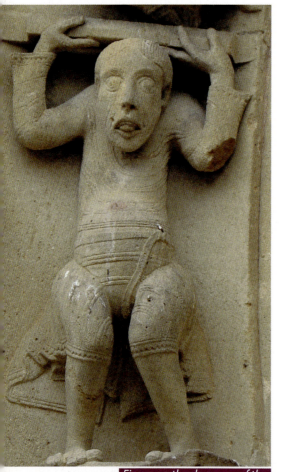

Figure on the doorway of the Église Sainte Foy, Morlaàs

Coming into Focus

These four routes now have official status – they are promoted by tourist authorities and recognized by UNESCO – but they are not authentically medieval, traditional or definitive. No detailed medieval itineraries survive and all that we know is that medieval pilgrims made for the western corner of the Pyrenees by whatever route suited them. They would zig-zag between shrines that attracted them and choose the exact road each day with expediency in mind. They might, for instance, make a detour to avoid some local conflict or skirt around an inhospitable town.

Gradually, the routes as we know them coalesced and became accepted standards but it is better to think of them as "corridors" rather than precise, narrow paths. Only in modern times have they become rigidly established and signposted.

Interestingly, there is some evidence to suggest that these routes that now link up Christian shrines actually predate Christianity. It is now thought that early pilgrims followed roads that dated from Roman or even Celtic times, and that these in turn may be based not on human will at all but on routes of prehistoric animal migration.

Together these routes cover roughly a third of France, even if there are wide gaps between them. Walking along any one of them – even a short stretch, even in your mind's eye – can be a good introduction to the country. To do so is to travel simultaneously across the visible and invisible geography of France.

France is immensely rich in all things mystical and there are great treasures to explore, both on and off the pilgrim routes.

To begin with, though, to get a clear view of the country uncluttered by all that we know or think we know about it, let us try to wipe away 40,000 years of human history and imagine a France that no human being has ever known, as it was in its pristine state.

See p246 for pratical information on following the pilgrimage routes.

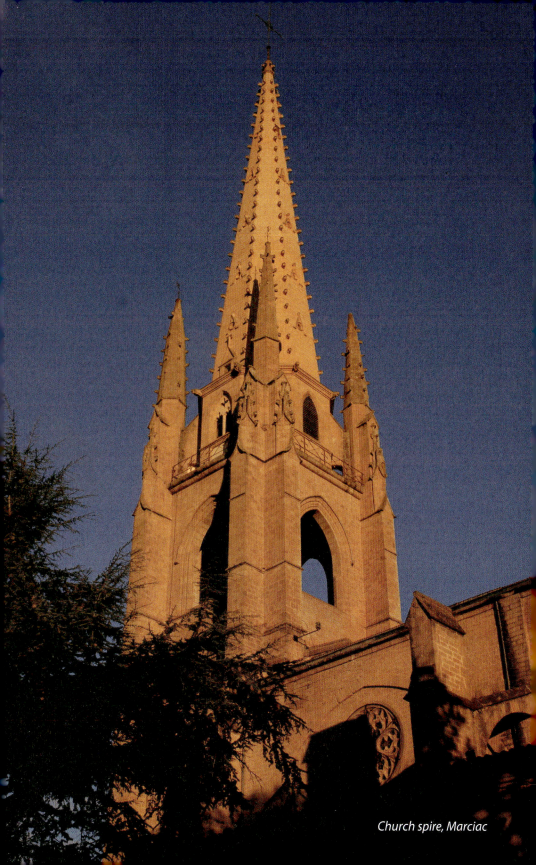
Church spire, Marciac

Destinations of Pilgrimage

There are over 500 destinations of pilgrimage in France, the vast majority of them dedicated to the Virgin Mary in her various forms, the rest to saints ancient and modern. Some of these places are known nationally or even internationally but many are merely small chapels with a local cult following.

The list below gives details of some of the better known and more distinctive Christian shrines (*sanctuaires*) that still draw pilgrims today. Other shrines, including those of other religions, are listed in the travel guide at the back of the book.

- **Ars-sur-Formans** (Ain, north of Lyon). The place of veneration of the "blessed priest", Jean-Marie Vianney (1786-1859), declared by the Vatican to be the "patron saint of all *curés* in the universe". The church dedicated to him receives half a million visitors a year. arsnet.org
- **Avioth** (Meuse, Lorraine). Small town next to the border with Belgium which holds a pilgrimage and procession on July 16 in honour of the 12th century statue of *Notre-Dame d'Avioth*. avioth.fr
- **Chartres** (Eure-et-Loir). Famous Gothic cathedral dedicated to the Virgin (see p214). cathedrale-chartres.org
- **L'Hôpital-Saint-Blaise** (Pyrenean foothills in the Pyrénées-Atlantiques). A small but fascinating church which is the object of pilgrimage on the Sunday closest to the feast of St Blaise, February 3.
- **La Salette** (Rhône-Alpes). Site of an apparition of the Virgin to two children. The shrine is at an altitude of 1800 m (6000 ft) on the edge of *Les Écrins* national park. lasalette.cef.fr
- **Laus** (Gap, Provence). A shrine of the Virgin Mary who appeared to a shepherdess, Benoîte, in 1664. sanctuaire-notredamedulaus.com
- **Le Puy-en-Velay** (Auvergne). One of the starting points of the pilgrimage to Santiago de Compostela but also a pilgrimage destination in its own right. (see p216). catholique-lepuy.cef.fr
- **Les Saintes-Maries-de-la-Mer** (Bouches-du-Rhône, Provence). Seaside shrine to two of Jesus's female followers, Mary of Jacob and Mary Salome who are said to have arrived here in a boat without oars or sails. In late May, the town hosts the so-called "Gypsy pilgrimage" sanctuaire-des-saintesmaries.fr
- **Limoges** (Limousin, central France). Once every seven years, the relics of saints are brought out of the churches of Limoges and fifteen other towns and paraded through the streets in a festival called the *Ostensions* ("ostension" comes from the Latin for "show"). The festival dates from the year 994 when a bout of ergot poisoning was cured by the first *ostension* of the relics of St Martial. UNESCO has recognized the *ostensions* as part of the "intangible heritage" of France. limoges-tourisme.com
- **Lisieux** (Normandy). The second most popular centre of pilgrimage in France. It has a shrine to "Little Teresa", Thérèse Martin (1873-97), author of *History of a Soul*. therese-de-lisieux.catholique.fr
- **Locronan** (Brittany). Every six years in July, a *Grande Troménie* is held, a mass circumambulatory procession over 12 km (7.5 mi.) which is thought to have Druidic origins. The route is divided into 12 "stations" marked by 21 granite crosses and 42 huts made of branches. It has two parts: a low part on the valley and plain dedicated to the cold, dark season of the Celtic calendar related to the female principle and the mother goddess; and a high part across the mountainside which is dedicated to the warm season, and the male divinity, the sun god Lug, now represented by St Ronan. A smaller *troménie* of 6 km (3.7 mi.) is held in the intervening years. locronan-tourisme.com

Rocamadour

- **Lourdes** (Hautes-Pyrénées). The most popular destination of pilgrimage in France and one of the most popular in the world. Pilgrims were first attracted here when a young girl, Bernadette, had visions of the Virgin Mary in the 19th century. Millions of people now converge on the town each year in the hope of a miraculous cure for illness (see p236).
en.lourdes-france.org
- **Mont Saint-Michel** (Normandy/Brittany). Picturesque church built on a tidal rock island. In the Middle Ages, it rivalled Rome and Santiago de Compostela as a place of pilgrimage. (see p198) mont-saint-michel.monuments-nationaux.fr
- **Mont Sainte-Odile** (Alsace). At an altitude of 753 m (2470 ft), this is the most sacred site in Alsace, along with **Strasbourg** cathedral. mont-sainte-odile.com
- **Orcival** (Auvergne). A statue of the virgin and child, kept in the Romanesque basilica church, is carried in procession at Ascension (in May or June).
terresdomes-sancy.com
- **Paray-le-Monial** (Burgundy). The 11th-century *Basilique du Sacré-Cœur* influenced by Cluny maintains the cult of the Sacred Heart of Jesus.
sanctuaires-paray.com
- **Rocamadour** (Lot). A dramatically located shrine built against a cliff, reached by a monumental staircase. The site of the hermitage of St Amadour was extremely popular in the Middle Ages where an image of the Black Virgin is venerated.
vallee-dordogne-rocamadour.com
- **Sacré-Cœur** (Montmartre, Paris). One of the famous sights of Paris and always swarming with tourists, this emblematic church is also a pilgrimage destination for many people.
sacre-coeur-montmartre.com
- **Sainte-Anne-d'Auray** (Morbihan). The prime pilgrimage site of Brittany receiving 600,000 visitors a year. In Brittany, pilgrimages are known as *pardons*, a form of community penance which may date back to pre-Christian Celtic times. A *pardon* takes place on the feast day of the patron saint and indulgence is granted to those who attend. Other major *pardons* include the Pardon of the Poor at **Tréguier**, the Pardon of the Singers at **Rumengol**, the Pardon of Fire at **Saint-Jean-du-Doigt**, the Pardon of the Mountain at **Saint-Ronan** and the Pardon of the Sea at **Sainte-Anne-la-Palud**.
sainteanne-sanctuaire.com
- **Saint-Maximin-la-Sainte-Baume** (Provence). Considered the third most important tomb of Christianity (after the church of Saint Sepulchre in Jerusalem and the tomb of St Peter in Rome). Pilgrims go to the cave where Mary Magdalene lived and prayed for the last years of her life, and the basilica, the largest Gothic church in southern France, where she is interred. There is a special pilgrimage at Pentecost.
mariemadeleine.fr
- **Vézelay** (Burgundy). The Basilica Saint Mary Magdalene is one of the rallying points of the Compostela pilgrim and a masterpiece of Romanesque art in its own right.
basiliquedevezelay.cef.fr

L'Aiguille and the Porte d'Aval, Étretat

II

Raw Landscapes
The Transcendental Power of Nature

Swans on the Eure river

Never far from the manmade environment of France is the wild world, and this is full of mystical inspiration if only we can see it. Nature is everywhere. It gives us the chance to put ourselves "in neutral"; to be more ourselves, more present and more open to insight.

Imagine if you can that as you walk across France you are also walking back in time and seeing the landscape evolve in reverse. Cities shrink in the first few decades of your regression and highways shrivel up. When you reach the 1950s, you notice a profound change as fertilizers and pesticides are removed from arable land and tractors disappear. Farming becomes labour-intensive, relying on the ox-drawn plough and weeding by hand. Field size is smaller – the size that a family or community can keep clear of ever encroaching weeds; hedgerows are thicker and more widespread, and there are many more woods and forests.

And this is more or less how it stays going back for thousands of years based on subsistence farming. As you stride down the centuries, France evaporates altogether leaving behind a series of territories, feudal holdings and then tribal domains. Life is dictated not so much by willpower as the whims of the climate and disease. Spaces are cleared for cultivation in one place and swallowed up by encroaching trees in another; the population rises and falls, but generally dwindles.

Gradually, in what we call prehistory because we know so little about it, agriculture fades to tiny clearings among the trees in which only a few semi-wild crops are grown. The land is not so much inhabited as roamed. People of the Old Stone Age migrate and hunt across the choicest parts of it but their presence is hard to detect in such a vast place as the earth. Then people are gone altogether, and soon the hominid races that preceded us are gone too.

You arrive, in your imagination, at a time before any human consciousness has looked on creation. You are left in a landscape containing nothing but its native fauna and flora. You are now somewhere other than where you are today, an ancient, underlying country that existed once but has been smothered by human activity.

In reality, of course, it is impossible to get away from the modern, industrial, populated country of France altogether, but the lost natural world is still there if you look for it. It exists beneath your feet and just out of eyesight and earshot.

Although it is occupied by 63 million people, France has a relatively low population density for a developed nation and has a good record of wildlife conservation.

For anything approaching wilderness, you need to get away from the over-populated Parisian basin, the flatlands of Picardy and the north, to those places which are useless for human needs because they are too steep, too infertile, too dry or too wet.

The high places, particularly where there is exposed rock, are the best places for uninterrupted mystical contemplation. Height gives perspective and the air is pure. Five of the country's seven mainland national parks (Cévennes, Ecrins, Mercantour, Pyrénées, Vanoise) cover mountainous areas.

Mostly, France is a managed landscape of plateaux, valleys and rolling hills with two elements predominating: woods and surface water.

Trees cover around a third of the land surface but not generally as extensive unbroken or ancient forests. Woods, hedgerows, plantations and plane trees on village squares and beside roads are the norm. Tree cover is increasing in places where the land is no longer farmed, or is too steep and unprofitable. Even a small wood can give you an immediate sense of seclusion from the world, of things moving unseen, of the rich tangle of life.

All this woodland is irrigated and drained by a network of grand rivers and tributaries that make up five great hydrologic basins. The Loire, Garonne and Seine flow into the Atlantic; the Rhône into the

---

"Nature is a labyrinth in which the very haste you move with will make you lose your way."
—Francis Bacon

Sacred Springs and Wells

Since water is essential to life and growth – and symbolically important in baptism and other initiation ceremonies – ancient people reasoned that the places where it issues from the ground must be sacred. The spring, or source, is an interface with Mother Earth, and as such is to be respected and protected. The Celts believed that every spring was protected by its divinity. An example of this is the extraordinary circular *lavoir* (public washhouse) of **Fosse Dionne** in **Tonnerre** (Burgundy), which is named after the Celtic water goddess, Divona.

Folktales often talk of pools of refreshing water inhabited by aquatic sprites or nymphs. In days past, offerings and votive gifts would be placed beside or thrown into the pools formed by springs. Over 1600 coins and other objects have been recovered from the depths of the *Fontaine de Vaucluse* in Provence.

Some churches are built over wells, notably **Chartres** cathedral and the church in **Limoux** (Aude). Other churches, such as **Bénévent-l'Abbaye** in the Creuse, are said by diviners to stand over underground streams carrying telluric energy that the building has to be attuned to.

Springs give rise to rivers and they too can be blessed. There are still the remains of a Gallo-Roman sanctuary at the source of the Seine, dedicated to the goddess Sequana, after whom the river is named.

Bains de Broca

Rivers in turn feed the landscape and there is something magical about places where water and land interpenetrate – such as the Camargue, at the sprawling Rhône delta, and in the Marais Poitevin on the Atlantic coast. Canals, too, although man-made, have an undeniable fascination. France has many of them, notably the *Canal du Midi* that flows across the Languedoc from **Toulouse** via **Carcassonne** to **Sète**.

Druidic medicine was based on water and many springs and wells in France are still venerated for their healing properties. Their former pagan guardians were long ago transformed into saints but the belief in the magical power of the water is still alive. Water is not all the same: each spring has its particular curative property. Spas in the Pyrenees, the Massif Central and elsewhere carry on this tradition while giving it a stamp of medical respectability.

The prime example of the cult of water is **Lourdes**, where an entire service industry exists to supply taps and bathing pools that serve the needy and faithful with water made holy and healing by the intercession of the Virgin Mary.

Fountain, Bétharram

Mediterranean; the Rhine, meanwhile, heads northwards through Strasbourg, on the edge of Alsace. These rivers have many different aspects. In the mountains they often create stupendous gorges. On the plains they slow down and widen. In between, in the valleys, they are often exquisitely picturesque and their banks make deeply peaceful places to sit or stroll.

Dispersed around the country, particularly near the coast, are wetlands that provide rich habitats for wildlife. Some of these are centered upon natural lakes and ponds but in places human actions have led to the creation of singular landscapes of canals and irrigated fields, notably in the Marais Poitevin and the Camargue.

The relative absence of water, meanwhile, leads to other attractive types of scenery around the Mediterranean, created by moisture-harbouring plants. The large tracts of garrigue and maquis in Languedoc and Provence have their own charm.

There are also magnificent coastlines in two varieties, the Atlantic and the Mediterranean. While the latter is characterised by sunlight, the cliffs of Brittany and Normandy can be dramatic and moody places to stroll. Offshore there are over 250 islands. The smaller and more remote of them are off the coast of Brittany. With luck, whales and dolphins can be seen in both the sea and the ocean.

What Nature has to Teach us about Mysticism

Every kind of landscape has its own quality but nature everywhere offers us the same potential for transcendent experience. The wilderness can be a source of wisdom. Wherever and however we travel, it always is conveniently close to hand. It could even be considered the primary reserve of mystical wisdom, a way into all other mysteries; and it requires no human interpretation. Why go to temples and spiritual teachers when you have the real thing in front of you and all around you?

Nature has commonly been compared to a book – one left permanently open to be consulted by anyone who chooses to do so.

Not that Nature itself is mystical. It is simply how things are; how the universe has come to be arranged. It is that which cannot be changed or argued about.

It is a great mechanism of outstanding ingenuity that obeys its own precise but often inscrutable laws governing the cause and effect of every event. Wisdom lies in understanding as much of this as is relevant to us, and recognizing those mysteries that must remain unfathomable.

Nature serves us spiritually in a variety of ways.

To look to the natural is to establish a baseline for the senses and the mind. It is a chance to recalibrate your human perception of the world; to remove straight lines; to set aside all that you think you know and understand; to remind yourself that names for plants and animals are not their real names; to suspend all definitions and judgements; and to see true non-sense. It is a whole and indivisible ecosystem, marvellous, bewildering and challenging in its every aspect.

Nature is the absence of what we do with our heads: explanation and justification, theory and analysis, of abstract ideas formulated and expressed, of records kept, of communication over impersonal distances.

Nature makes us uncomfortable and that is good for us. To go to nature, we must leave our familiar, artificial environments behind and accept conditions as we find them. This means that for a time we may be ill-at-ease in alien surroundings. This can be disconcerting, even threatening, but it frees us from habits of thought which keep us stuck in old ways of being. Disorientation inevitably lets in the new. We leave behind our daily routines and enter a space apart in which there is no human logic and in which different rules apply.

Nature also provides a lesson in suppressing our selfish, short-term desires and learning instead adaptation and submission. It denies us the easy amusements and distractions of the human world and this facilitates contemplation.

We also experience insignificance and anonymity. I am not myself in nature. I have no name. My identity disintegrates. There is less reason to be self-conscious and self-obsessed. This can be a lonely experience but also an illuminating and humbling one. In nature, I am just another organism, and potentially some other organism's food.

Nature reminds us that time is not so much a discovery as an invention and, although it is a necessary myth to live by, sometimes we need to break free of it. We need to be able let go of our anxieties about wasted time and the perceived shortage of it.

Nature makes use of time in another way, without measuring it or recording it. We can regain a sense of time as something instinctive and unanalysed.

To see nature, to place ourselves delib-

Sacred Trees

Symbolically a tree is a mediator between heaven and earth, with its roots in the rock and the crown in the sky. It also represents longevity such as we cannot expect to know: an old tree that was here when we arrived will be still there when we depart. A hardy oak or yew can know both the ancestors we never knew and our descendants that we will never know.

Venerated trees in France include:
• Two yew trees in **La Haye-de-Routot** (Eure, Normandy) that are said to be 1500 years old. One contains a chapel, the other an altar.
• An ancient, hollow oak tree, *le chêne millenaire*, in **Alouville-Bellefosse** (Seine-Maritime, Normandy) that is said to have been planted in the time of Charlemagne. It contains two chapels connected by a staircase.
• The tree shrines of the Houtland region of Flanders which are set into the trunks of limes. If a tree dies, a new one is planted beside it because it is said, "If a tree in this spot had a chapel in it, it obviously needed one."
• Six sacred oak trees in the *Forêt de Chaux* (in the Jura and Doubs *departements*) dedicated to the Virgin Mary, a vestige of the Celtic belief that these trees were the columns of a temple dedicated to the earth goddess.

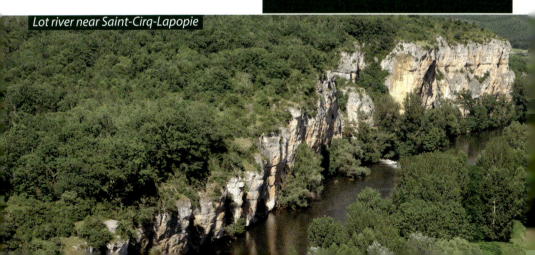
Lot river near Saint-Cirq-Lapopie

Lac de Gaube

erately in it, is to remind ourselves of the true non-existence of time. When there are no clocks and no one to remind us of the passage of time, we can make of it what we want or ignore it altogether.

Another quality of nature is to prompt us to think about the nature of change. Nothing stays the same. It is folly to rely on constancy. As time is at work, everything is in decay. We have our lifespan and it is not as long as some other beings. Trees, in particular, give us age and perspective. Foresters, it is said, always plant for their sons and daughters.

This reminds us of the folly of taking our enterprises too seriously, of getting caught up in the dramas in which we invest so much importance. Nature erodes what we do and undermines our definition of solidity and endurance. Everything has its lifespan. Barring misfortune, I will live longer than a butterfly but I am also aware that every tree higher than a house is older than me already and still growing. I will get consumed in the end and vanish: that is the truth. It does us good to relativize our awareness and this may make us more modest in what we hope to achieve.

Nature also teaches us that time can be perceived not as linear but cyclical. Only the determination of our memories interferes with the truth of this. If we learn to live with the seasons, and not count them and compare them, we observe a kind of reincarnation taking place. We perceive an endless appearance and disappearance of souls. Perhaps we too will be back, forgetful, concentrated on the new task in hand rather than looking backwards for information.

This thought leads to us questioning the nature of the individual and speculate on the soul. Who is to say that even though my world-given personality will disappear on my death, my consciousness will not continue in some form? Is it only our human sense of apprehension that sees death as so final and terrifying, and that urges us to create consoling myths about the afterlife?

Change also prompts the question of chance. In nature, everything has its place and its time and way. Things work to precise laws and, even if we cannot see every link, there is always an arrangement of cause and effect. Doesn't this mean that chance is only a human way of saying that we lack a complete explanation for the phenomena we are experiencing?

The weather is an additional layer of change, shifting mood from day to day and hour to hour. No two days at any given point on earth are exactly the same. In mystical terms, what we see with the weather are the four elements in play creating different moods of meditation. Even inclement weather can be enriching if you allow it to be. The rain which so frequently drives people indoors can be experienced as soothing and cleansing. Inclement weather gives you the country to yourself. A storm can be both frightening and exhilarating at the same time. In fog you could be anywhere. It's a chance to uncouple yourself from all the reassuring sources of orientation.

The alternation of day and night provides another change. They are not two separate things but a continuum punctuated by the fading or building light of dusk and dawn. Nature is always there but it is very different in its aspect depending on the time of day. At night, very often, you have the world to yourself and the immensity of the night sky to enjoy – and the stars have plenty to say for themselves. Astronomers have taken over ownership of the universe from those astrologers who at one time informed much mystical thought over the centuries. And yet, for all that our rational brains know about what we are seeing above us, there is an irrational part of us too that responds to the immensity of open space that becomes visible when night defeats our attempts to keep the world lit up.

Night is the absence of emphasis on light. It wakes up a part of us when the everyday part of us goes to sleep. Nothing is wilder or more mysterious to us than the night. Most of us forget to go out at night without lights and see what we see or do not see. In the late evening and early morning, it is possible to come across deer or wild boar wandering across a country road; or the spectral light of a glow-worm beside a garden path. Ghostly barn owls are a common sight and sound. Bats are plentiful around rural buildings where there are neglected spaces for them to roost in.

Nature doesn't make sense. It takes away meaning and demolishes human knowledge. Animals don't reason, as far as we know. The planet functions without explaining itself to anyone on it. We impose sense on everything. We try to see patterns of cause and effect in the behaviour of animals without being able to ask them how things really are when experienced inside their brains. Only the starling knows why it flies in one direction at a given moment and not another. Often we are forced to adapt our theories to account for exceptions and the inexplicable.

There is nothing wrong with trying to interpret nature and hypothesizing on what we see, but it has its limitations. All

Damselfly, Pyrenees

sense ultimately is reduction and delusion. The human brain and human science can never have the last word.

We do not need to understand nature in an intellectual sense and there is a great incommunicable value in uncomprehending delight. We should allow ourselves simple admiration, awe and wonder. We may want to know everything about the life of the wolf, but there is just as much to be gained by going the other way, retreating from meaning.

Nature obliges us to think about who we are in relation to it. We always get back to ourselves, and spending time in nature may well lead to an inner contemplation of existence, the nature of yourself and what you are doing here, both in the cosmic sense, and here in this spot at this time.

There are many further questions to dwell on when I am sitting on a rock or beneath a tree. How far am I "natural"? Can I defy the laws of nature if I am clever enough? Are we humans different from other animals, perhaps special in some way? Do I know who or what I am beyond my own skin, and what my relation is to the remainder of existence? Do we have the courage to see that we are special but not better, responsible for what we do but not necessarily dominant? Is all creation for our benefit? Does any other creature appreciate beauty? We are in an absurdly paradoxical position. We are part of Nature and apart from it at the same time, somehow special.

This recognition tests our empathy. It also begs questions about the morality we have created. Nature has no ethics. It is neither cruel nor kind. Should I, though, behave in an ethical way and, if so, how do I know what to do?

To immerse ourselves in nature and submit to it is to find a missing part of ourselves; to restore a broken connection that we once had. We have gained so much by becoming modern but we have also lost much. In pre-industrial, pre-consumer society, our forebears understood much more about nature. They had to know about the properties of wild plants and the behaviour of animals for their own survival. They looked at the hedgerow and saw not a clutter of unidentified greenery but a library of curative powers and folklore.

Sacred and Magical Plants

Before industrialization, urban living and synthetic medicine, every country dweller knew at least something about the power of plants. Some were to be sought out for their curative or magical powers or association with deities; others to be avoided for their diabolical connotations. Knowledge of such things was best left to sorcerers who knew all about poisons, aphrodisiacs, bewitching spells and hallucinogens that could put a person into an altered state. A little information about traditions associated with plants makes a walk in the countryside much more interesting. One common plant in France, for instance, is mistletoe (*Viscum album*, *gui* in French), which was considered sacred by the Druids because it grew in the branches of trees out of contact with the earth and produced fruit at the time of the winter solstice. Less easy to find is mandrake (*Mandragora officinarum*, *mandragore* in French) which is grown in botanic and medieval gardens. It was held to be a potent plant mostly because its root system was said to resemble a human being. There was a belief in the Middle Ages that to pull it out of the ground was to court certain death.

Star-shaped fungus

Lichens growing on a stone

Ice pattern

Leaf seen against the light

Seeing the Extraordinary in the Ordinary

None of this depends on seeking out the purest, most unspoilt tracts of wilderness. All of it is available everywhere, even in wasteland on the fringes of a modern shopping centre or industrial park or beside a highway.

If you want to lose yourself, or temporarily change the way you see the world, any wood or field will do. Wildlife is often surprisingly closer than might be expected and quickly found. Sometimes, all we need to do to see what is there, but initially invisible to us, is to look again – but this time to refocus our gaze so that we see into the parallel but ever present world. We must look at not the concrete but what is beside it; not the asphalt but the grass that breaks through.

One way back into nature is to start with manmade objects in their ancient and remote forms. Most megalithic monuments, monasteries and shrines do not stand in towns but out in the countryside, often at the end of winding lanes, where they are surrounded by nature.

An even simpler way is to wander away from the village, or out of the suburbs, and look for uncultivated land, steep slopes and river banks.

There is plenty of nature on display wherever you are with, of course, local variations. Plant life is always easy to see. France has an immensely rich flora which includes spectacular gentians in the mountains and multiple species of insect-imitating orchids, especially on limestone bedrock. In autumn, woods and fields sprout an extraordinary variety of fungi, some species being quite wonderfully bizarre.

Birds are everywhere, too, although generally keeping their distance from people. Buzzards wheel over ploughed and fallow fields. Solitary herons and bright white egrets are often seen standing by water or flying with slow wing beats overhead. Where there are high crags, vultures wheel silently around them.

Be patient by a shady river and you may well see the electric blue flash of a kingfisher. Other shy birds that can be seen are jays, green woodpeckers and hoopoes. You

Gardens for Meditation

If the wilderness isn't to hand, a garden can make a good alternative for communing with nature. As well as municipal parks and the grounds of châteaux, monasteries and other monuments, there are 50 recreated medieval gardens around France, around 150 botanical and herb gardens, and 160 arboretums. Although cultivated and not purely wild, every garden is still a co-creation between man and nature. One good way to find a nearby garden to meditate is to go to: parcsetjardins.fr.

Garden inside the Château de Carcassonne

"There are always flowers for those who want to see them." —Henri Matisse

come across them rather than find them.

In spring and autumn, huge flocks of cranes fly in high v formations north and south. Alsace is populated by storks that easily cohabit with man. Flocks of flamingos stand in the lagoons of the Mediterranean coast.

Ground dwelling animals are more cautious of people than birds but one can come across them unexpectedly. Coypu, for instance, live in the banks of streams and drainage ditches, even close to town centres.

In summer, butterflies, nervous dragonflies in fluorescent colours, grasshoppers and other insects are everywhere in the air over vegetation, water or the ground.

At the other extreme are the animals that only rarely let themselves be seen – wolves, bears, eagles – super predators that show the health of an eco-system. We need them to be there.

The best way to find and be with nature is to slow down, to adjust to the pace of the instinctive and fearful animal world. The best way is to stand or sit and watch without expectation. That is the way to see what there is to see, however big or colourful it is, and whether or not it has a name.

It helps to look up and down. The skies that seem at first vast and empty can hold great interest. At our feet is always nature in microcosm. What at first passes unnoticed can turn out to be extravagantly beautiful if you get down on the ground and look at it at its own level. We may wish for the big and dramatic but the small can also be dramatic, and just as compelling. A lichen or a moss can become a work of abstract art when you are on your knees looking at it close up.

To look at nature with non-judgemental eyes, even for a moment, is to wipe away all human analyzing, discarding thousands of years of civilization and progress at a stroke. We need to declutter our minds occasionally if we are to put ourselves into the minds of our ancestors who went into caves to paint.

Pas de Peyrol, Auvergne

The Sacred Heights

Certain hills and mountains of France are held to be sacred – the homes of gods – and humans of old used to ascend them with reverence in order to commune with the deities and to gain perspective over the lands below and the affairs of people. Many have been Christianised since pagan days by placing a church or chapel on the summit. Some can be ascended by car but it is always better to walk where possible. Whether or not you meet the gods in residence, you may find a sanctuary or monastery to visit, or a quiet spot to meditate. You will certainly get an incomparable view. Many holy hills are dedicated to the archangel St Michael who keeps a watch over humanity from a high vantage point.

- **Chapelle de Saint-Michel-d'Aiguilhe**, Le Puy-en-Velay (Haute-Loire) 82 m (269 ft). A 10th century chapel built on top of an exposed volcanic plug. On another crag overlooking the town stands an iron statue of *Notre-Dame de France*.
- **La Rhune** (Pyrénées-Atlantiques) 905 m (2,969 ft). Lonely hill at the western end of the Pyrenees and straddling the Franco-Spanish border. Cromlechs, tumuli and dolmen suggest that it was sacred to prehistoric society. It is also said to have been gathering place for witches. A cog railway ascends the steep slope.
- **Ménez-Hom** (Finistere, Brittany). 330 m (1,083 ft). Sprawling hill overlooking the Bay of Douarnenez. Considered to be one of the "seven sacred hills" of Brittany. The others are *Saint-Michel de Brasparts* with a chapel on top, *Mané Gwen*, *Ménez Bré*, *Bel Air*, *Mont Dol* and *Mont Saint-Michel*.
- **Mont des Cats** (near **Godewaersvelde** in French Flanders) 164 m (538 ft). A Trappist monastic community lives in an abbey on the summit.
- **Mont Saint-Michel** (offshore, on the border between Normandy and Brittany). 92m (300 ft). Small rocky island in a vast tidal bay, bearing a Gothic abbey and a cluster of other buildings. See p198.
- **Mont Sainte-Odile** (Alsace) 753 m (2,470 ft). A Catholic place of pilgrimage named after the 8th century patroness of Alsace. The monastery on the summit includes a basilica and restaurant, a cloister and a chapel. Also on the summit is the *Mur païen*, a giant rampart built of large blocks, 10 km (6 mi.) in length in 3 loops.
- **Montmartre** (Paris) 130 m (426 ft). Archaeological remains show that there was

Pic du Canigou

pagan temple on the "Mount of Martyrs" thus called because, according to legend, St Denis was decapitated here. The Basilica of the Sacré-Cœur looks down on a monumental stepped garden.

Montségur (Ariège) 1,207 m (3,960 ft). This isolated hill in the Pyrenean foothills is topped by a ruined castle. The ascent is steep. It has become a symbol of the resistance of the Cathar heresy to the Catholic church. See p234.

Notre-Dame de Fourvière (**Lyon**) 287 m (942 ft). The "praying hill" above Lyon has been sacred since the earliest days of Chrisianity. The Virgin venerated here is believed to have saved the citizens from the plague. The view extends to Mont Blanc on a clear day. Photo: p 218.

Notre-Dame de la Garde (**Marseille**) 162m (531 ft). This conspicuous, neo-Byzantine church topped by a massive gold Virgin and child stands on a high peak overlooking the port and the city.

• **Pic du Canigou** (Pyrénées-Orientales) 2,784 m (9,134 ft). Emblematic peak of the Catalan people in the eastern Pyrénées. A fire is lit on the summit on June 23. Below are two Romanesque monasteries, *Saint-Martin-du-Canigou* and *Saint-Michel-de-Cuxa* and the *Priory of Santa Maria de Serrabone*.

• **Puy-de-Dome** (Auvergne) 1,465 m (4,806 ft). Distinctive volcanic peak overlooking the city of **Clermont-Ferrand**. Just below the summit stands the ruins of a Roman temple dedicated to Mercury.

• **Sion-Vaudemont** (Meurthe-et-Moselle, Lorraine) 545 m (1,788 ft). The Celts venerated their war god Wotan, and Rosmerta, goddess of fertility and abundance, on top of this isolated hill. Now there is a basilica, *Notre-Dame de Sion*, which is the object of a pilgrimage.

• **Tumulus Saint-Michel** (**Carnac**, Morbihan, Brittany) 10m (33 ft). An artificial mound built in the 5th century BC, now crowned by a chapel. See page 196.

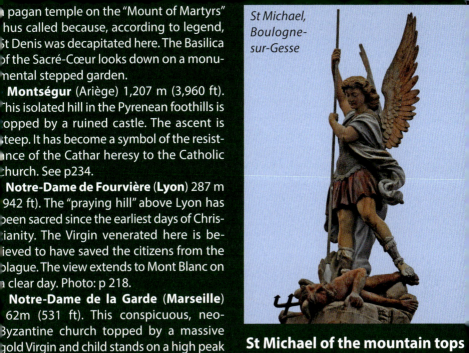

St Michael, Boulogne-sur-Gesse

St Michael of the mountain tops

The high places belong to the archangel St Michael (*St Michel*), the prince of all the angels, holy warrior of God and the leader of the celestial armies. He is depicted everywhere in France in statues and paintings. One of the most dramatic portrayals of him is in a splendid fountain, not on a hill but in the middle of **Paris**, at the bottom of the Boulevard Saint-Michel.

In art, he is shown as a beautiful and severe young man with wings, dressed in white or shining armour and a helmet, and concentrating on the task in hand. Armed with a lance or sword and shield, he subdues a dragon or snake (representing Satan) that writhes at his feet in submission. When France was being Christianized the high hilltop temples to Celtic war and thunder gods, as well as the Roman gods Mars and Mercury, were rededicated to the cult of St Michael. If the devil must be driven to the lowest places in defeat, St Michael must occupy the high ground from which he can survey the battle and keep the souls of men and women safe

Grottes de Lascaux II

III

Artists of the Underworld
Visions in the Darkness of the Painted Caves

Prehistoric rock shelter, Aurignac

Why and how did so called primitive prehistoric people create such extraordinary works of art deep under France? Science continues to amass data but has come up with no definitive explanations. There is, however, another approach. Go into the cave, turn out the lights, stand still, wait, and see what you see.

One day, around 13,000 years before today – it is impossible to be more precise – a primitive man or woman whose name we will never know was walking through the pristine landscape of southern France, around where the city of Toulouse now stands. He (let's assume it was a man) watched bison grazing the steppes beside the River Garonne, had an idea, and developed a compulsion to make that idea real.

He may have been alone or in company. He certainly formed part of a society; but his visual memory was experienced in his own private world. Seeing is an individual act, as is reproducing what we see, but all human activity takes place within or with reference to groups.

It is possible he made a sketch of the animal on bark, or even sculpted it in stone; but it is just as likely that he committed the shapes and anatomical details to his memory.

Having seen what he wanted to see, he carried the memory of it 100 km (60 mi.) southwest as he travelled on foot into the hills beneath the Pyrenees.

He made for a particular valley in what is now known as the Ariège, which he presumably knew about and had probably left some time before. Arriving at the mouth of the cave of Niaux, he prepared a rucksack containing brushes, pigments and water, and sufficient torches for a long underground journey. He then crawled through a narrow opening in the rock, walked 800 m (875 yd) along a cavern in pitch blackness, illuminated only by the weak flickering light of a tallow lamp, until he came to a particular spot. There he reproduced the bison that he had seen several days before on the underside of a rock overhang, along with and often on top of existing pictures left by perhaps ten generations of his ancestors. He recreated his view of the animal with accurate attention to its form, depicting its musculature, hair and even its facial expression.

We know about the result because it is still there, almost as fresh and vivid as when it was painted. The steps leading up to the painting of the picture we can surmise. What we don't know is how primitive man learned to do this and, more importantly, why he did it in the places he did it.

The Nature of Caves

As modern people, we have lost contact with the cave and, before we approach the art, we must first try to imagine how our attitudes towards the subterranean world might differ from those of Palaeolithic people.

We don't choose to spend much time underground. Why should we when we need the light and everything we have is on the surface of the earth? We think of everything out of sight or beneath our feet as an alien environment. We don't go there except for functional reasons – to retrieve stored items, to take a metro or stow a corpse – or as sport.

We are at home in "positive", extruded, inorganic architecture, entirely under our control, and wary of the "negative", introverted organic architecture of the caves.

We do visit certain caves that have been equipped to receive us, but only with a guide. Mostly we send recreational or scientific explorers to tell us what the underworld is like and send up photographs.

This makes it hard for us to imagine how prehistoric men and women would have experienced caves, both literally and symbolically.

Whereas we generally see caves as dis-

"Who are we to say that intelligent, communicative, non-physical 'entities' encountered on…trance journeys are just figments of consciousness that have no real existence? What do we really understand about the place shamans call the 'spirit world', or of the states of trance that they must enter in order to explore it?" —Graham Hancock, *Supernatural*

Horse, Labastide

Cave Paintings in France

Half the painted caves in Europe are in France, mostly in the Dordogne but also in the foothills of the Pyrenees. The Vezère Valley has 147 prehistoric sites including 25 decorated caves. The greatest caves, Lascaux and Chauvet, are closed to the public and replicas have been built nearby, but there is nothing like the real works of cave art at Niaux, Gargas, Font-de-Gaume and Pech-Merle.

• **Grotte de Lascaux,** Montignac (Dordogne). The most famous cave in France is closed to the public but a replica, *Lascaux II*, has been built in Montignac, close to the original. semitour.com

• **Grotte de Chauvet-Pont d'Arc,** Vallon Pont-d'Arc (Ardèche). This cave contains 30,000–32,000 year old paintings from the Aurignacian period, including drawings of horses, but it is closed to visitors. A replica cave can be visited. cavernedupontdarc.fr

• **Grotte de Niaux,** Niaux (Ariège). You have to carry your own torch to visit this cave which fortunately hasn't been equipped for visitors, rendering the experience of contemplating the bison in the cave floor, or the long-haired horse sketched 15,000 years ago, much more authentic. grands-sites-ariege.fr

• **Grotte de Gargas,** Aventignan (Hautes-Pyrénées). This cave contains over 200 mysterious negative hands, painted some 27,000 years ago, as well as Paleolithic animal engravings. grottesdegargas.fr

• **Le Mas d'Azil,** Pamiers (Ariège). There are two caves in one here: a massive natural tunnel lets the river and the road pass through the hillside, and the prehistoric cave leads off from this tunnel. The galleries decorated with paintings and engravings are inaccessible but the visit gives an idea of the atmosphere of the cave. grands-sites-ariege.fr

• **Grotte du Pech-Merle,** Cabrerets (Lot). This cave contains drawings of bison and mammoths, disk-like concretions of unexplained origin, prehistoric footprints, an engraved head, negative hands and imaginary creatures. pechmerle.com

• **Font-de-Gaume,** Les Eyzies-de-Tayac (Dordogne). This is the only cave with polychrome paintings still open to the public. It contains more than 200 paintings from the Magdalenian period, circa 15,000 BC. These include bison, horses, mammoths, reindeer and stylized human figures. font-de-gaume.monuments-nationaux.fr

• **Abri du Poisson,** Manaurie (Dordogne). Several caves near Font-de-Gaume can also be visited by arrangement with the ticket office including a rock shelter that contains one of the oldest representations of fish in the world. font-de-gaume.monuments-nationaux.fr

• **Rouffignac,** Rouffignac-Saint-Cernin-de-Reilhac (Dordogne). An electric train takes you down this immense cave in the *Périgord Noir* to see more than 250 line drawings and engravings of mammoths and other animals. grottederouffignac.fr

concerting and quite possibly dangerous, they may well have thought the opposite. A cave has a stable microclimate and even temperature all the time. It is a safe place: wild beasts do not venture far into the dark away from their sources of food.

Then or today, a cave is the same peculiar kind of space. It is indescribable, difficult to map or even to visualize. It is unfamiliar territory to anyone brought up on maps, compass points, longitude and latitude and units of measurement. Enter a cave and you are immediately disorientated. You leave behind all reference points: landmarks, sun, moon, stars, wind, sky and clouds. Your one point of certainty is the entrance but after a few twists of the path and ascents and descents, you don't know where that is any more. It is soon hard to tell how far you have walked or how deep you are.

A cave is organic; irregular in all senses and you are inside it with your sight restricted to the distance a lamp will throw light. There are few smells, except of rock and moisture. Your sense of touch is not much use without your eyesight to back it up.

You either organically adapt to this free "weightless" environment by surrendering yourself, admitting your control is slender and there is nothing you can do about it, or you risk bewilderment and panic.

A cave has obvious symbolic connotations. Going into a cave is a way of reminding ourselves that we have a triple relationship with the planet. We are on it, in it (including the atmosphere) and of it. Life comes from underground. It is the source of rivers that

Grotte de Niaux montage

irrigate our lands; and it is the source of us, the uterus. Ultimately we are creatures hatched out of the earth.

Secret societies frequently use caves for the purpose of initiation: entering and leaving represents a ritual death and rebirth. He or she who enters does not leave the same person. The cave also represents our concealed anatomy: rock is akin to bone and the cavern is "the bowels of the earth".

Until the end of 19th century, it was assumed that all caves were empty, natural spaces. It was also assumed that prehistoric man was primitive: a hunter-gatherer with only a rudimentary social organization, culture, language and interior life. To think otherwise would have been to contradict the narrative of civilization, progress and the improvement of man that people lived by.

Mysterious Art

The discovery of the cave of Altamira in Spain in 1879 changed everything. At first respectable scientists didn't believe the paintings were authentic, but as evidence accrued it became beyond dispute. By 1940, when the most famous painted cave, Lascaux, was discovered in the Dordogne, the archaeology of prehistoric art had become an established discipline.

Prehistoric art has now been discovered on the walls, ceilings and occasionally floors of around 350 caves and rock shelters in Europe. Almost half of them are in France, mostly in the southwest. The art is extraordinarily varied. It includes not only the well-known depictions of animals but also thousands of inscrutable, non-pictorial signs that have yet to be deciphered. A great deal is known about the extent and nature of cave art but, in over 130 years of scholarship, no progress has been made on the central questions: what do the cave paintings mean? Why would anyone want to draw, paint or engrave on a cave wall? Surely people in primitive societies had

Handprint (modern imitation), Gargas

other priorities? What gave the artists the idea to make them? Why did we – humanity – start doing this and then stop? All we can do is approach the subject with as much common sense as we can muster.

There are several reasons why human beings make marks. Mostly we make them to communicate, between one person and another, or one person and a group, or between human beings and a deity. We also make marks to keep records for future use. We record stores, debts, decisions or actions taken or experiences (e.g. a successful hunt). This can be done by a person for his own use, or by one person for another. Then we can also use marks as ornamentation, in simple or elaborate forms, to beautify the human world. Art, it could be said, exists in a particular category: the making of art for the sake of it. Finally, we make marks such as doodles without meaning to, spontaneously, for no good reason. Such unintentional marks have no meaning – at least no deliberate, conscious meaning. Many marks are made for a combination of two or more of these reasons so, for example, writing can also be decorative. Where in this scheme of mark-making do we place cave art?

It is possible that prehistoric art has no great meaning, but this is unlikely because of the inaccessible locations of many of the paintings. Prehistoric artists chose particular sites to place their work. These are not the first sites to hand when you enter a cave. Often they are deep underground, requiring a long walk to get to them. Sometimes the particular rock surface is difficult of access. Some paintings are so high that the artists must have had to construct ladders and scaffolding to do them. At times, the paintings are on ceilings as little as 50 cm (20 in) from the ground meaning that the artist had to be lying uncomfortably on his back to do them or squeeze into some awkward crevice. Nor are the paintings on the most obvious rock surfaces. They showed no interest in flat "canvases" but painted in places where the contours of the rock complicated the composition. Very often they incorporated the features of the rock in their work.

It was as if they were trying to be as discreet and as quiet as possible, marking the earth as little as possible in the most hidden corners of it.

The choice of work surface and the attention to detail rules out impetuous sketching or decoration. There was too much effort involved for anything frivolous. It also discounts the idea of "art for art's sake". If you are moved to draw or paint, you look for the nearest place for your work – a cave mouth or a scrap of wood. You don't care about its ephemerality; and you don't involve anyone else in your scheme. There is nothing spontaneous about most cave art. It shows purpose and preparation.

The trouble taken by the artists indicates some compelling reason to paint where and how they did it, and a serious intention either to record or to communicate their individual thoughts. Given the tribal, pre-individualistic nature of hunter-gather societies, it is safe to assume that the artists were not keeping personal records or visual diaries on the stone.

Nevertheless, we mustn't be fooled into oversimplification: there may be different motivations behind the various works of cave art; variations from region to region; and variations over time.

Many hypotheses have been put forward. It would seem obvious that they had a limited world view compared with ours and this must be reflected in their art. These, as far as we know, were people living in close contact with nature and in a constant struggle for survival. Their paintings of animals must be related to hunting. Perhaps they were appeasing the spirits of slaughtered animals or invoking good hunting for the following season. Possibly they were recording the kills of the best hunters or of the tribe. The trouble is that they depicted some animals that they didn't hunt, and some animals that they did hunt are not shown. They also painted much else beside animals: innumerable inscrutable signs almost like an ancient language that we cannot decipher.

Bison, Niaux

Ibex, Niaux

Another suggestion is that they had some sacred or ritualistic reason for making the paintings. The sites they chose must be somehow "holy" and the paintings must be associated with shamanic visions or ancestor worship. This is potentially a good explanation, but vague. The South African archaeologist David Lewis-Williams notes that the animals seem to go into and out of the rock as if were a membrane between worlds. The art, he says, must have been the product of shamanic trance.

How Are We to Understand?

There are only three ways we can approach cave art as modern human beings: through science, through art, or directly through ourselves as complete and complex human beings, without any filter. Science, the dominant approach to cave art, can only take us so far. The scientific consensus on rock art is that we can learn a great deal about it but only ever speculate on its purpose: we will never know for sure.

There are three great obstacles to understanding the purpose of cave paintings.

The first and most obvious is the remoteness of the people who made them and our disconnection from them.

The second obstacle is the lack of context and corroborating evidence. We can study bones and other finds in the caves but we cannot be sure that they are associated with the paintings. Even then, they tell us little except about lifestyle. They do not tell us anything about the consciousness that must have been at work. It truly is as if we see a primitive hunter-gatherer society that left few traces of its existence and an extraordinary art gallery, but no connection between the two. Essentially the evidence we have to go on is in front of us, on the cave walls.

The third great problem of cave art is that there is so little for us to get hold of with our brains. It is almost as if the artists

Natural Caves

Caverns are strange, atmospheric spaces whether or not they were frequented by human beings. Many can be visited to get the sensation of being in the womb of the earth – even if you are part of a guided group. Most of the caves in France – prehistorically painted or not – are in the southwest. The most interesting include:

• **Gouffre d'Esparros, Esparros.** The speciality of this cave in the foothills of the Pyrenees is a kind of intricate white crystal formation. The highlight of the tour is the astonishing *Salle du Lac* where visitors hear a short piece of music played on stalactites.
gouffre-esparros.fr

• **Gouffre de Padirac.** Legend says that this impressive hole on the ground in the Lot department was created during a fight between St Martin and the Devil. The cave consists of several subterranean lakes and most of the visit is undertaken by boat. Access is via a lift or stairs.
gouffre-de-padirac.com

Grotte de Labastide

• **Grotte de L'Aven Armand**, Hures-la-Parade. A funicular takes you down more than 100 m (330 ft) into the ground to this enchanting cave near the *Gorges du Tarn* to contemplate a forest of 400 stalagmites, including one 30 m (100 ft) high.
aven-armand.com

Grottes de Bétharra

want to deny us anything definite, as if they are defying every rule and theory. Everything is irregular, disorganized. The paintings float without base lines and horizons. It is all otherworldly and dreamlike, difficult to catalogue and categorize. Even naming the paintings is difficult: sometimes we are not sure what species an animal is or what a scene shows. Some paintings acquire names on the basis of what an archaeologist thinks he sees (e.g. "wounded man") but later acquire more ambiguous names along with question marks.

Faced with these problems, all science can do is compile data. Scientists working in the field are honest about the nature of the task and are aware that the scientific method imposes its own limits to progress. Any hypothesis can only be tested against the available evidence, never by reference to prehistoric society because it no longer exists. The scientific approach is very good at tackling some particular aspects of cave art but very bad at tackling cave art in general.

Science approaches cave art with a notion of superiority – albeit, perhaps, for the noblest of reasons. Through science, it is assumed that we can explain them because we have modern tools and a rigorous methodology with which to analyze their remains. More than this, we believe we should understand cave art for our own sense of pride. Cave art and the people who created it, though, do not need any explaining. They don't need anything from us.

We expect all knowledge to fit into molds that we devise and to be supported by material evidence. We don't like knowledge that straddles more than one category, or that fits into no category at all. We are uncomfortable with the notion of knowledge that defies science, and is therefore not provable. There is a difference, however, between ignoring or contradicting the evidence and respecting the evidence but trying to go beyond it.

We must be wary or at least aware of ourselves. Even the way we formulate our thoughts and questions is suspect. Words, which enshrine concepts we have inherited or developed, can mislead us. The ones we choose to use may be inappropriate to the world of cave art. We can easily get used to using definitions that are more for our own comfort and convenience than understanding the phenomenon before us.

We must also be wary of over-analyzing what we see with our hyperactive left brains. And we must be aware that, because we are imperfect human beings, we are involved with the phenomenon we are studying, not detached from it.

To put this difficulty another way, the biggest obstacle to understanding cave art may be ourselves and our way of looking at reality. If we are the obstacle, we also hold the key.

To understand cave art we may need to put science aside temporarily, or explore ideas in parallel with it. This does not mean ignoring or misinterpreting the evidence. We simply need to make cautious but expansive use of our intelligence.

If we are to make any progress we have to take one step away from our normal way of understanding, which is wrapped up with our obsessive search for certainty.

To understand a symbol it is necessary to think like the symbol-setter. If we are to understand the cave paintings, we must think like the artist who made it.

The first valid response to cave art is not to question or analyze it and try to explain it but accept who we are and free our minds from all our preconceptions as far as we can. We need to begin by putting our brains into neutral and allowing cave art to be non-sense. We can then simply appreciate it and see what thoughts flow from that.

Recreation of prehistoric paintbrushes, Labastide

ment now to another present moment long gone. It could be said that art is the opposite experience to the shamanic trance. The doing of it is a way of fixing us to reality, to the planet. The contact with the utensils, the materials, the ground or surface is not a way of flying off elsewhere but being here in the immediate now: "I art therefore I am".

While visiting a cave it is difficult to create art, but we can allow ourselves to have an immediate emotional response to what we see; perhaps even to sing in the cave if that is what we feel like doing. In so doing, we decouple the cogs of rational thought in our minds and quiet the measuring, counting, judging, logical brain. This gives us at least a sideways glimpse at the art before us, impressionistic, wordless, psychic.

There is a step before that, however, and that is to see exactly what prehistoric people saw when they entered the caves: nothing.

Being in Darkness

Inside the cave the dark is absolute, just as it was 30,000 years ago when the first cave paintings were done. We have to ask: why would they retreat from the light, which furnished them with visual images, to a place utterly devoid of light? The answer has to be that they were seeking the darkness itself.

To step into the darkness (or extinguish your torch) is to deliberately handicap yourself. It is to shut down one of your senses. All visual information disappears – all shapes and colours and dimensions.

What you have left is your sense of hearing, which serves for nothing in the silence, your sense of touch which feels only cold, neutral cave walls, and your visual memory and imagination. The cave, above all, away from the all-pervading, all-interfering light, is a place without distractions where it is possible to concentrate on seeing with your inner eyes. If there are other

Making our own art is the best way to do this. If we want to know what was going on in the mind of a cave artist we could, by observing a bison, walk for a week, crawl down a cave and draw it on a rock wall using tools we have made ourselves and natural pigments.

Short of that, simply looking at and drawing any animal, and making paint marks ourselves on any surface at least takes us a step towards the experience of that unknown artist.

When I draw, I enter a feeling of timelessness and egolessness. Nothing matters except the doing of the art. It doesn't matter whether anyone ever sees it, whether it endures or not. This sets up a direct link across the millennia, from the present mo-

realms, it is in the darkness of the cave that we come closest to them.

The dark of the cave represents perpetual night and the inner life of man. You open your eyes and they may as well be shut. It is almost as if your head is disconnected from your body and in another dimension. Time becomes meaningless. Place disappears and you could be anywhere in the universe. The dark makes and keeps secrets. Closing your outer eyes allows your inner eyes to open. Darkness leads you into dreams and the unconscious; being in it is already to be in an altered state of consciousness.

This is far away from how we see the dark in the modern world. All too often we see the absence of the sun as something terrifying, representing evil and death. We need to know what time it is and where we are. We crave light both in the sense of scaring away superstition and prolonging the day. We spend a great deal of our time and money lighting the interiors where we live and the cities which contain our homes. The alternative – a blackout – is disconcerting. And yet we also crave the darkness. There are ever fewer places on earth where night guarantees true darkness away from the glow of artificial light.

In the dark, you are removed from the habitat that sustains you and makes you human, and you revert to your animal self. This is borne out by prehistoric art.

Observe an animal. Only some aspects of its behaviour are explicable and predictable. Mostly it is erratic in its movements. It may or may not follow a straight line, taking a logical course from where it is to where it wants to be. Nature certainly "knows" about geometry but doesn't always obey it.

Similarly, the ungraspable irregularity of cave art is animal in nature. It may have taken a human mind and hand to execute it, but the state of mind that propels it is connected to a part of us beneath the intellectual. It follows neither logic nor any human-devised rules but an animal sixth sense.

It is as if it were done before some leap or shift in human consciousness towards the deliberate organization of space, building from a baseline and the calculation of the right angle. We need to realize this before we look at cave art. We need to see it not with the human part of us, but with our animal nature.

To return to our original question, if the cave artists were recording or communicating subjects important to them, who were their marks intended for? There are only three possible answers: other men and women; their gods, spirits or ancestors; or us.

That the art is located in particular places often of difficult access suggests that access to it was restricted to certain people. If it was for other living people, it may only have been available to those who

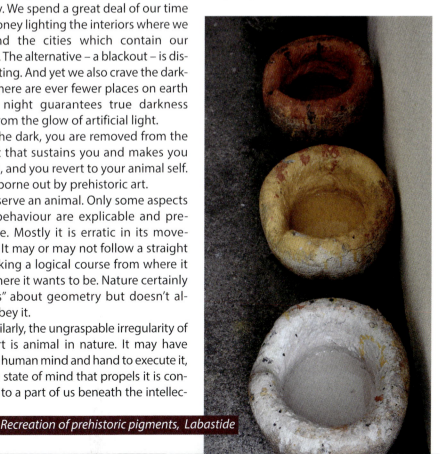

Recreation of prehistoric pigments, Labastide

knew about it, had a right to see it, or who made the appropriate effort. It may have been reserved for an elite of the tribe, other artists, chiefs or shamans. Or was it part of a rite of passage with only initiates allowed to walk into the cave after appropriate training and tests, and in the right frame of mind?

If the art was not intended for other human beings, it may have been directed at deities or their ancestors. We have no way of knowing.

A further intriguing possibility is that it was not for their forebears but their descendants, us. We consider ourselves irrelevant to the story, chance viewers of art whose meaning died with its makers. But what if those makers were sending a message through time to us? "Inside the cave; inside yourself it is safe," they could be saying.

At Gargas, in the Pyrenees, the whole tribe holds up their negatively silhouetted hands in greeting, projected across time to us, as if time doesn't matter. This is the same gesture as seen on the plaque fixed to the interstellar probe Pioneer 10 launched in 1972 intended as a greeting for any future extra-terrestrial who comes across it. Could the hand prints at Gargas serve the same purpose? "We know you," they are saying, "we are the same". Maybe we just have to answer back, hold up a hand in return and ask no more questions.

If they were communicating with us or keeping records that we haven't yet managed to read, that will interfere with our views of the past. There are still all those enigmatic signs on the walls of the caves to be translated. It could be that they comprise a language and a literature we are unable to read, even a holy book that has been conveyed to the safest of places. One definition of prehistory is time before records were kept. It may be that we have to reclassify the Stone Age as a historical period.

Could it be that humanity was preparing psychically to leave the cave, to leave behind its animal nature, emerge from the mother and start to build on earth beneath the sky? If so, the cave paintings could be seen as a dream of the destiny of man or a symbolic blueprint for his life to come. This is the starting point, they are saying, where you come from. This is who you were, don't forget it.

There is a final possibility to consider. Perhaps this holiest of holiest texts was not meant to be seen – or to be seen only rarely. The last light in the cave might have been that of the departing artist as he committed his work to eternity. After that, the paintings and the marks remained in darkness. Those who entered subsequently knew that they were there like ghosts in the darkness and that was enough. The invisible and mysterious have great power and set a riddle for us: if beauty is not seen by a human with the ability to appreciate it, does it still exist as beauty? Would our lives be poorer if we closed up all the caves and left the paintings unseen? What if there are other paintings, more extraordinary than those we know of but never to be discovered? Should we dig everywhere in France; wriggle down every hole in the ground; invade every cavern? Or should we leave the under-realm, as prehistoric human beings eventually did, and concern ourselves instead with mysteries on the surface?

Original entrance to Niaux

Grottes de Bétharram

Subterranean church, Aubeterre-sur-Dronne

Subterranean Spaces

One way to define a building, especially a church, is as an imitation cave. It may be a natural cave, or a structure scooped out of the rock, but it is still an enclosed space with walls and a ceiling.

A purpose-made building has many advantages but it lacks certain qualities of the cave. A cave is a safe, intimate, mysterious place with its own peculiar acoustics, smells and irregular contours. It is surprisingly suited to human activity despite its lack of light: the temperature inside stays even day and night, throughout the year.

The darkness and greater or lesser accessibility makes it an ideal place for concentrating on the divine, holding secret rituals, and for conducting initiation rites.

Small wonder then that early buildings often combine the two, linking a human structure with a natural or excavated cavity. Across France, there are a great many subterranean or semi-subterranean structures used for sacred purposes that are invisible unless you know they are there. Some are not open to the public but many are.

Going back to the first buildings in France, megalithic chambers were often buried under artificial mounds or tumuli (see p74). Other early structures – *hypogeums* (found in the Marne, at Poitiers and in Provence), *souterrains* (Iron Age galleries) and *Mithraeums* (sanctuaries to Mithras) are mainly of interest to archaeologists. Gallo-Roman semi-underground buildings include the *cryptoporticums* of Arles and Reims and the *horreum* in Narbonne.

Many early churches were built, for convenience or safety, partly or entirely underground. Such a church is known as an *église monolithique* or *rupestre*. The largest in Europe is at **Aubeterre-sur-Dronne**, in Poitou-Charentes. Its nave reaches 20 m (66 ft) in height and is looked down on from a rock-hewn gallery.

A similarly large *église monolithique* was hollowed out of the rock in the 11th–12th centuries at **Saint-Émilion** near **Bordeaux**. It connects the town's lowest point with its highest, the bell tower above, ascended by 196 steps.

Even more charming to visit is the church of the tiny village of **Vals**, in the Ariège, which is only semi-subterranean. It has the advantage that it can be visited at any time you please and, being out of the way, you may well get it all to yourself, which is the best way to get a real sense of the atmosphere.

Other monolithic churches, or at least churches that are partly underground, are at **Fontanges** (Cantal); **Les Baux-de-Provence**; **Chaudon** near **Domme** in the Dordogne; **Bieuzy** in Morbihan (Brittany); **Gurat** in Charente; **Peyre** (near **Millau** in the Aveyron); **Haute-Isle** in the Val d'Oise, an underground village with two underground churches. The Abbey Saint-Roman at **Beaucaire** meanwhile is the remains of an underground palaeochristian monastery.

The old abbey at **Brantôme** in the Dordogne has a set of troglodyte chambers, one of which contains a depiction of the Last Judgement (see p228).

Chapels were also included in larger underground complexes built for other purposes, as in the **Paris** catacombs, and in the "underground city" that lies 33 m (108 ft) beneath **Naours** (Somme, Picardy). Its 300 chambers can be visited on a tour.

In addition, many churches have crypts beneath them, providing an entirely different space to the nave or choir above. **Chartres** (see p214) has the largest crypt. **Dijon** cathedral also has a fine crypt, as do the Abbaye Saint-Maur in **Bleurville** (Vosges, Lorraine); **Boulogne-sur-Mer** on the English Channel coast (decorated with murals); **Vézelay**; the *Basilique Saint-Victor* in **Marseille** and the Abbaye de Montmajour (Bouches-du-Rhône). In the middle of Montmartre in **Paris**, steps lead down to the crypte de Saint-Denis, the site of the saint's martyrdom in the 3rd century. Beneath **Caunes-Minervois** (Aude) lie the cavern remains of a Carolingian church.

A corner of the Anjou, south of the Loire river around **Saumur**, has Europe's highest concentration of excavated caves, past and present, adding up to more than 1000 km (600 mi) of excavated passages carved out of the soft tufa limestone. Some of them are used as houses, hotels and restaurants, or for maturing wine, or growing mushrooms. Some of them are particularly interesting. The *Cave aux Sculptures* at **Dénezé-sous-Doué** stands out among them. It has a gigantic erratic frieze of over 230 faces and figures emerging from the rock. It is thought to date from the 16th century but no one knows who sculpted it or why. Various theories make the cave a pagan temple, a refuge of heretics during the Religious Wars, or the site of a colony of fugitive stonemasons giving free reign to their skills.

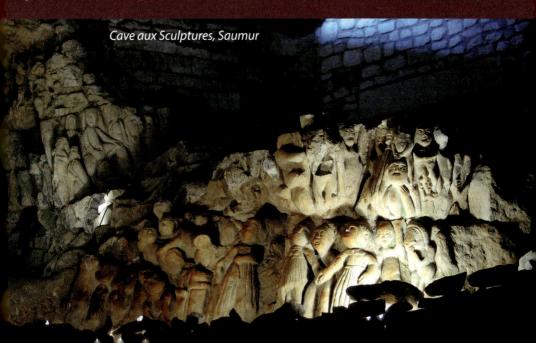

Cave aux Sculptures, Saumur

Menhir in a field outside Ger

IV

Silent Stones
The Riddle of the Megaliths

Dolmen, Finistère

Interwoven with the cities, towns, villages and roads of France, there is an alternative, forgotten landscape of giant stones that were planted in the ground in ancient times for inscrutable reasons. How far can we go in interpreting the dolmens, menhirs, tumuli and other prehistoric constructions left to us like time capsules by the unidentified people of long ago?

Two strangely juxtaposed constructions stand in the valley of the Tarn River where it flows through the department of the Aveyron. At first sight, they could not be more dissimilar. The **Millau Viaduct**, a sleek motorway suspension bridge, designed and engineered to perfection, was opened in 2004. It exemplifies our age: a grandiose building project built for convenience and speed. Every last fact about its purpose, construction and operation is public knowledge.

from large components brought from somewhere else and put together in a precise pre-calculated way. Both stand somewhat incongruously in the countryside, placed in a precise spot carefully chosen by someone and painstakingly constructed by a collective effort.

Each was built to endure beyond a human lifespan, demonstrating an intended investment in the needs of the future. The Millau Viaduct has a guaranteed lifespan of 120 years. The dolmen has so far

Standing stones alignment, Carnac, Brittany

In contrast, we know almost nothing about the Neolithic dolmen of Soulobres, a little to the north of the bridge, except that it is stubborn, discreet and somewhat mysterious.

Yet the two structures do have some common traits. Both are strangers in the organic green landscape. Like the dolmen, the modern bridge is essentially a structure of verticals and horizontals assembled

survived at least 4000 years of weathering, which is 2000 years longer than any other non-prehistoric building in France.

The dolmen is neither exceptional nor rare. There are megalithic monuments in most – but not all – parts of France but they are most concentrated in a broad belt stretching from southern Normandy southeast across the western Massif Central to the Languedoc. Together they form an incoherent parallel human geography of enigmatic landmarks that were clearly placed for some great purpose but fell into disuse 100 generations ago sometime before the inception of history.

The peninsula of Brittany is especially rich in ancient stones. In the Morbihan department alone, there are 750 megalithic sites including the famous massed megaliths of **Carnac**. Elsewhere, the stones tend to occur in local concentrations. Salles-de-la Source, for instance, has almost 270 prehistoric monuments within its municipal area.

These prehistoric sites are in various states of weathering, preservation and access. Some are conspicuous, cared for, signposted and easy to get to – they even stand conveniently at roadsides, at crossroads, or have been incorporated into picnic areas. Others are out of the way, unspectacular, overgrown and only found if you know what you are looking for. The less well-known sites are not always the least interesting. There is a good chance that you will get the place all to yourself and can take your time to ponder on the nature and purpose of the stones.

Classifying the Unclassifiable

Megalithic monuments have been given names and classifications by tradition and scholarship and these may have nothing to do with their construction or use. The most common, basic structure is the dolmen, or portal tomb, typically a table top on a tripod, made of uprights supporting a capstone. This was usually covered with a mound of stone or soil to make a tumulus. An elaboration of the dolmen is the passage grave or barrow, a corridor with one or more "burial" chambers, the whole thing covered by a tumulus.

The three oldest buildings in the world

are in France – Barnenez passage grave in Finisterre dated at 4850 BC; the *Tumulus de Bougon*, 4700BC; and the *Tumulus Saint-Michel* (a grave mound near **Carnac**), 4500BC. They predated the pyramids of Egypt by 2000 years.

Altogether more inscrutable are *menhirs* or standing stones. These are most often seen individually but in places they occur as stone circles (often called *cromlechs*) or in straight rows, known as alignments.

The Great Broken Menhir of Er Grah at **Locmariaquer** in Brittany, put in place in 4500BC and toppled many years later, now lies on the ground in four pieces. The original block of stone would have been 20 m (67 ft) long (making it as high as a five-storey building) and weighed 280 tonnes. It was transported here from perhaps 12 km (7.5 mi.) distance and shaped with stone chisels. It is now thought to have been part of an alignment of 18 menhirs. Where the other stones went, no one knows.

Unlike cave paintings, which were rediscovered by accident, these outdoor prehistoric monuments have stood without history in plain view. For most people they were either a matter of mild curiosity, a structure on which was hung a legend about giants, devils or petrified armies – or they were in the way of the plough or road. Those that could be shifted were used as building materials in houses or bridges. For Christianity, they were an unpleasant remnant of paganism that had to be owned or neutralized. Some were Christianized by placing a crucifix on top or moving them next to a church. One stands outside the cathedral of **Le Mans**.

In the 20th century, they were seen not as obstacles but as treasures of national heritage to be preserved and argued over by professional archaeologists, who subjected them to scientific analysis, and megalith enthusiasts who tried to get at their secrets in any way possible.

Empty Centuries

The trouble for both groups and anyone else looking for the secrets of the stones is that there is so little to go on. There is not much you can say about stones that have few distinguishing marks or corroborative evidence. The megaliths are as much a mystery as the cave paintings but we can make sense of them if we approach them in the right way. The first problem is when we refer to the builders of the megaliths to know whom we are talking about.

Prehistory is an unimaginably long and vague time comprising 95% of the time that humans have inhabited France. It is also a judgement. When we say "prehistory", we mean "history before our history" or "the history we know little about." We know that today no country on earth is the same as it was a hundred years ago and yet we find it impossible to think of prehistory in the same way, dynamic and changing. Perhaps nothing happened in the undocumented centuries but it would do us no harm to assume that many events took place.

It is unlikely that the megalith builders were the direct descendants of the cave painters. Around 10,000 years separated the last cave paintings from the first megaliths, equivalent to five times our sense of recorded history. It seems the human beings of France made themselves conspicuous with their achievements at least twice, and vanished twice.

However, to think of the people of the Neolithic as some kind of uniform and continuous community is misleading. The megaliths were built over roughly 3000 years, perhaps longer. That is something like 150 generations. And there are almost certain to be regional variations in their constructions if only we could perceive them.

From cave to megalith was not so much a disconnected chronological step but a conceptual transformation. The prehistoric

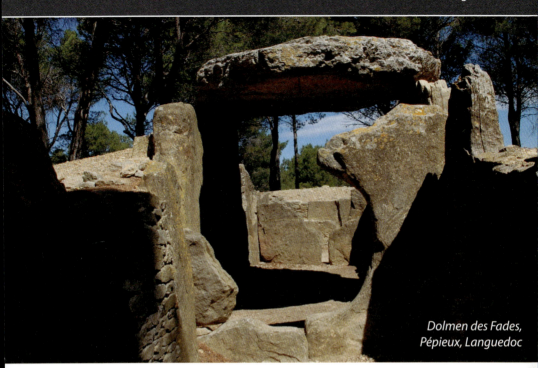

Dolmen des Fades, Pépieux, Languedoc

people who built the megaliths had abandoned their hunter-gatherer nomadic lifestyle, settled and developed a civilization based on agriculture. In that, they were not dissimilar to us.

Whereas the cave paintings could have been done – and probably were, given the shortage of space – by individuals or small groups, the megaliths must be the work of masses of people. Considering the scale of the stone blocks deployed, these monuments were collective creations. It must have taken both a strong sense of purpose and an impressive social organization. It has been estimated, by modern experiments with moving stones, that a modest megalithic structure would take 50,000 man hours to build, and a complex one at least 500,000.

All this was accomplished without vast resources of labour. The Neolithic population expanded and shrank and the best estimate is that the population of France varied between 500,000 and 1 million, the equivalent to 1–2 people per square km (1/3 to 2/3 people per square mile), or no more than 12,000 people living in the equivalent area of a modern department on average. Clearly there would have been some concentrations in certain areas compensating for virgin territory elsewhere. Discount the very young, the very old and the sick and that doesn't provide a large workforce. The workers had to travel where they were needed. They had to be fed and perhaps defended. This was long before Egypt managed the same task with the benefits of having a god-king, centralized power, and a system of writing.

We can assume that they did not go to so much trouble for trivial reasons. Various hypotheses have been proposed from the mundane – that megaliths were landmarks to facilitate trade – to the sophisticated: that the alignments and circles were part of an elaborate system to keep track of astronomical events and the passage of time. Mostly they are agreed to be ceremonial, religious, sepulchral, and related to rites to do with death and the dead. These, however, are speculations and assumptions. Even if they are tombs, we should be wary of assuming that they are tombs in the sense we think of this word.

Menhir-Statues: Prehistoric People in Stone

The *Monts de Lacaune*, an upland area east of Toulouse, are renowned for an unusual and mysterious type of prehistoric monument, the statue-menhir. These erect monoliths made of granite or sandstone differ from standing stones elsewhere in that they are carved on two faces in bas relief to represent the back and front of human figures – men and women.

Their purpose is unknown, as is their age. Experts believe they date from the Chalcolithic, around 3500–2300 BC, making them the earliest examples of statuary occurring in Europe.

The stones reach up to 4.5m (15ft) tall. Some of them have been removed to the *Musée Fenaille* in **Rodez** – including one well-preserved stone known as the *Dame de Saint-Sernin* – and there is a museum at **Murat-sur-Vèbre** (east of **Lacaune**) dedicated to them.

Around thirty statue-menhirs still stand where they were put, unfortunately exposed to the erosive power of the weather. The best known of the *in situ* stones is *La Pierre Plantée*, just outside **Lacaune**. There are also a few elsewhere in France, held in private collections.

No one knows who these people-stones are supposed to be. They could be divinities, shamans, ancestors or commemorated warriors.

A statue-menhir has certain features

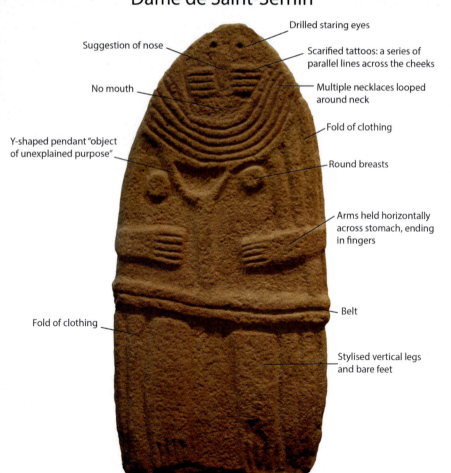

Dame de Saint-Sernin

- Suggestion of nose
- No mouth
- Y-shaped pendant "object of unexplained purpose"
- Fold of clothing
- Drilled staring eyes
- Scarified tattoos: a series of parallel lines across the cheeks
- Multiple necklaces looped around neck
- Fold of clothing
- Round breasts
- Arms held horizontally across stomach, ending in fingers
- Belt
- Stylised vertical legs and bare feet

and is etched in a particular style, although where the stone is worn, the details take some imagining. Copied from the stone to paper, the design looks sketchy and impressionistic like a doodle, a child's drawing of a person, or a piece of modern art.

The average statue-menhir is a large oval or pointed stone with the suggestion of the outline of a disproportionately small face at the top. This has eyes shown as two circles (perhaps with drilled holes as pupils) and a nose but no ears or mouth, as if the artist wanted to tell us that the stone is not intended to talk or even betray an expression. It stares but does not hear or speak. Across the cheeks are sometimes a series of horizontal lines, presumably scarifications or tattoos.

Below the face the figure has crudely drawn arms ending with fingers shown as six parallel lines. Round the waist is a belt that may be ornamented with parallel lines or chevrons, with a buckle in the middle.

The legs hang down below the belt, again with no attempt to show them anatomically, and end in vertical lines depicting feet without shoes. It is impossible to know whether the figure is meant to be standing on the ground, or floating in the air, or emerging from the stone itself.

Indications of folded cloth suggest that the figures are robed or otherwise clothed. They usually wear some sort of sash or shoulder strap, which may indicate their function or status.

Beyond these common characteristics, the two sexes are treated differently. Female statues have small circular breasts and multiple pendant necklaces.

Male statues include weapons or emblems of power drawn symbolically below the shoulder rather than realistically: a bow and arrows, an axe or what may be a boomerang or sickle. Intriguingly, the male statues also have an object placed at the level of the chest and possibly hanging by a sash or shoulder strap. The nature of this object is a mystery and may be key to explaining the statue's identity.

Interestingly, the backs of the stones are also carved, showing hair, the shoulder blades, cloths and belts. This suggests that the stones are not meant to be two dimensional pictures on rocks but three dimensional people.

Personal Approach

Archaeology will only ever be partially fruitful, adding details without expanding the overview. There must be something intrinsic about the individual stones because they were chosen with care, dragged from far away and laboriously worked on.

If we cannot see or measure this special quality, we can perhaps feel it if we put ourselves in the required receptive state. Does stone have a smell, a sound, even a taste to it that we can detect if we can be sensitive enough? Ultimately one has to make sense of the stone personally and intuitively.

The stone stands in context, in a particular place in the landscape itself. While the cave painting is contained in an intimate space of limited access and looks inward, the megalith stands exposed in the open air. There must be something significant about the placing of each stone but we don't know what it is. Perhaps they are intended to tap into some kind of earth energy.

Contrasting with the early megaliths, barrows are "imitation caves", discreetly covered over to make them part of the earth. Menhirs stand unmistakably proud, rooted but connecting the surface of the planet to the sky as if it were a lightning conductor, possibly acting in reverse. It is as if humanity has psychically emerged from within the earth and planted itself on it. The painted caves are symbolically female; the menhirs are undoubtedly male: the shift from one to the other is the child's progression from dependence on the mother to becoming the companion of the father.

We can assume that, because the stones stand conspicuously in the open air and involved so many people in their erection, they were for communal use, or at least for an elite of "priests" on behalf of the community. They probably had some ceremonial role and communing with them was not a solitary experience – although they may have served both purposes, public and individual.

Megaliths are buildings without an obvious function and we can be certain of two things about them. They were built with a sense of permanence if not immortality. The people who made them must have had a notion of the distant future. They have survived all human habitations built. Anything else built before the Romans hasn't survived intact, only as ruins. I can stare at the same stone periodically all my life and it will still be there when I die. Stone megaliths stand there resisting and insisting. "Surely," they seem to say, "you can see what we are trying to tell you; take your time. Try harder. Think about time unimaginable without simple answers."

The megalith builders were also more concerned with structure than with decoration. There are exquisite, puzzling Neolithic carvings at the island Cairn of Gavrinis and elsewhere, but they are more the exception than the rule. Gavrinis combines both structure and decoration in a way that prefigures the church.

There is nothing human about the stones and yet they are certainly the hard remnant of a civilization. Presumably they are a concrete expression of a belief. What must their culture and way of thinking have been like? Again, archaeology is more suggestive than categorical but we can imagine our way into the minds of those people if we start off by seeing them not as remote from us in time and life experience, but as essentially the same as us.

If history is the story of recorded events and identifiable people, prehistory is the story of unidentified people. We homogenize these people in our mind. They are nameless and shapeless groups that are not composed of individuals like us.

Not only do we assume them to be people in the collective rather than the singular sense, but we assume they lived uneventful lives. The centuries of prehistory are vague, flat and featureless.

All of this makes it possible for us to construct generalizations about them, which is tantamount to dismissing them as unimportant to us, and this has the side-effect of making it impossible for us to comprehend them. In our ignorance and lack of interest, we look no further than our absence of knowledge about them.

Dolmen des Fades, Pépieux

There is no reason we should deny identity to people just because we do not know their names and prefer to treat them as faceless masses. It is a challenge to us to re-create them as people like ourselves, to see them as more than archaeological reconstructions, that is to say caricatures and stereotypes.

Those people must have had names, positions in society and job descriptions just as we do. They must have mattered to each other. They must have loved, suffered, given birth to children, dreamed, schemed, expressed selfish urges, doubted, and wondered. Were their worries about their kin similar to ours? Did they think about the future? Did they have abstract, imaginative ideas? Did they have their own oral literature, as rich as ours even if it is lost down to the last trace?

The "empty" centuries in which they inhabited France may really have been full: packed with drama and variety, with a deep reflection on the nature of existence. They may well have had their own history – an entire history before history begins – transmitted orally and perhaps recorded in the stones.

They must have had their reasons for doing things which made sense to them and perhaps, if we are willing to shift our angle of view, it can make sense to us. It may also help us to see ourselves better.

Religions Purposes?

It is quite possible that many or most of these things are to do with a belief in the supernatural – religion for want of a better word – but probably not in the way we think of it. There is an unmistakable similarity between a dolmen and an altar, and the Cairn of Gavrinis has echoes of an early church in which the tomb of a saint provides a sanctified enclosed space in which to hold ceremonies.

Even if we allow that they were religious and that we know what that word meant, we are forced to ask why were they so religious? Why did they feel the need to make such an extraordinary effort on behalf of their gods?

It may be that they knew something we do not know, or that they gave their own expression to the same perennial questions that beset all of us on the planet, in whichever era we live.

If we want to know what they were thinking, we need do no more than look at ourselves and ask what makes life on the surface of the planet possible in settled farming communities. What do we require of our gods (taking that word in its widest metaphorical sense)? If the megaliths are inspired by religious motivation, our perennial human preoccupations could be the key to understanding them.

We would do well to focus on a megalith, from time to time, to reconnect through stone with our roots and remind ourselves that we are part of one great system of forces about which our understanding can only ever be partial.

We belong to a universe that, like everything in it, is at once an indivisible whole and its constituent parts. All parts

Menhir at Mancioux

are interrelated and they interact. Sometimes we can see the mechanisms at work; often we can't. Inevitably, all of us ask what humanity is doing here and how anything came to be. We look around for the answer and at each other, but the answer is not in the faces of our equally mystified fellow beings. So we look up and wonder whether the answer is in the sky that dominates our earth in two different guises by day and night. What information could there be for us? How are we connected to the heavenly bodies we see? How do they influence life on earth?

Chief of all bodies in the sky is the sun, which provides light and warmth to the earth. Human life depends on plant growth and that requires just the right amount of sunlight harmonized with a suitable amount of rainfall, at the right times of year. This is as true today as it was 6000 years ago. Life and growth are not to be taken for granted. The climate does vary – perhaps there was a folk memory of the ice age still lingering in people's minds – and it was natural that prehistoric people should want to mark the winter solstice in the middle of the hungry season when the light began to return to the fields and the shadows lengthen. If anything is a cause for celebration, this is it.

The sun is one unpredictable power that can (as we perceive it) overheat the earth or cool it down. We are also rightly fearful of all other forces beyond our control, including the weather and parasites.

We have replaced a belief in the gods' ability to order these things with a trust in scientific knowledge which has given us mechanization and chemical control of the fields and the preservation of food. We are not, however, immune to the vagaries of nature.

A conscious human life with the power to decide the fate of the other elements of terrestrial existence is clearly something sacred. We have duties which are not to be taken lightly. We must learn how to behave as thinking components of the universe and we must devise ways to pass on "the rules" of being here. A human life has a set course and involves several transitions, some of them abrupt. We need to be steered through each of these rites of passage in order for us to shift gear in an appropriate way. This is another function of religious practice: to show us the way to do this.

Our final rite of passage is death. This involves obvious mysteries and poses certain challenges. What do you do with the body of a dead person: dispose of it as if it were lifeless meat or treat it with ceremony? What happens to the invisible part of the person who dies? Does the "soul" need some special care taken of it?

Maybe the megaliths are, as is often suggested, part of some obsessive death cult but, if they were, death was not dealt with as some separate experience but as an essential part of the universal experience of life.

We who have not yet died have no right to disparage any primitive idea of the afterlife as wishful thinking or gullible nonsense. Even if we are convinced that death is a meaningless, random event, we cannot avoid the great implied question it poses. We cannot ask "where do we go?" without simultaneously asking "where do we come from?" One good way to begin to answer that is to telescope forwards through history to more recent events.

Statue of a prehistoric man, Les Eyzies-de-Tayac-Sireuil

Cromlech above the Ossau valley in the Pyrenees

Lands of the Dead

"Me today, you tomorrow," says a Breton funerary inscription, reminding us that there can be no mysticism without facing up to our mortality – or immortality. To put it another way: why waste time with other mysteries when the biggest one is there in front of us all the time? As well as visiting more uplifting sites, a tour around mystical France also involves visiting places of death to see what feelings they inspire and what we can learn from earlier generations.

The Celts believed that death was at the centre of a good long life; that the dead must be honoured for what they had lived and what they were yet to live. It serves us well to sometimes stand in appropriate places, those set apart from daily life, and contemplate the role death plays in our incarnation.

Some places of the dead in France have become tourist attractions. There is always a queue for the Catacombs in **Paris** and the "celebrity" cemeteries of *Montparnasse* and *Père Lachaise* are also popular. More atmospheric and less busy (especially on an overcast day) is *Montmartre* cemetery, which, too, has its share of tombs of the famous.

The country's most historically renowned cemetery – barring the prehistoric monuments which may or may not have had a funerary purpose – is *Les Alyscamps*, in **Arles**, a stopover for pious and penitent travellers from Roman Times into the Middle Ages. It was alluded to by Dante and painted by Gauguin and Van Gogh.

Even in obscure small town churchyards there can be a wealth of monumental funerary art to contemplate. It is often rich in tile work, stone carving, wrought iron and stained glass – and filled with symbolism. There are also some surprises. In the middle of the cemetery of **Rieux-Minervois** in the Aude, for instance, there is the sepulchre of a prominent 19th century Freemason that stands out in its details from the standard Catholic imagery around it.

Dating from more recent times are memorials to the dead of the two world wars. Every village has its own such memorial, usually the focus of a ceremony on November 11. Closer to the battlefields, there are vast cemeteries containing the remains of the hundreds of thousands of soldiers who died. Most of them are in Normandy and northern France and they pose questions not only about death but the manner of dying, of sacrifice and the nature of strife and peace. The D-Day beaches, too, where so many men died, are poignant memorials in themselves. Back in Paris is the most conspicuous war memorial of them all, raised above the most humble victim of conflict, the Tomb of the Unknown Soldier. It lies beneath the *Arc de Triomphe* and is in stark juxtaposition to the glorification of battles one can see above and all around it.

At the other extreme from the sepulchre of the unidentifiable everyman are the tombs of the very identifiable and vain aristocrats and kings that are covered with images

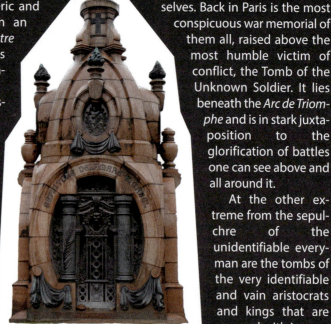

Mausoleum, Montmartre cemetery

Discoidal gravestones, Lacommande

speaking of temporal power, lineage and earthly achievements.

The Revolution made the dead more democratic, commemorating achievement rather than riches. The *Panthéon*, up the hill from the Latin Quarter in **Paris**, is a place of veneration for the nation's heroes in all fields of endeavour.

Most monumental tombs to the great, good, powerful, rich or clever are impressive but nothing more. One of them, however, stands out. The mausoleum of Francis II, duke of Brittany, in **Nantes** cathedral is a masterpiece of Renaissance sculpture. With the four virtues placed at its corners, it is said to be fashioned according to esoteric symbolism.

Several cemeteries have funerary chapels standing in them, such as the *Octagone de Montmorillon*, and at **Chambon** in the Auvergne. Others have curious towers, known as *lanternes de morts* – their purpose has yet to be explained. They may be beacons to guide the souls of the deceased and, while some were equipped to show a light from the top, others show no sign of having served such a purpose. The best examples are at **Cellefrouin** (Charente), **Fenioux** (Charente-Maritime), **Felletin** (Creuse), Sarlat-la-Canéda (Dordogne) and **Saint-Agnant-de-Versillat** (Creuse).

Finally, there are works of art to contemplate on the theme of death. The Middle Ages were preoccupied with the subject, with good reason. The Last Judgement was a favourite theme of medieval craftsmen and their patrons. The best carving is to be seen on the *tympanum* at **Conques**. **Albi** Cathedral in the Tarn has a large and graphic wall painting of it.

The Plague, famine and the Hundred Years War gave rise to a peculiar French subject in art, the Dance of Death or *Danse Macabre*. In it, death is shown leading a dance of men and women towards the grave. Particularly good examples are to be seen on the walls of *La Chaise-Dieu* Abbey in the Massif Central; in a cave of Brantôme Abbey in the Dordogne; and in churches at Brianny (Côte-d'Or), Kernascléden (Morbihan in Brittany), Kientzheim (Alsace) and Plouha (Côtes-d'Armor). All is futile, says death: don't get attached to worldly things and don't believe that power, wealth and prestige in the world will count for anything when the time comes.

The 13th card in the tarot deck is Death. It shows a skeleton wielding a scythe but, depending on the method of interpretation, it doesn't have to be taken to mean physical death. It can also mean the death of one kind of life and transition to another.

Dieu de Bozouls, Musée Fenaille, Rodez

V

Idols Unknown
The Evolution of the Gods of Old

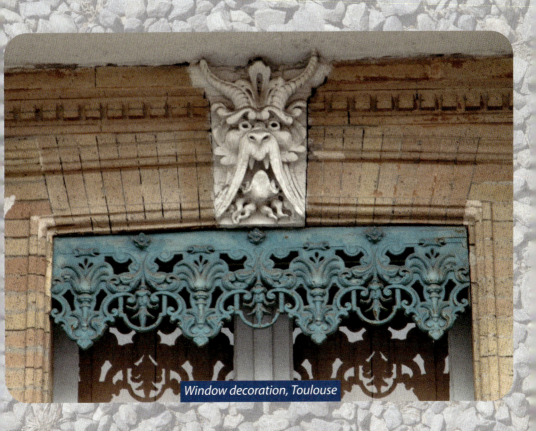

Window decoration, Toulouse

How many deities has France been home to? Most of them we know nothing of at all. Some are reduced to archaeological artefacts sitting in museums with vague labels attached. Others have acquired Christian names. All of them represent the perennial needs of the human soul to be in contact with the supernatural.

One day in December 1957, a team of workmen were laying pipes in a hamlet of Aveyron when they unearthed a small statue in pink sandstone. They had a job to finish so they put the statue in a field and forgot about it for a few days. When they came back to look for it, they realized it might be of some historical interest and they reported what they had found. Since then, it has been classified as an archaeological discovery and it has made its way to the *Musée Fenaille* in **Rodez**, where it sits in a case behind glass against the wall on an upper floor. Most visitors give it no more than a casual glance, mostly because the label beside it gives so little information.

The statue is 95 cm (38 in) high and well preserved. It sits on a rectangular base and is roughly pyramidal in form. It shows a man (according to the official description, but it could be a woman) with an elaborate hairdo coiling around the ears and a plait hanging down one shoulder. Round his neck is a torc – a stiff decorative ring. In his right hand he holds a dagger pressed against his chest, and in the left hand is the sheath.

Without any context to go on, nothing can be known about the age of the statue or who or what it represents. Everything is perhaps. For want of a better description it is labelled, "The God of Bozouls", after the place where it was found, and attributed to the Gauls.

There are many such unidentified figures in the museums of France: surviving fragments from pagan religions we know nothing about.

If the "God of Bozouls" is a deity, it is a displaced and forgotten one. It must once have mattered to someone, perhaps to a whole tribe. It would have had a name, a biography, a home and a cult surrounding it.

Now there is no one who cares about it or even knows what it is and it can no longer be considered sacred. It is redundant, buried long ago along with those who made it and adored it. Who knows how many gods have been worshipped in France, central to someone's life and now without power or consequence to anyone?

What we make of it says much about our attitude to the past and religion. A century or two ago, it would have been reburied or broken up with a hammer. The modern fashion is to treat everything old as information and so we keep it in the hope that we can decipher it.

We treat it as precious but not in the way its original owners would have thought of it. For us the value of this figurine is artistic, historical, cultural. It is the object we prize, not

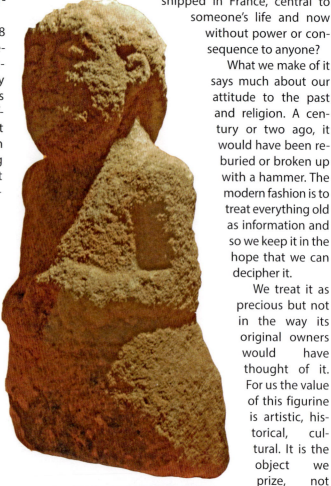

Dieu de l'hôpital, Musée Fenaille, Rodez

what it once meant.

This once-god is treated as lost property that will never be reclaimed, so it has been placed in a museum. This seems disrespectful somehow, although it is hard to see where else it could go. It would not be welcome in a church or another temple because they are reserved for living, identifiable gods.

What is a God?

For the archaeologist, appointed custodian of orphan gods, the statue is just another object to be described and catalogued, even if it is less interesting than a cooking utensil or the contents of a latrine. "Religious artifact" is the default description of anything dug out of the ground that does not have a strict utilitarian purpose, or which is not decorative, or a toy; but the phrase is uninformative. It is a term that mystifies rather than explains. It deliberately ignores the central questions raised by the unearthing of an ancient god: what has such a god to say for itself, if we are willing to listen? What exactly are gods and where do they come from? Are they human inventions, fantasies based on superstition and ignorance, or is there some reality to them?

Looking back at the gods of ancient times, we need to be careful not to make a fundamental error by assuming that there has always been a category of human thought and belief that is religious. It is probable that for a long time in man's development – tens of thousands of years – there was no separation between the sacred and the non-sacred, the supernatural and what we would call reality.

When humanity was in its earliest phases, haunting caves, they almost certainly did not set aside time and specific spaces for sacred practices. All experience would have been mixed together seamlessly in their minds. The spirit world passed freely through the cave walls and human imagination was similarly free. The universe was one, multifaceted but an indivisible substance. Creation was all equally marvellous and inexplicable. A god could be anywhere and everywhere. For this reason, it didn't need a name or an effigy.

At some point of prehistory, the gods were invented or discovered as something apart from the rest of life. Why were they needed? Because people began to feel their individuality. They felt detached very slightly from each other and from the universe they inhabited. They perceived the passage of time and they needed explanations for that for which they had no inner, instinctive understanding. Early gods must certainly have had to do with those concerns that went beyond common sense and everyday routine.

"How did nature come to be the way it is?" they must have asked. "How can we know what is coming tomorrow?" "What will the weather be like in the growing season? Will this be a year of abundance or hunger?" "How is it decided when a man or

Fountain, Auch

Druids Ancient and Modern

Almost nothing is known for sure about the priesthood of the Gauls, the Druids, a professional elite that advised and steered tribal society from around the 4th century BC to the 2nd century AD. More than merely intermediaries between the people and the gods, they seem also to have performed the functions of judges, soothsayers, teachers and natural philosophers.

They deliberately passed their wisdom down by word of mouth, both to keep their mysteries in chosen hands and to train the memory – what use is tradition if it isn't held in the mind? A lack of writing also limited embellishments and rhetoric.

As a result, a sophisticated culture has been entirely lost to the collective memory of humanity.

All we know about the Druids is what we are told by Greek and Roman writers who were all outsiders and sometimes hostile to native culture. Details in these writings are scarce and not necessarily reliable. The only description of a Druidic ceremony comes from Pliny the Elder who explains that, on the sixth day of a new moon, a Druid in white robes would climb an oak tree to cut the sacred mistletoe plant down with a golden sickle. The mistletoe was caught below the tree in a white cloak and two white bulls would be slaughtered.

Since their disappearance there has been much speculation about them and a great deal of invention.

In the 18th century, concurrent with the inception of freemasonry and other secret societies, a Celtic revival began and new Druidic groups were formed. They aimed to satisfy a growing need for spirituality and a re-connection with nature, to emphasize that man is not the centre of the universe but a part of it, and to re-establish the nature of sacredness. There are now around a dozen organizations operating in Brittany, considered to be the remaining Celtic homeland of France, claiming to be the heirs to ancient knowledge.

They celebrate eight great festivals a year, four to do with the sun and four with the moon:
- **Samhain:** early November, the living meet the dead;
- **Alban Arthan** (winter solstice): around December 21, the festival of the great birth;
- **Imbolc:** early February, the festival of the mother goddess Brigantia, and of fertility;
- **Alban Eilir** (spring equinox): around March 21, the festival of the Seed Sowing;
- **Beltaine:** early May, the festival of the father Fire;
- **Alban Hefin** (summer solstice): around June 21, the festival of the Sun and the god Belenos;
- **Lughnasadh:** early August, union of heaven and the earth, the festival of the god Lug;
- **Alban Elfed** (autum equinox): around September 21, the festival of the Harvest and of prosperity.

It can be hard to know where traditional knowledge ends, and "invented" or contrived knowledge begins – but perhaps it doesn't matter.

---

woman dies; when woman or an animal conceives and gives birth; or when a sick person is consumed by disease or cured by a witch-doctor's spells and medicine?"

Intellectually there developed a distinction between that which was predictable and explicable, and the supernatural, between the comprehensible and the mysterious. To ask "what causes these things?" was too abstract a question. "Who causes them?" made much more sense to the human mind. We ask many of the same questions today and, for all our modern knowledge, we cannot always be sure which cause goes with which effect. Instead we prefer to suppose that the answers must be to do with forces or laws at work rather than deities.

Stories and Writing

This separation between the sacred and profane must have happened first in storytelling. The tribe's ancestral lore would be passed down in tales. Oral tradition, however, does not bring gods fully down to the ground.

Storytelling keeps the gods alive, fluid, ethereal, changing and slightly detached from the earth. It draws on the imagination of the shaman and the devotee, and remakes the divinity at each recital of his deeds.

A crucial development in religion was the introduction of deliberate, meaningful image-making. The earliest pictures and statues may well have been nothing more than figurative representation of reality. As a result over the course of prehistory, we can suppose, the human mind learned to think on two levels at once. The artist's hands produced images that were more than superficial appearance: they were metaphors, visual packages with meanings used for precise purposes.

A statue reduces a god to human terms

Door decoration, Toulouse

and forces change upon religion. It fixes his appearance outside of the storyteller's imagination and gives him a permanent, concrete form. It also occupies space. The image of the god must be kept somewhere and so a home (shrine) is created for it. This leads automatically to the notion of special sacred places being set aside in which to worship the gods, or question them. These locations needed protecting and managing, and they had to be overseen by priests, an elite like the Druids, who devised their own rules for the cult.

All this happened before the introduction of writing, which had an even more tectonic effect on the spirit world.

Writing pins the ethereal story down; it records it and stores it. Once written, it cannot be spontaneously remade with each new telling of the story. Even the briefest inscription on the base of the statue of a God summarizes him for human convenience.

We find it hard to understand the enormity of this. We cannot remember now how to think without words and the abstract concepts they enable us to formulate. We rely so much on writing ourselves that we base our judgements on it. If it is not written down, we reason, it cannot matter much. We belittle tales that were told around firesides long ago because we cannot know anything about them. Their memory is lost. Texts, however, we can study and argue over for eternity.

We thus concentrate on understanding religion in its recorded forms while forgetting that this always implies that someone was keen to own and control the gods, and to perpetuate an official version of them. "Institutionalized" religion and science both make the same mistake: analysis changes the human relationship with divinity. It pins down, objectifies it; it makes it concrete and dogmatic when it was never any of these things.

The culture of Gaul before the arrival of the Romans was entirely oral and visual.

What we know or think we know about comes almost entirely from the writing of the conquering civilisation. Roman authors – Julius Caesar in particular – saw and reported what they wanted to, in their own interests. They compared the religion they found to the one they had brought with them and did what they could to replace indigenous gods with their own superior pantheon.

As a result, we know very little about the specific gods worshipped in Gaul before 58 BC. We have various names, attributes, effigies and traditions which do not always go together – yet a great deal can be inferred by looking at the evidence and inside ourselves. We all have our blind beliefs.

Even if we regard religion as irrational or even ignorant, it can still make sense because it is a manifestation of the human condition.

The Preference for Polytheism

The Gauls were polytheistic. To believe in more than one god is more natural for human beings than monotheism. Existence has many aspects to it and our lives are fragmented; how could one god cope with everything all at the same time? How could he possibly see and hear everything? Even if there were only one god, he would have to delegate tasks to subordinates and that would mean lending them godly powers. Besides, what are you supposed to do if you don't get on with the only god available? It was logical that there must be a team or panoply of gods to choose from. And so we see a range of gods so that there would be one to suit each tribe, family, household and person.

In any society living close to the earth, the gods must correspond to the same set of archetypal, pantheistic concerns. For instance, there has to be a deity associated with the sun, the moon, fertility, death, and the sky – to personify the unpredictable violence of thunder storms and lightning.

To be of use, a god has to be amenable. He must be somewhat like us, otherwise he would not understand our concerns; but he must not be too like us. If he is remote – living in some distant galaxies – he won't be able to hear us or take an interest in our affairs. If he is too ordinary, he won't have the supernatural power to help us or to influence other gods when we need him to.

A balance of plausibility needs to be struck. To make him real, a god must have a life like we do. He needs a place of residence, a companion, a family, a slot in the celestial hierarchy and a back story, including an origin.

This quasi-humanness gives the god his personality. If he can feel what we feel, then he is capable of having likes and dislikes, moods, caprices and weaknesses and emotions – anger, jealousy etc., – on the higher plane on which he lives.

The gods must be able to provide a complete explanation for birth, death, famine, conflict, and all the other ingredients of human life.

Gods, however, are not static entities; they are fluid and adaptable. They migrate from culture to culture and evolve according to the needs of those who inherit them, changing their names and appearances

Doorknocker, Marciac

but keeping their essential personalities and attributes.

For example, the Romans inherited some of their gods from Egypt, Persia and Greece, and they spread knowledge of these gods to the territories they colonized.

The outward-form religion is syncretic, built by absorbing elements of previous faiths, and Christianity is no different. Religious mythology is always hybridized and entwined with earlier stories; it is never entirely original.

The accepted story is that Christianity supplanted all existing religions in France during the first millennium; in effect, that it out-competed them. In fact things were – and are – not that simple.

The process of establishing the new religion was not a smooth transition from a chaos of multiple beliefs to a simple single belief.

Any colonizing and proselytizing religion – as Christianity was in its first millennium – must either eradicate pre-existing belief systems, by force if necessary, or adapt them to its own end. It must also adapt itself to seem more appealingly familiar.

The Arrival of Christianity

When Christianity arrived in Gaul around the 2nd or 3rd century, it found a land of multifarious paganism, a quaint inchoate patchwork of faiths.

Christianity itself was not a fixed and unified creed with all the details agreed. It did not offer a "take it or leave it" replacement of one God for all the existing deities.

The Christianization of France was an *ad hoc* arrangement that required compromise on both sides and, it could be said, ended in only a nominal victory. The question is: did paganism adapt itself more to Christianity or did Christianity adapt itself more to paganism?

The people of Gaul already had a deep rooted set of beliefs which they didn't abandon altogether. These beliefs had been shaping and reshaping themselves in the collective psyche from the time of the cave dwellers through the period of megalith buildings to the development of the tribes of pre-Roman Gaul. They had been carried by an invisible perennial thread of belief from the earliest people to the present, communicated verbally through myths and tales and imagery.

Statue, Albi

The Gods Become Decoration

For centuries, the Catholic Church worked hard to eradicate paganism from France. In church art, non-Christian deities were converted into saints or else shown as monsters. Everywhere, though, were remnants of the Gallo-Roman civilization that had left behind representations of its gods.

In the Middle Ages, paganism began to creep back into Europe. The teachings of Plato and Aristotle fascinated scholars and, if they were to become respectable, the heathen worlds that had produced them had to be accommodated by the Church. Soon a comprehensive knowledge of Greek and Roman mythology became an indispensable part of western education – as long as the educated person continued to pay lip-service to the one permitted religion.

The Renaissance made free use of pagan gods for its own artistic ends. Stories about them were more dramatic and colourful than the lives of saints. They provided useful metaphors for human affairs and Renaissance artists regarded mythology as a source book of allusion and allegory. Representations of the Christian God were discouraged at this time – they are rare in churches (see p194) – but depictions of pagan gods on secular buildings soon became commonplace.

Classical deities achieved a new immortality in the decoration of mansions and palaces. The Château of Versailles has rooms named after Venus, Diana, Mercury and Hercules, and the Sun King equated himself with Apollo or Phoebus, the shining one. The *Île Feydeau* in Nantes is particularly known for its mascarons, sculpted faces of often hideous or wild spirits of the sea, bearded winds and classical personalities such as Bacchus with grape vines in his hair.

In the Enlightenment, the ancient gods fitted in comfortably with rational thinking. They were safe because they were obviously fictitious. They provided a useful source of metaphor, and a fascination with them did not feed popular superstition or prop up the power of the Church.

Gods are still everywhere on the buildings of France, although most people have lost the ability to identify them. They appear on doorknockers; keystones above windows; and caryatids holding up the balconies. A basic knowledge of mythology is indispensable for perceiving the deeper layers of meaning in any decorated château, art gallery or even a grand public monument such as the *Arc de Triomphe*.

La Depêche du Midi building, Toulouse

Fountain, Saint-Savin, Pyrenees

Polytheism is persistent. Attempts to reduce the number of gods and simplify them rarely work. Everywhere in France, people had specific deities to whom they turned in times of need. These became saints, many of whom are entirely mythological and thinly disguised versions of nature spirits that have been personified.

The solution to this was "Christian interpretation". Elements of the old religion that could not be eradicated were incorporated into Christianity under assumed identities. Gods became saints – especially those with scant or vague biographical details. Shrines became churches, cults continued with only a little modification to make them acceptable.

Christianity thus systematized what was there before and added its own ingredient. The forces of tradition do not just wither away to be replaced by something entirely new. Tradition remained in the minds and mouths of the people; they didn't care about the particular names they had to use. Christianity, like any religion, is about the same basic concerns of life as always: fertility, enough to eat, freedom from illness. Much of the earlier, ancestral religion flowed into Christianity and has never gone away.

At the same time as absorbing existing beliefs, Christianity was honing its own story. Not everything we think of today as being indisputably Christian is in the New Testament.

There were many gaps to be filled in by the church fathers and the development of religion was steered by human decisions as much as divine revelations. Problems of faith – such as what was and was not heresy – were decided by powerful individuals or church councils, or by reference to apocryphal documents written long after Biblical events. Some lengthy reasoning was necessary if the religion was to makes sense.

Eventually the church established a monopoly on superstition with a coherent narrative. The same eternal needs therefore had to be channelled through it, in its language, directed to the cast of characters it appointed and sanctioned. But it couldn't stamp out all the old ways completely.

Today Christianity in France could be described as a polytheistic heterogeneity masquerading as monotheistic conformity orthodoxy, with the accepted formulae of words disguising a complexity that never went away. Christianity is not something outstandingly new and discontinuous but part of a theological thread stretching back to prehistory.

Keystone head, Toulouse

Caryatids, Toulouse

From Goddess to the Black Virgin

The Goddess tradition seems to go back to the beginning of human consciousness and, although it derives mainly from the Near East and North Africa, it also has its endemic counterpart. The people of the Paleolithic left behind them puzzling little statuettes of women known as "Venus figurines". Made of carved wood, bone, or fired clay, they are often rounded, naked, explicit in their anatomical detail and sometimes pregnant. For want of a better explanation, they are assumed to be female deities. Several of these figurines have been found in France, including the Venuses of **Lespugue** (in the Pyrenean foothills, **Brassempouy** (the Landes) and **Laussel** (Dordogne). All of them are now in museums.

The goddess stands for certain traits that complement the masculine. She is, above all, a deity for planet Earth, our home, and Nature. As such, she champions not mere survival here, but thriving. Sex and fertility, vital to the health of any community for both human beings and animals, is also within the domain of the Goddess.

In the heavens, Venus and the moon are also symbolically feminine. The latter provides us with a natural measure of the passing of time, not in the linear way that prevails in the modern world, but as cycles that repeat. Time, she reminds us, is not something in short supply, to be wasted and regretted, but to be experienced as a repeating rhythm.

The goddess, of course, also represents all other female qualities, including being rather than doing; acceptance of what cannot be changed; respect for life; compassion; co-operation in groups rather than focusing on individuality and competition; relationship with other people and other beings; holism; the senses; intuition and other ways of knowing; humility (but not

Vals church, Ariège

humiliation) – in other words everything to do with the difficult balancing act of being a conscious human being.

Along with being nurturing, the feminine is also healing. The principle of all healing is to tune into the natural, the autonomous, the self-restorative, the sensitive, and so to restore balance throughout the organism.

The goddess also has two great pieces of wisdom to complement the dictates of masculine gods. We must always strive for balance, she says. It is important to correct a faulty course and mitigate folly rather than persist in it. The goddess is also about mystery. She is about not knowing and not being able to know. She is the awareness of the paradoxical wisdom that much of life is incomprehensible.

The Virgin Mary

The Virgin Mary is far from being a straightforward figure with a simple identity. We think we see her in sharp focus because we have seen so many paintings of her; but all of these deceive us. In art, she is always depicted as a grown woman, serene, centred, unselfconscious and in control as if she is the model of a wise and experienced mother, yet it would be more in keeping with Jewish tradition of the time for her to be around 14 years old, the age of Bernadette Soubirous when she saw her visions.

That is, if she existed at all. She is not a historical character. As far as we know, she exists only in the pages of the New Testament. Even then, there are only a few mentions of her, mostly to do with the birth of Christ. We first hear about her when she is betrothed to be married to Joseph. The angel Gabriel appears to her to tell her that she will miraculously conceive a son. For the rest of Christ's life, she is in the background of events, a minor character whose main purpose in the story is already achieved. There is virtually nothing in the gospels about Jesus's childhood when Mary must be assumed to have played an important role, and she plays no part in the development of the early church, which was entrusted to men, the Apostles.

Gradually, though, in the first centuries of Christianity, her identity solidified and amplified as if it were necessary to make her more real. The cult of Mary flourished in Byzantium, in the east. The scant textual details in the gospels were turned into a rounded personality and biography. Dates were set for the main events in her life – Purification, Annunciation, Visitation – and she was allocated a birthday (September 8, no one knows why). She was also given a mother of her own, St Anne, and a suggested lineage.

The finer logic of doctrine was argued out. If she gave birth to divinity, it was reasoned, she must be "the Mother of God" as confirmed by the Council of Ephesus in 431, and from that it followed that she was divine herself. It was therefore ruled by the church that she did not die a mortal death but that her body and soul were "assumed" into heaven intact. Another theological loophole was closed in 1854, shortly before Bernadette's apparitions, when she was declared to be of "immaculate conception", that is born biologically but in such a way

Virgin, Musée de Cluny, Paris

Mosaic, Lourdes

as to make her soul free of original sin.

Today, she is revered in French Catholicism as much as Christ himself. There are around 600 holy sites – churches, chapels, country shrines, convents and monasteries, pilgrimage centres – dedicated to her cult as universal and perfect mother, and mediator between humanity and God.

One aspect of Mary that often confuses non-Catholics is her multifarious manifestations. She is not one thing but many things. Seldom called simply The Virgin Mary, she is usually referred to as "Our Lady" of whatever it is that she watches over. While she always remains a virgin mother, the characteristics of her identity shift each time.

There is an "Our Lady" for hermits, cyclists, sailors (and another when they are ship-wrecked), travellers, the poor and rugby players. She is also the sacred figure for high places, low places, fields, vineyards, woods, the end of the bridge and the end of the earth, islands, rocks, heaths, marshes and the underground. There are Virgins offering hope, joy, succour for the afflicted, compassion, consolation, mercy and good health. The Virgin is also associated with a range of other subjects including snows, storms, bread, solitude, work and victory. Each has a story to tell which begins with the common Christian dogma and ends with some tale of miracles and particularly of powers that inspire local devotees and set her apart from all the rest.

In almost every case, Mary is not just an essence, an ethereal being who is believed to have lived once but is now in heaven interceding from on high. She is also an effigy, a statue of wood, carved in three dimensions, painted and dressed. This statue is not a representation of her but is her, or, more correctly, an aspect of her. Many of these statues date from the Middle Ages (or are copies of medieval statues) but others are of more ancient and obscure origin.

One aspect of these statues is particularly intriguing. Mary is often shown as a black or at least very dark-skinned woman. Some of the most venerated effigies of Mary are Black Virgins, as at Chartres, Le Puy-en-Velay and Rocamadour. There are thought to be 450 Black Virgins in Europe of which 180 are in France.

Why the Virgin Mary should be shown as being black, no one is certain. For a long time no one was much interested in the phenomenon. For art historians, it wasn't a subject worthy of serious study, and for the Church, the question of skin colour is irrelevant. Some priests would deny that their virgins were black or played down the importance. "Blackened by centuries of candle-smoke" or simply the process of wood ageing was a common explanation.

It is now clear that Black Virgins were not coloured by circumstance but by deliberate intent. It has been suggested that

Mary is shown as black because she was from the Middle East and the colour of the statues shows ideas brought back by returning Crusaders; but this theory does not stand up to examination. In the Middle Ages, when the Black Virgins were carved, it was widely known that Middle Eastern Jews were not black-skinned. Could the images not have come from Africa then, where it would be only natural to show Mary as a black woman? There is simply no evidence for any ancient image of the Black Virgin being made outside Europe; besides, most of the images are known to have been made near where they now reside, out of local wood by local craftsmen.

These statues hint that there is more to Mary than the woman at the centre of the Christian nativity story. It is probable that she is a blend of the Biblical figure and traditions of the goddesses of the ancient world. This synthesis came about to meet a need. There was a glaring imbalance in the Christian religion. The name Mary would be given to an existing goddess and the qualities and personalities of the two merged.

Christianity is essentially a male religion and its deity would have been seen by pagans as a version of the sun god, reborn each year around the time of the winter solstice when light returns to the world. What was lacking was his female counterpart and, as Jesus was unmarried, his mother had to fill this role. The goddess in paganism is the deity of the night, darkness, the cave, unknowing, mystery, and also of wisdom. This goddess is not a single figure with just one aspect, but multifarious which explains why there can be so many "versions" of Mary. Black Virgins almost certainly derive from dark-skinned depictions of ancient goddesses passed from culture to culture until they arrived in medieval France. In her, we can see especially Isis, Cybele and Diana but also, plausibly, Lilith, Lamia, Inanna, Kali, Neith, Anath, Hathor, Sekhmet and the Queen of Sheba.

There are matters which you cannot discuss with a male deity. Mary/the goddess is more approachable than her son. Traditionally she provides an ear to mothers, especially, and to those who do not feel that a man can comprehend their suffering.

Black virgin, Chartres

Saint-Bertrand-de-Comminges

VI

Awake in Dreams
An Initiation to the Temples of the Romanesque

Detail of the porch, Moissac Abbey

Just after the turn of the millennium, the people of the Middle Ages began building extraordinary churches in great number. What was behind this urge to house their religion? Romanesque churches nowadays may look quaint and naïve but do they enshrine wisdoms if we can only approach them in the right way?

Just after the turn of the first millennium, something extraordinary happened in France. Church-building fever took hold of the land. Between 1050 and 1350, according to the medievalist Jean Gimpel, 80 cathedrals were erected, together with 500 large churches and tens of thousands of parish churches. In three centuries, the country quarried more stone than Ancient Egypt in a thousand years. It was as if Christianity had emerged from the first millennium with a new source of energy and a determination to make its presence permanent.

There had been earlier churches but there were never that many of them and they survive mostly as parts of later buildings. Mostly they were baptisteries (designed for the mass baptism of adults), oratories or funerary chapels. They seem now like the tentative steps of a new religion finding its architectural way. They are, in the main, unsophisticated but nevertheless atmospheric buildings that soon became redundant or else were incorporated into later churches, sometimes as crypts. Good examples can be seen in **Poitiers**, **Metz**, **Fréjus**, **Aix-en-Provence** and **Grenoble**. The oldest church in France is believed to be *Saint-Pierre-aux-Nonnains* in Metz, built in 380, although subsequently altered.

From the mid 11th century, however, new churches appeared as if they were coming off a medieval production line. With many of them being built simultaneously, the country must have resembled a fragmented building site. How France was able to mobilize itself to this extent we can only guess. Some of the necessary architectural knowledge must have come from studying remaining Roman buildings, or else was imported from Italy and Byzantium; but this doesn't sufficiently explain how so many trained master builders, stonemasons and artists could have become available at the rate needed to keep the works going. Much must have been achieved by determination and trial and error. Each generation of craftsman tried to improve on the work of its predecessors. Their achievements with what we would consider rudimentary tools of measurement and construction are nonetheless magnificent today.

While some churches are copies of others, and influences clearly travelled from building site to building site, there was also a huge impetus towards innovation and developments in architecture followed each other at an extraordinary pace.

What we see now are the finished buildings that have endured and it is easy to forget that medieval ecclesiastical construction was not just a matter of executing a vision with the right calculations, but also required experimentation. Structures could and did fall down through faulty design, robbing us of some wonderful architecture.

To these disasters must be added the losses to the effects of fire and weathering; the attacks of Protestant forces during the Wars of Religion; the anticlerical demolitions of the Revolution – in which much building stone was pillaged or sold off; the trade in antiquities which saw many exquisitely carved cloister capitals shipped to the USA; and the explosive power of two World Wars. In sum, what we see today is only a fraction of what there once was. Too

> "A church is a precise instrument with a length, width, height and contents determined in harmony with the heaven and the earth. If one of these things is missing, is inaccurate, the church doesn't work: it would be as if you were stepping into a barn. If the building is not sited where it should be or turns its back on the current of this world, then the bread remains bread, the wind remains piquette and men remain pagans." —Henri Vincenot

many fine abbeys and their cloisters now stand in ruins, or have vanished altogether.

Despite all this, there are an estimated 100,000 religious buildings in France, around two thirds of which are medieval. In parts of the country they are so common that the less distinctive ones barely get remarked on, yet even these are extraordinary buildings full of interest. Most are open to the public: if the door is locked, the local town hall will often furnish the key.

Shedding Preconceptions

Churches are usually described according to their status in the ecclesiastical hierarchy, century of construction and, above all, style. Every medieval church in France can be classified either as essentially Romanesque, Gothic or as a transition between the two. These are terms invented and applied after the Middle Ages for the convenience of architectural historians and, if we place too much weight on them, they reduce a church to one material dimension. They are, in any case, often misleading since most churches are an accumulation of building projects in different styles from different periods of history.

To approach a church with a textbook of architecture in your hand, however, is to miss something fundamental about it before you step inside. A sacred building is not just a structure built at a particular time and place for a particular patron and in the service of a particular variation of a particular religion. It is more than that, more even than its function or how it has been used over the centuries or is used today. Before all that, it is the embodiment of an intention. It is a symbol and an idea.

It is hard not to approach a church loaded with preconceptions. We are influenced, in a general sense, by the times we live in. Today, we very often see a church first and foremost as a tourist attraction, or at least somewhere to while away a time in a state of disinterested curiosity. Some churches stand out for their architectural reputations – the guidebook tells us how much we should esteem them – but others simply seem like nondescript anachronisms occupying valuable space in the town centres: under-frequented remnants of an age before consumerism and freedom of belief.

Former abbey church of Larreule

Added to the cultural context are our personal beliefs and feelings. Whether we arrive with faith or atheistic scepticism (or even cynicism), we are armed with expectations about what we will find within. We freely generalize about religion and by extension, about the house of religion; it is easy to forget that a religion is not the same everywhere, at all times, in all its manifestations. Every church is both part of a pattern and a one-off. If we don't remember this, it will be impossible to see the church as it is, as all that it is.

The time and conditions of a visit also matter; not just the time of day or year but the time of life. A church is completely different when entering as a young person on a sunny morning, rather than as an ageing person on a gloomy, overcast, stormy evening.

If we are to see the church as it is, not how we perceive it to be, we must become aware of all our preconceptions and everything we have heard or read (however expert the source) and put all this information to one side. This way, you can allow yourself to see the church afresh, both its visible and invisible aspects, using your outward and inward senses. The aim is to have your own direct, singular personal experience of the church in the present. Visit it in any other moment and it will be different again; you will be different; and you will see more.

The next step is to try to see the church as it is, in its totality: in more than one dimension. A religious building cannot be reduced to its architecture, the works of art it contains, or even the ceremonies undertaken within it. To see it in any one of these ways alone is to miss the essence that unites its parts. It is everything it is at the same time: its shell, adornment, contents, history and use. It is the static structure and the shifting activity in and around it; the stale and the living; death and human commotion. It also now contains you. When you enter a church, you too become a small, temporary part of it.

Characteristics of the Temple

Going one step beyond the totality of the building, the church is, of course, a Christian house of prayer with a name, address, dedication and other attributes. But before, that it is something more universal, a temple, an archetypal sacred space.

A temple is unlike any other building in its function. It does not supply a purely earthly need; it is only half to do with this world.

Unlike the painted caves and megaliths (if we assume these had a religious purpose) and the sacred hills, springs and groves of prehistoric pantheism, a temple is a permanent, enclosed, roofed construction structure set apart from ordinary lives for the

Tympanum, Moissac

Champagnolles church, Charente-Maritime

purposes of communing with the divine. It works on two levels – as an exoteric or physical structure, and as an esoteric entity.

In metaphor, the temple has been described as a book or a ship in which to travel to the supernatural realm. It can also be thought as a bridge between the mundane and the sublime. Although this temple has been fabricated by human beings, if it has been made well and properly maintained, it is a repository of knowledge, a giant battery of wisdom.

There is a clear division between space outside and inside the temple. Outside is the common, familiar world, but inside is a place in which secrets and mysteries are kept, and gods are offered a home on earth. It is where contemplation is possible,

and rituals can be held.

The temple does not appear the same to all people who enter it. Someone who is initiated into the mysteries of the temple knows how to cross its threshold in a suitable way in order to "activate" the building and communicate with it.

Once inside, there are rules of behaviour to be observed. Thoughts, speech, action and group interaction take on particular meanings and human consciousness is different to the outside. Whether you are initiated or not, it can take time to adjust to the temple and tune in to its rhythms. You need to settle yourself inside and open yourself to the space in which you now stand or sit.

To understand and appreciate the tem-

Chi Ro

Often seen carved in stone over country church doorways, the Chi Ro (*chrisme* in French) is an ancient Christian symbol made up of the juxtaposition of the Greek capital letters P (ro) and X (khi), standing for the name *Christos*. Usually, the letters for alpha and omega are added to denote the beginning and end of everything, and the letter S winds around the bottom part of the vertical line through the centre. Most Chi Ros are enclosed by a circle but some are set in a square frame. They all follow this basic pattern but each one is slightly different.

The meaning of this symbol seems simple and clear – "this is a place dedicated to the cult of Jesus Christ". Constantine is supposed to have seen it in a dream, and had it emblazoned on his standard, the *laburnum*, before winning a decisive battle on 312 AD.

It seems, however, that the juxtaposition of the Khi and Ro predates Christianity and there are suggestions that it is of pagan origins. What looks like a "P" may be an adaptation of the Egyptian symbol for immortality, the *ankh*. The "S" is not easy to interpret but it suggests the serpents that wind their way up the Caduceus symbol.

The writer and mystery-hunter, Louis Charpentier, questioned whether the Chi Ro was meant to be read alphabetically at all and if it is, whether it doesn't spell out some word other than the name of Christ. Several symbols can be perceived within the Chi Ro including St Andrew's Cross (composed of two diagonal lines) and a six-pointed star.

Another theory is that the Chi Ro encodes astronomical information. In some early versions, the lines of the "X" do not form neat right angles but in fact constitute a diagram of the crossing of the two great circles of heaven: the imaginary lines which trace earth's elliptical orbit around the sun and the celestial equator.

For Charpentier, it is a sign carved by initiated craftsmen to be read by brothers who come after them. It may, he says, show a particular variation of the pilgrimage route to Santiago de Compostela for those who can decipher it. Another possibility is that it is a quality stamp placed on the church to show that the building has been constructed according to the traditional sacred methods, as it were, a cosmic signature of approval.

Lintel, Lemé church

ple (especially as a non-initiated outsider), it is important to know that everything about it and in it is deliberate, even if this is not at first obvious. The temple is an accumulation of the purpose, intention, hopes and desires of those who planned and built it. Nothing is casual or spontaneous; or included by chance, frivolity, or merely out of a desire for beautification.

This intentionality begins with the site, which was chosen, often before records were kept, because of some feature or property. The temple may stand over a spring, on a mound, over a current of earth energy or some other place imbued with spiritual qualities.

The temple is not meant to be a place that is quick and easy to understand, either inside or out. It does not serve up blatant, superficial truths. It is a place of hidden things and ambiguities. It speaks through symbolism. Everything you see in it is not to be taken literally but to be seen through and interpreted.

There are two reasons for "hiding" information in symbols. One is that it is impossible to talk about the other world in any other way. Truths about it cannot be named, summarized and reduced to words. Instead, symbols allude to it.

The other reason for rendering the sacred using symbols is that metaphysical insights are only understood and digested if it requires some effort of mind to reach them. A church is to be visited slowly; to be gazed at and meditated upon, first without questions, then, perhaps, with questions which may have no answers. Disengage the questioning brain and we may just perceive the numinous in some corner or detail.

Everything about the church is symbolic, beginning with its orientation which has been chosen for geomantic reasons. All churches in France "point" east. In the west, this is usually said to be a way of indicating Jerusalem but it is also, of course, the direction of the rising sun. Many churches do not point precisely east and, where there is a variation, it is usually to mark the position of the rising sun on the feast day of the saint to whom the church is dedicated.

Romanesque Churches

As temples, the Romanesque churches of France are not just places of Christian worship but sacred enclosures in the universal sense. Indeed, Romanesque was used almost purely as a religious style of architecture. Of all the many hundreds of buildings that survive hardly any – less than half a dozen – are civic buildings.

Romanesque churches are found throughout France but not everywhere. They have a distinct geographical bias to them, being heavily concentrated in Burgundy and the south. This distribution probably indicates areas that felt a greater sense of security and stability in the 11th and 12th centuries, and it coincides with the pilgrimage routes to Santiago de Compostela, which carried Romanesque ideas from northeast to southwest France along with the tide of travellers.

The most important Romanesque buildings were the churches of abbeys. The largest Romanesque church in Europe – and perhaps the world – is Saint-Sernin, the remnant of an abbey in Toulouse. Sadly, the great and influential monastery of Cluny is no more than a ruined remnant of its former self but the church of the Sacré-Cœur in Paray-le-Monial gives an idea of what it was once like. Another large abbey church in Burgundy is Vézelay, a place of pilgrimage and starting point for even longer pilgrimages. Provence has three great Romanesque abbeys: Silvacane, Thoronet and Sénanque. Also worth visiting is the royal abbey complex of Fontevraud even if it is also now a hotel, restaurant and entertainment venue. Beneath Gothic superstructures, meanwhile, there are often Romanesque crypts to be discovered, as at Dijon, Chartres and Mont St Michel.

The best Romanesque churches, however, are not those which are large, conspicuous and urban but those which are more modest. Romanesque excels outside the limelight and it is a true delight to come across some out-of-the-way church that is not discussed at length in architectural encyclopedias and travel guides.

In some regions, small, uncelebrated Romanesque churches are thick on the ground. Within a 25-km radius of the town of Saintes in Poitou-Charentes, for example, there are around 150 Romanesque churches, many of them elaborately sculpted. Very few of these churches are known beyond the region, or much visited. There are many small country churches in other parts of France, often not large enough to require a resident priest.

The charm of such a church may not lie in its being an outstanding piece of architecture but in its defiance of categorization and its atmosphere of undisturbed spiritual peace. To get an obscure church to yourself for as long as you like can be more rewarding than visiting a cathedral in which every last detail has been pored over by an art historian and which is always overrun with visitors.

Romanesque churches show a blend of pious and pagan influences in their architecture and decoration. Self-evident Christian iconography mingles with imagery that is bewildering and inscrutable. Many churches are quirky, puzzling, intriguing and idiosyncratic. Several of them stand out for some feature or other: *Lescar* (near Pau) for its mosaics; *Saint-Savin-sur-Gartempe* in Poitou-Charentes for its paintings; *Conques* and *Autun* for their *tympanums*; *Talmont* for its location above the low cliffs on the bank of the Gironde estuary near **Bordeaux**. Some Romanesque churches – *Jumièges* in Normandy and *Alet-les-Bains* in the Aude – are now picturesque ruins, but decay adds something to their appeal. While all Romanesque churches have an esoteric story to tell, some stand out from the rest in this sense, such as the *Église Saint-Barthélémy* in Bénévent-l'Abbaye (Creuse).

There may be similarities between some of these buildings – influences that have travelled with itinerant builders – but no two churches are the same. Every Romanesque church could be said to be at once an experimental and experiential building: step through the door after 800 years and you feel something even if you are not sure what.

Too often Romanesque is seen as the precursor of Gothic, almost as if it were an apprenticeship that comes before a masterwork. To see it like this – as primitive, naïve, somehow lacking – is to get caught up in architectural techniques and fail to see Romanesque as it really is. The elements of a Romanesque church and the atmosphere they create do not necessarily amount to anything less than a Gothic cathedral; they are simply of a different nature. Romanesque does, however, presage a transition that eventually led Western Europe from one vision of spirituality to another. At the same time, it conserves something valuable that must not be lost: the dark, cool, quiet, intimate sacred space that is the echo of the cave of the earth goddess.

Angel, Saint-Sernin, Toulouse

Axiat church, Ariège

Romanesque Sculpture: dreams, nightmares and monsters in stone

Capital, Église Sainte-Croix, Oloron-Sainte-Marie

"What are these fantastic monsters doing in the cloisters under the very eyes of the brothers as they read?" wrote St Bernard of Clairvaux, the great promoter of the Cistercian order in the 12th century, referring to the art he saw around him in churches, cathedrals and abbeys. "What is the meaning of these unclean monkeys, strange savage lions and monsters? To what purpose are here placed these creatures, half beast, half man? I see several bodies with one head and several heads with one body. Here is a quadruped with a serpent's head, there a fish with a quadruped's head, then again an animal half horse, half goat... Surely if we do not blush for such absurdities we should at least regret what we have spent on them."

St Bernard was not referring to Biblical subject matter. Most Romanesque stone carving depicts people and events from the Bible, or at least draws on Christian tradition. Nowadays, we may need some information to explain what we are seeing but to medieval eyes the carvings would have been recognisable renderings of familiar stories repeated in church and out of it. The Seven Deadly Sins, Adam and Eve, the Wise and Foolish Virgins, the lives of the saints, and events in the life of Christ were all the standard homilies of how to live a good life.

These scenes adorn facades (Notre-Dame-la-Grande in Poitiers, Vézelay, Saint-Gilles-du-Gard, Angoulême); portals (Autun, Saint-Trophime in Arles, Saint-Gilles-du-Gard, Saint-Sernin, Moissac, Charlieu); capitals in naves and around choirs (Serrabone, Rieux-Minervois, Chauvigny, Saint-Sernin in Toulouse); cloisters (Moissac, Saint-Trophime again, Saint-Bertrand-de-Comminges); apses (Rioux); lintels (Saint-Génis-des-Fontaines); and columns (Souillac, Souvigny) can be seen in various lumps of stone now standing in museums such as the Musée de Cluny in Paris.

Neither was St Bernard complaining about the decorative details that accompanied these stone illustrations – floral motifs, knot and scroll work – nor those subjects with a precise, Christian symbolic value such as animals, human heads and signs of the zodiac.

What perplexed and outraged St Bernard is what makes Romanesque stone sculpture so remarkable. Along with the religious iconography is a great deal of

Face puller, Oloron-Sainte-Marie

Corbels, Lescar

graphic content that seems to have nothing to do with Christianity. Monsters and nightmares abound and male and female figures expose their genitals or disport themselves in lewd or even erotic postures.

Such subjects are often, but not always, placed way above head height on corbels – blocks of stone protruding from beneath the eaves, particularly around the apse (the rounded east end of the church). A pair of binoculars or a telephoto lens helps to see them in more detail.

Many out-of-the-way country churches, particularly in the southwest, have such mini-masterpieces that would be considered great art if they were signed by an ironic, iconoclastic, atheistic modern day sculptor and placed in a fashionable art gallery.

If an explanation is given for these incongruous, very unchristian sculptures, it is usually that they are strictures against bad behaviour - a catalogue of dependable ways for the already-fearful medieval peasant to get to hell. The trouble with this idea is that it is not usually clear whether the artist is condemning sin or celebrating it. The sculptures suggest that there was another side to medieval life, one that revelled in earthy pleasures rather than trying to avoid them. Perhaps the stone mason was commissioned to supply moralizing sermons but used his skill to deliver titillating works that could be read either way: as warnings or winks to his fellow villagers below.

This ambivalence may be the reason why Romanesque art is much described by experts in general terms but little interpreted or explained. Decoration is, by definition, superfluous to the architecture and, if it is not easily intelligible, then we must accept it as an enigma and ignore it.

The trouble is we don't know how to look at it. We never know whether the artists are naïve or knowing in their work; whether they are being serious or frivolous or both at the same time. We don't know if they are playing with us and teasing us with private jokes that we can never hope to get. Indeed, we don't even know whether they have anything or nothing to say. In this, the church sculpture of the 11th and 12th centuries is much like modern art: it defies us to react in some way to show that we "get it" or to surrender and concluded that this art and all art is what it is and is ultimately unfathomable.

To judge it like this, however, may be to make the mistake of assuming that because it is nonsensical it is without meaning. There is another possibility: that the intriguing stone sculptures are encoded wisdom. The carvings challenge us to keep looking at them until we see past our first, superficial response. Could they be the remnants of pagan folk knowledge that communities wanted to write up on the walls of the church, along with the stories of the "new" religion? While Christianity dominates the most obvious ground level parts of the church, the esotericists place their work in positions that we don't notice at first. We have to crane our necks, look hard and repeatedly, and go beyond our first smile and bewildered shrug. Only then, gradually, we may perceive the hidden meaning. At the very least we have to allow ourselves to go on looking without understanding, gradually releasing all our assumptions about Christianity, the Middle Ages, art and heritage – until we can simply see what there is in front of us or above us, in this moment.

Christian Iconography

Churches, inside and out, are full of symbols that the faithful know – or at least knew – how to read. In the early days of Christianity certain symbols, such as the fish, enabled Christians to recognize each other without betraying themselves to their persecutors. Later, when Romanesque and Gothic churches were being decorated with paintings, stained glass and sculptures in wood and stone, symbols provided a concise lexicon for conveying items of faith.

The Middle Ages were highly ritualized in their form of expression and nothing was done simply because it looked good. Everything that we see today – every object, every hand gesture – was the product of a deliberate decision dictated by orthodox belief. Only later, with the advent of the Renaissance, did stylized iconography give way to more realistic art in which aesthetics competed with meaning.

- **Anchor.** An early Christian symbol denoting the dependability of Christian faith.
- **Angel.** See p144.
- **Biblical characters.** All images of Biblical characters, including Jesus and the Virgin Mary, are symbols rather than portraits. Their appearance depends on many artists and their patrons. The way they were depicted changed over the early centuries of Christianity until an accepted version was decided upon. Jesus, for instance, began as a smooth shaven very young man and later (from around the 6th century) became older and grew a beard. Both Jesus and Mary are shown in a variety of roles, each with a specific name such as Christ in Majesty or Christ in Judgement.
- **Chi Ro.** See p108.
- **Christ in majesty.** This image is often placed in the tympanum of a church doorway as in the Portal Royal of Chartres. Christ, with a beard, is shown sitting on a throne as ruler of the world. He holds a book, the gospels, in his left hand and raises his right hand in the gesture of benediction taken from a Roman sign to "speak well", with the thumb and first two fingers pointing upwards (the trinity) and the last two fingers closed (duality). Christ is enclosed in an almond-shaped mandorla (the *vesica piscis*) and surrounded by the Tetramorph.
- **Cross.** See p201.
- **Devil.** See p146.
- **Dove.** It represents the Holy Ghost or Spirit.
- **Dragon.** Mythical monsters, see p126.
- **Eye (in the pyramid):** God. The Bible proscribes images of God, who is impossible to visualize, but he is represented in three elusive ways. He is the eye high up on a wall or on the ceiling that sees everything without moving. In a similar way, he is also seen as a hand that created and controls the world. God is also shown more directly as The Ancient of Days, an old man with a white beard in the clouds.
- **Fish.** An ancient Christian symbol for Christ and hence one of his followers.
- **Last Judgement.** Another favourite subject for tympanums shows Christ as Judge sorting out the saved (on his right side) and the damned (on his left). The best example is at Conques.
- **Pelican.** A pelican stands over the gateway of Saint-Wandrille monastery, near Caudebec-en-Caux (Seine-Maritime) and also appears on altars in many churches.

Pelican and chicks, Montségur church

Romanesque 115

Montaner church

According to legend, the mother pelican is willing to sacrifice herself by giving her own blood to feed her starving chicks, an allegory of Christ's gift to humanity.
• **Phoenix.** Death and resurrection of Christ.
• **Saints.** Each saint has his or her emblem, an object that he is associated with or that indicates the method of his martyrdom. St Peter, for instance, carries the keys to Heaven, St James is dressed as a pilgrim and Saint Lucy carries her eyes (put out by her murderers) on a tray.
• **Sator** or **Rotas Square.** A curious word-grid (five rows by five columns) known as the Sator square (after the letters in its first line) or Rotas Square (referring to the last line). It has been found in many places associated with early Christianity including the ruins of Pompei. There are examples in France in a funerary chapel next to the ruined chateau of Rochemaure (Ardèche) and at Loches, Chinon and Tarnac. It lightly conceals the letters for Paternoster (our father) but other meanings have been read into it.
• **Scallop shell.** The scallop shell is a symbol of the pilgrimage to Santiago de Compostela (see p30).
• **Ship.** The whole church symbolizes a ship that conveys the faithful to salvation.
• **Signs of the Zodiac.** Pagan in origin, long assimilated uneasily into Christianity. See p217.
• **Snake/serpent.** This animal normally stands for the devil and hence evil but it can also be a signifier of knowledge, as in the story of the Garden of Eden and the caduceus symbol.
• **Tetramorph.** Four winged figures are often shown over church doorways around the figure of Christ in the Vesica Pisces. These are the symbolic representations of the four evangelists as described in the Book of Ezekiel, and echoed in the Book of Revelations. The eagle represents St John, the bull St Luke, the lion St Mark, and the man is St Matthew. Together they are known as the Tetramorph. They are seen on the Portal Royal of Chartres and in many Romanesque and Gothic churches around the country.
• **Trinity.** The perplexing concept of three beings – God, Jesus and the Holy Spirit – making up one entity is represented by an equilateral triangle. It is also associated with some unusual stone carvings called trifrons in which three faces (one looking left, one straight on and one right) are joined together (see p232).
• **Virgin Mary.** The sketchy details of her life in the New Testament have been amplified by tradition and given an iconography of their own. See p97.

Portal, La-Ville Dieu-du-Temple

The nave, Condom cathedral

VII

Babel Revisited
The Grounding of the Gothic Enlightenment

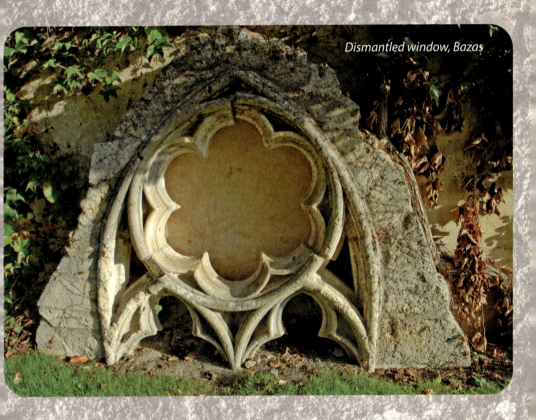

Dismantled window, Bazas

Feverish experimentation and innovation around Paris in the 12th and 13th centuries gave rise to an architecture of verticality and splendour that has never been excelled. The great Gothic cathedrals of northern France are rich repositories of sacred geometry, numerology and stained glass, and also testament to a shift in human consciousness from the celestial to the terrestrial.

Mystical France

In one way at least, Gothic architecture is like rocket science: they both depend on the same point. The defining feature of the Gothic style is the ogive arch in which two lines curve away from the vertical to reach a rounded point. This is the same sharpened, aerodynamic shape seen in ballistics and rocket design. It is almost as if the cathedral – like a bullet, plane or missile – is designed to move through the air with the minimum of wind resistance.

The ogival arch was used before the first Gothic buildings were conceived. It can be seen on some otherwise Romanesque buildings and ultimately it may have been imported from Islamic architecture in the east.

It was, however, extensively deployed and perfected by the master masons who built the Gothic cathedrals and it transformed the possibilities of architecture. Along with other key innovations, especially the flying buttress, it enabled great things to be done with the building that had hitherto been impossible. Vaults over the nave, transepts and choir could now soar while the weight and width of the walls could be reduced and masonry replaced with large areas of glass.

Gothic architecture was a combination of all these new construction techniques and the possibilities they unleashed. From the mid 11th century to well into the 14th century, there was fever of cathedral building. The first truly Gothic cathedral is the Cathedral of Saint-Denis (mid-12th century) now in the northern suburbs of Paris. The epitome of the style is considered to be Chartres cathedral (see p214), built in a relatively short time (begun after a fire in 1194 and consecrated in 1260) and very little altered over the subsequent centuries.

Gothic was not just a gradual evolution of Romanesque; it was a spiritual and architectural revolution. The nature of the temple changed, almost as if religion itself had changed its nature. This raises a question:

Albi cathedral

did the new techniques available enable a different way of thinking about how a cathedral should be conceived, constructed and used - or did these techniques come about because of some pre-existing way of thinking? Was it the desire or the ability to put the desire into practice that came first – or did they arise simultaneously? Did architecture bring about a shift in consciousness or facilitate it?

A Technique of Time and Place

The answers lie partly in the way that the Gothic style came to be. Gothic archi-

tecture may have something sublime, timeless and universal about it, almost as if it were divinely inspired, but it arose in a particular time and place for very worldly reasons.

Gothic is principally a style of northern France. It originated and was perfected in the Paris basin. The early cathedrals were all in or around the capital: Notre-Dame itself, Saint-Denis, Sens, Noyon, Senlis, Laon, Soissons. In a second High Gothic phase, it spread further out to Bourges, Chartres, Reims, Troyes, Le Mans and Strasbourg. Whereas Romanesque had implanted itself almost everywhere but the north, and was especially associated with the southwest pilgrimage routes, Gothic represented Paris and the Ile de France, the hub of the growing country of France, over which the Capetian dynasty was gradually asserting its power.

Climate played an influence too: in the south of France there was a need to keep an oversupply of sunlight out of church buildings, but in the north the need was opposite, to make the most of the sun and illuminate dark interiors. Later, Gothic spread both as Flamboyant Gothic and

Labyrinths

A few medieval churches in France still have labyrinths incorporated into them. Chartres has the most famous one but there are also labyrinths in Amiens (Picardy), Bayeux (Normandy), Mirepoix (Ariège) and the modern cathedral of Évry near Paris.

Before the 19th century there were many more but they were destroyed during and after the Revolution, as modern thoughts replaced medieval ones. What was it about them that offended so much? Was it that their purpose and use had been lost? That they had become old, cracked, untidy as well as being antiquated, inscrutable and unnecessary?

The labyrinth as a motif has been found etched into prehistoric rocks and therefore long predates Christianity. It is almost certainly a pagan device that was brought into the church to satisfy some long standing tradition that has now been forgotten.

A labyrinth has nothing to do with a maze in which the aim is to find the right way to the goal using trial and error, memory and intelligence. In a labyrinth as opposed to a maze, there is only one path from the rim to the centre so there is no getting lost.

Such an arrangement militates against the modern notion of directness. If you are going somewhere, we reason, you go there by the straightest route possible. Why take a devious path?

The labyrinth, instead, maximizes the length of the route within the space allowed and is as indirect as it is possible to be. It involves, on the face of it, a deliberate decision to meander and waste time.

The labyrinth uses space in a more ingeniously efficient way. More than that, it mesmerizes and numbs the sense-making capacity of the eye-mind that likes to make instant sense of patterns and designs. A labyrinth demands to be stared at and studied.

To walk a labyrinth requires commitment and obedience to the path. If you do it for amusement, you quickly tire. It takes a certain amount of time, and that is time that could be spent in prayer or meditation. It distracts the body in a higher cause: by enslaving the feet, it frees the mind.

That, precisely, is the point of the labyrinth. It slows you down, tests your perseverance and disorientates you, temporarily disengaging the brain's notion of forward motion and progress. You double back and repeat your last trajectory in reverse, then change direction yet again.

In its twists and loops, the labyrinth recalls the human brain and the intestines (said to be our second brain). It is a metaphor for thought and digestion; or to put it another way, the healthy digestion of thought.

The former labyrinth of Reims cathedral, from a book by Jules Gailhabaud

southern variations, but its home was always the north.

The Gothic cathedral is also a reflection of the economics of its time. It is very much an urban building. There was no longer any need to build castles, and suddenly the bourgeoisie, aristocracy and church had wealth to spare for pious works and a plentiful labour force at their disposal. It was implanted in a well-to-do-city on an important road or river trade route.

In the international context, religion was being brought home. By the late 12th century the Crusades were failing in their objective and the Christian God had been repatriated. Jerusalem had to be mourned forever or a version of it erected in France. The Crusade against the Cathar heresy (see p133), however, succeeded, reinforcing the power of the kings of the north.

The pilgrimage to Santiago de Compostela was a southern affair. The burghers of northern France believed they could make their own places of pilgrimage. They had no need of distant cathedrals reached by exotic journeys and their skilled workforce should not be encouraged to go wandering.

At the same time, there were new ideas circulating in Europe. Contact with the east through the Crusades, and with Muslim Spain, had re-introduced the philosophy of the pagan ancient Greeks to Europe. There was great interest in sacred geometry (see p22), numerology (see p23) and symbolism. Masons and other artists-craftsmen who had honed their skills on Romanesque churches were looking for fresh challenges.

> "Medieval Christianity redefined the human sense of space. In antiquity the great distinction was between right and left; in the Middle Ages it was between low and high." —Jacques Le Goff.

Political and economic conditions combined with intellectual and spiritual aspirations to create an atmosphere of competition. The great Gothic cathedrals literally arose out of an atmosphere of frenzied competitiveness: everyone involved wanted to see how much higher naves and spires could be built, how much more overwhelming the next cathedral to be finished could be.

The Distinguishing Marks of Gothic

Gothic architecture has six principle distinguishing marks. One easy way to identify a Gothic cathedral is by size. Architects strove to build large, partly to impress the viewer (and God) but also to create immense assembly spaces where the mass congregation could be preached to. The volumes of Gothic buildings are grandiose, not intimate. It is as if the building has been magnified without regard to the scale of a human being. The structure talks down to the individual. It is not an architecture suited to the parish church, where the whole congregation knows each other, but for the town or city with its greater and more loosely allied population.

It is not just overall size that Gothic is concerned with but height. The vertical axis dominates the horizontal axes below. The spire or spires of the building rise above the surrounding rooftops and point skywards, away from the earth, in "a-spiration". If a church symbolically expresses a spiritual journey, in Gothic the direction is not east to Jerusalem for salvation but directly upwards, straight to heaven.

The next distinguishing quality of Gothic is weight, or lack of it. A Gothic cathedral is a "light" building. It is the result of a leap of technical understanding by the master mason by which he is able to transmit the weight of the vault down through the piers and columns to the ground, thereby reduc-

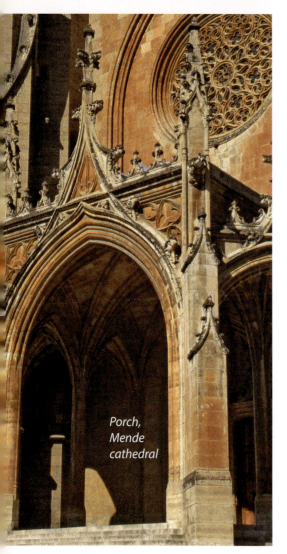

Porch, Mende cathedral

the subconscious. Gothic took this thought further: it was never interested in the plain when it could be made elaborate. Clear glass would only half glorify God; coloured glass would do an even better job and hence the cathedral is illuminated with great amounts of stained glass arranged to tell Biblical stories. Advances in glass making and stone working meant that the windows of Chartres, Bourges and the Sainte-Chapelle in Paris could become immense jigsaws of coloured glass divided up by ingenious designs of tracery.

Another hallmark of Gothic is its planning. For the most part Gothic cathedrals are not haphazard constructions but meticulously co-ordinated affairs. They are products not of religious instinct but of the human mind. A cathedral conforms to a scheme and every detail can be worked out in advance. Thus, for example, the three rose windows are not separate compositions but ingredients of the cathedral narrative.

In the 19th century, the great restorer of ancient monuments, Viollet-le-Duc, fantasized about the ideal Gothic cathedral which the master masons of the 12th and 13th centuries were working towards. "It would," he said, "have been an immense and perfect house of God with seven spires."

The sixth trait of Gothic is invisible. The building incorporates two abstract or ephemeral qualities. One is acoustics, particularly how it responds to music. The other is time. A cathedral is not made for present use but for posterity and eternity. If we are 25 generations from the cathedral builders (approximately), it is an interesting exercise to ask how a Gothic cathedral will be seen in 25 generations from now.

Although there are transitional buildings, a High Gothic cathedral is very different from a "routine" Romanesque cathedral or church. The ogival arch has different symbolic properties to the semi-circular

ing the thickness of the walls and making a building which is solid but slim.

This structural weight loss enabled the building to be light in another, more literal sense which becomes obvious when you step inside. The walls have become less important to the structure and large areas of them can be replaced with windows.

Gothic architecture indulged a desire to bring as much light into the interior as possible. Light, in the Middle Ages, was considered synonymous with God: it brightened the darkness and drove away demons from

Stained Glass: the light of heaven

The windows of thick-walled Romanesque churches had to be so small that no ray of light could be wasted on frivolity or else the interior would be impenetrably gloomy. With its technological innovations, Gothic architecture removed this limitation. The audaciously large openings in the walls meant that windows need not be cramped and discreet. There could be light to spare and creative things could be done with it.

Coloured glass was probably first made by accident when impurities found their way into the viscous, molten mix in the crucible. Hesitant experiments with stained glass were made in Byzantium and later in the west around the 9th century, but they only ever resulted in rudimentary compositions.

By the early 12th century, however, the technique of colouring glass to precise degrees using various oxides had been perfected, as had the method of joining coloured shapes of glass together by means of lead connectors called cames, and setting the whole intricate design in the frames of stone tracery. Glaziers, supported by masons and blacksmiths, pushed the possibilities of their art to the limit in making brittle transparent jigsaws along the naves and transepts and around the altar.

This was more than merely a new possibility in architecture. God was light and glass was a magical material. The Gothic building could be illuminated in spectacular fashion at the same time as glorifying God. Windows grew larger and more complex, telling stories about Biblical characters but also depicting medieval life.

The stained glass window reached its apogee in the circular rose windows placed high up in the walls, half way to heaven, of the great cathedrals of northern France. The name likens them to the flower with its radiating petals.

A cathedral typically has three roses corresponding to the three facades and their doorways. The north is the cold direction and represents the past. The south represents the warmth and the present. The west is the direction of the setting sun and the future, typically encapsulated by the Last Judgement.

The great medieval stained glass windows, brittle transparent jigsaws, invariably recount Biblical anecdotes in picture form for the benefit of the illiterate. They are generally designed to be read from left to right and bottom to top, with the conclusion of the story pointing towards heaven.

Stained glass is seen at its most glorious in the cathedrals of Chartres and Bourges, among others, and also in the Sainte-Chapelle in Paris.

Rose window detail, Troyes cathedral

Romanesque arch. The rounded arch derives from the circle and therefore is associated with the cyclical nature of life and continuity. It is "here" and self-contained. It leads the eye gently up to the vault, around the heavens and back down to earth. It reassures and brings the mind back down to earth with it, creating an intimate human space reminiscent of the cave beneath it. However, it could also be seen as unadventurous and confining.

The Gothic arch can never be complete. Its two vertical lines, left and right, meet only briefly but do not merge. If they are continued with the eye they go off to separate infinities. They thus suggest "elsewhereness", restlessness, allowing the viewer to float away with them. The ogival arch creates a mood of aspiration and wishing, of dissatisfaction. The Romanesque arch is feminine; the Gothic arch masculine.

The history of art tells us that Gothic took over from Romanesque and was an improvement. The history of mysticism should remind us to question this: perhaps the people of the Romanesque period would not have wanted the "benefits" of Gothic had they been offered to them.

Why Bother to Build a Gothic Cathedral?

The political, economic and intellectual conditions may have made cathedrals possible but that didn't mean they had to come into being. A cathedral was an enormous undertaking that took more than one generation to build. The aims of providing a place of worship and a building to glorify God could have been achieved with a much lesser building. Why did the society of the time decide to build Gothic cathedrals? What made so many people dedicate so much time to such grand projects knowing that they would never see the complete fruits of their works?

The ostensible answer to these questions is faith. A Gothic cathedral has been described as a "sermon in stone", embody-

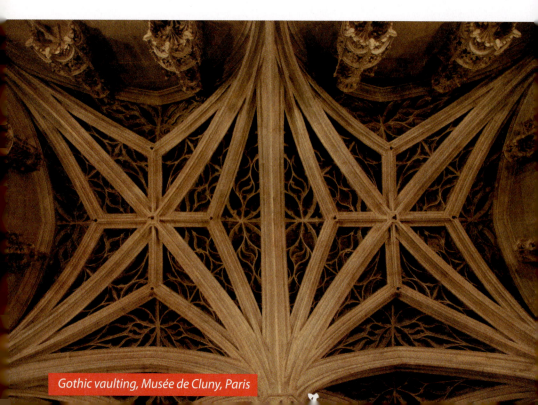

Gothic vaulting, Musée de Cluny, Paris

ing the devotion of the people and preaching the tenets of Christianity to an illiterate population. Its layout, stone carving, stained glass and other accouterments all celebrate the Christian mystery. It was built by the community, driven by a belief in the possibility of salvation. If they were committed Christians, how could they build anything less than what they were capable of? The local cathedral had to be the most beautiful structure on earth; no task could be considered too arduous, too extreme for the glory of God. All this is true but it is not the complete answer. Romanesque was also a testament of faith, but something else is going on during the Gothic period.

Comparing a pure Romanesque church with a mature Gothic cathedral, it is obvious that something has shifted in human consciousness – at least in France.

The change could be summed up as a step from unknowing to knowing; from reaction to action; from revelation to innovation: a stride out of the darkness and into the light. Old doubts and fears have been left behind and new ideas have been embraced.

If the Romanesque church looks back to the cave and in some instances is still physically attached to the earth and half inside it (see p68), the Gothic cathedral stands entirely on the earth without strong attachments to it. A phase of uncertain humility has ended and with it a sense of fear of impending doom and disaster. The Romanesque church is a place of dreams and nightmares, the Gothic cathedral is a place to walk awake. Superstition has been left behind and with it the ambiguity which permeates Romanesque sculpture.

The Powers of Heaven on Earth

The foundation of the Gothic cathedral is the notion, tentative at first but increasing in confidence, that man can do what he

> "Where shall we begin? There is no beginning. Start where you arrive. Stop before what entices you. And work! You will enter little by little into the entirety. Method will be born in proportion to your interest; elements which your attention at first separates in order to analyze them, will unite to compose the whole. In the calm exile of work, we first live patience, which in turn teaches energy, and energy gives us eternal youth made of self-collectedness and enthusiasm. From such vantage we can see and understand life, this delicious life that we denature by the artifices of our enclosed, unaired spirit, surrounded though we are by masterpieces of nature and art. For we no longer understand them, idle despite our agitation, blind in the midst of splendours. If we could but understand Gothic art we should be irresistibly led back to truth."
> —Auguste Rodin, *The Cathedrals of France*

wants in the world if only he allows himself to dare and experiment. The earth (but not heaven) is his to shape. The Gothic cathedral is built to glorify God but glorify man at the same time; and man has discovered his will and declared himself an instigator and designer in his own right.

To do what he wants, man must know. Previously he relied on divine revelation to supply him with knowledge but that is no longer enough. He wants to investigate reality further on his own terms. By the 12th century, he has acquired a sense that the Tree of Knowledge can be shaken without fear of punishment and the fruit gathered.

In this new spirit of unchecked learning, man comes to realize that he no longer has to regard himself as a part of nature; he can see himself as a separate, special kind of being with an objective viewpoint. Nature is a resource to be studied and

Dragon, Bétharram

Mythical Monsters

As if in deliberate counterpoint to the grace and beauty within, the Gothic cathedral sprouts monsters on the outside. These are not the same terrifying beasts that devour sinners in Romanesque sculptures (see p112) by way of warning, but tamed monsters that serve a purpose or are simply decorative. Most obviously they take the form of gargoyles: waterspouts protruding horizontally from the building to direct rainfall from the roofs away from the walls. Other animal sculptures are known as chimera, after a mythical creature in Greek mythology. By far the best known of these is the Styrge, a 19th-century addition to the skyline of Notre-Dame in Paris (see p205).

Back in medieval times, a great and varied menagerie of unusual animals inhabited France. Most of them have now been reduced to the catch-all term dragon, but models and statues of them show that not all were alike. The dragons of Bayeux cathedral are not the same species as the graoully housed in the crypt of Metz cathedral in Lorraine or the tarasque that stalked Tarascon, in Provence, until St Martha intervened and tamed it.

Mythological beasts serve to stimulate our imaginations and to remind us that our animal natures are always lurking within us, whatever the higher intentions of our minds and hearts. We have to accept our bestial nature and let it have just enough free reign to satisfy our needs without letting it control us. Snarling animals were put on Gothic walls and roofs so that what we fear in ourselves is somewhere we can keep half an eye on.

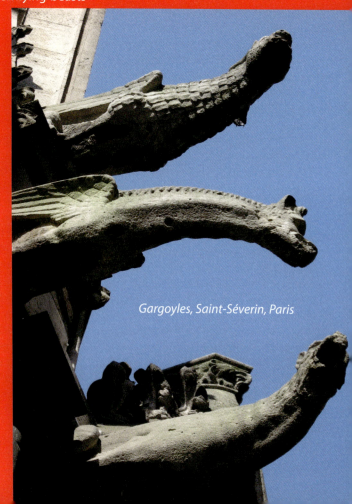

Gargoyles, Saint-Séverin, Paris

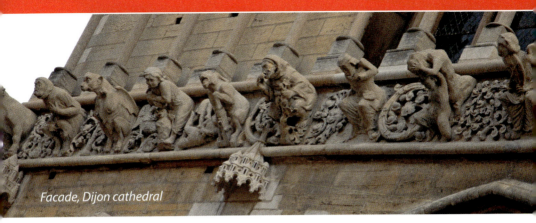
Facade, Dijon cathedral

drawn on as needed; and eventually dominated.

Man divorced from nature takes on god-like qualities. It is almost as if in the cathedral we can see the progression of man: he has in a century or so gone from being in awe of God to believing that he can put God in his place. What starts off as bold adventure on behalf of God ends up defying Him. Eventually the thought will dawn on him that he can do without a divine protector altogether.

It has been rightly remarked that the era of Gothic was the true start of the Renaissance. It could also be called the dawn of the *Anthropocene*, the age in which man takes over the world. What we see in Gothic is the first stirring of an ostentatious cleverness that is still with us and which has generated problems that we have not yet learned to solve.

Seeing the Future

In the late 11th century and early 12th century we see three surprising conceptual inventions. One is the future. Hitherto, mankind has looked back to the Crucifixion and distant past and depended on inherited traditions. Now, with Gothic, there is a forward direction with time and this invokes the other invention: progress – an inevitable and desirable movement in a particular direction, with or without God's blessing.

The third new idea is that perfection can be created on earth by devising and following a plan. Nothing need be done which is not deliberate. The cathedral on earth, in the midst of urban, temporal affairs, becomes more important than heaven and a new centre of the universe. Man can now begin to dream of manufactured utopias.

From a mystical point of view, this awakening of man is an essential part of his evolution. He must grow up and leave the cave but, at the same time, he must not forget where he comes from and what he is.

How Not to Build a Castle

The people who built the cathedrals must have thought that the advance of skills and knowledge could go on forever, that each generation would take over the baton and carry on the conquest of the world – but they were wrong. Events in the 13th century, mostly beyond northern France, were already undermining the favourable conditions that had enabled Gothic to flower. The Holy Land had been lost, causing Europe a moment of self doubt. The Cathar heresy in the south had been suppressed and France unified under

Gargoyle, Saint-Séverin, Paris

the Catholic Church and the Crown, which together suppressed the order of Knights Templar (see p149). During this time the Papacy was French, based in Avignon.

The 14th century saw the end of the Capetian dynasty, in favour of the House of Valois, the start of the Hundred Years War and the arrival in Europe of the plague.

Meanwhile, there were cultural changes in the air. The spread of paper and printing meant that there was less need for "books to be written in stone". Art increasingly became something that the wealthy could enjoy privately rather than place in a church to prove their piety. The anonymous medieval craftsman became the identified artist and the sense of communal, selfless working together for the greater mystical good was lost.

Churches and cathedrals continued to be built and modified after the decline of the Gothic, but the same level of achievement was never going to be reached again. This is made clear by an ambitious building project underway in an abandoned quarry in the forest of Guédelon in Burgundy where a team of craftspeople and volunteers are constructing a 13th century castle using authentic medieval tools, techniques and materials. It is a slow, labour-intensive folly but a convincing castle is gradually appearing.

No one would think to reproduce a 13th century cathedral in the same way. It would be too difficult: too expensive and too complicated. Even given unlimited modern resources, metal scaffolding, powered vehicles and electrical tools, it is not certain that another Chartres (see p214) could be raised in the middle of a town within 66 years. Chartres was built to an intricate geometric plan and elevation involving an organized scheme of iconography and including three ornately sculpted facades, two spires, the largest area of stained glass windows in the world (of which, three are large rose windows) and a circular labyrinth laid into the floor. If such a project were undertaken, like Guédelon, as a learning exercise, would the result be a convincing Christian temple or a sham? Supposing we were to copy Chartres, detail by detail and run out all its components on a 3D printer to build a "Chartres II" alongside the real thing, would the air smell the same inside it or would it lack the authentic sweat, sacrifice, commitment and endurance of the 13th century? Maybe we are better off keeping our ogives for rocket science.

Beaumarchais church iron gate

Gothic

Bourges cathedral

Monasteries

The idea of monasticism – withdrawing from the world in order to be as good as you can be in as good company as you can manage — was born in the deserts of the middle east in the 4th century, but was given its distinctive form in France, particularly in Burgundy, during the Middle Ages.

Hymn book, Montségur

The Irish missionary St Columbanus set up three early monasteries in the foothills of the Vosges at the end of the 6th century and St Benedict of Aniane created an abbey in the Languedoc in the 8th century. None of these institutions survive.

From the 8th to the 12th century, almost all monasteries in France were run according to the monastic rule of *ora et labora* (pray and work) created by Saint Benedict of Nursia. In particular, the Bendictine abbey of Cluny grew immensely powerful, spreading its religious and cultural influence along the pilgrimage routes to Santiago de Compostela.

Curiously, a number of "lay monasteries" were established at this time in the western foothills of the northern Pyrenees. They were created by feudal lords or landowners, partly as a bulwark against the threat of Islam coming from Spain, and each was supported by a number of dependent farms. Barely a trace of any of them is left today.

Monasticism has a number of tensions inherent within it. Every prevailing orthodoxy is gradually undermined by movements of reform. So it was with Cluny which had grown conspicuously wealthy in contradiction to the three vows taken by any monk: chastity, poverty and obedience. The Cistericans (the "white monks" as opposed to the "black monks" of Cluny), especially under the direction of St Bernard, sought a return to a simpler and more rigorous life in accordance with the Rule of St Benedict. The Cistericans were themselves subject to reform by the Trappist movement that began at La Trappe (near Soligny in the Orne) in 1662.

In parallel to Cluny, St Bruno set up his own monastery of Grande Chartreuse in the mountains of the same name north of Grenoble in the 11th century to offer his own concept of monasticism.

In the late Middle Ages, monastic orders proliferated and religious houses were set up by Augustinian Canons, Franciscans and many other orders. The Reformation, the Wars of Religion and the Enlightenment meant that the population of some monasteries dwindled and even died out altogether. The dechristianizing forces of the Revolution forced the abandonment of yet more abbeys and the dismemberment of their buildings, often leaving only an abbey church and possibly its cloister – Moissac being the finest example – but free of other dependencies.

While some monasteries were put to other uses in the 19th and 20th centuries – either run as monuments or even turned into hotels as at Fontevraud in the Loire Valley – others were revived or reoccupied. In recent years new monastic orders have been created and new abbeys built such as Randol in Puy-de-Dome and Le Barroux in Provence. Less than a quarter of the monasteries that were built in France in the last thousand years are still occupied by religious communities.

Today, monasteries can be divided into those that are active and those that are merely monuments visited by tourists or used as cultural venues. Fontenay in Burgundy, Fontevraud and the Abbaye-aux-Hommes in Caen all give a good idea of how a complete monastery looked in the Middle Ages.

A visit to an active monastic community can be a source of great insights into spiritual life. Many functioning monasteries today have accommodation for anyone who wants to stay and participate in the life of the community. Some only accept men or women, and all have particular regulations which guests are expected to respect. Religious communities that offer accommodation for those wishing to undertake a retreat include:

• **Saint-Martin-du-Canigou** in Catalonia
stmartinducanigou.org
• **Solesmes** in La Sarthe near Le Mans
www.solesmes.com
• The twin monastery/convent of **Belloc et Urt** in Pyrénées-Atlantiques
www.belloceturt.org

It is easy to underestimate, misunderstand or idealize the urge to live in a religious community. It is also easy to fall into the trap of thinking that monastic life in the present is exactly the same as in the past, when many monks and nuns were obliged by their families to enter an order so that there would be one less mouth for the farm to feed.

To take monastic vows today (always after a suitable period of preparation) is not to escape from the pressures of the "real world" but to enter another world which is, in many ways, more demanding. Every monk or nun subjects him or herself to a rule intended to ensure stability and predictability through regular work and prayer; and he or she submits to the will of a superior, the abbot or abbess. It is a humble, secluded life. Paradoxically, this giving up of everyday freewill is seen as liberating the mind and soul to concentrate on other, "higher" things. Without the distractions of consumer life, the monk engages in a struggle with his thoughts, doubts and temptations.

Cloître des Pénitents, Louviers

Chateau de Quéribus

VIII

Heresy of Perfection
The Doomed and Enduring Belief of the Cathars

Cité de Carcassonne

What is it about a 13th-century dissident religious movement confined to a corner of rural France that has such emotive appeal today? The crusade unleashed against the Cathar heresy is no more than a footnote to history and yet it encapsulates some perennial spiritual themes and dilemmas.

Mystical France

The department of the Aude, in the Languedoc, is a good choice for a quiet country holiday – as long as one keeps away from touristy Carcassonne. The climate is mainly dry and sunny, the countryside is beautiful. Not much happens to disturb the silence. Strangely, though, the Aude's chief selling point is an episode of extreme violence that took place 800 years ago, but which still has emotional resonance today.

The Aude is branded as "Cathar Country" after the Cathar or *Albigensian* heresy that briefly flourished in the 13th century. There is barely anything to see that is directly related to the ill-fated heretics who were persecuted into oblivion by an alliance of the Catholic Church and the French monarchy. "Cathar Country" is more a place of associations and evocations, demanding an effort of imagination and empathy from the visitor.

The story of the Cathars is usually told as a series of events involving certain named personalities. It can be summed up as a military campaign by the powerful (the king of France and the Pope) against the less powerful (the feudal lords of the Languedoc) with the aim of bringing the errant souls of the region in line with the Church's teachings. It consisted of a series of threats, negotiations and sieges followed by summary trials and executions.

To see it like this, however, is to ignore the complexity of the situation and the humanity of the participants – most of whom were without titles or positions of influence. The real story of the Cathars is not about deeds, statistics and generalizations; it is about thousands of intermingled biographies that history has not had the time or the means to explore. If there is any point in revisiting the Cathar period, it is not to repeat the facts but for us as individuals to reach back to the individuals of that time, so we can learn what may be useful for us today.

> "You cannot please both God and the world at the same time. They are utterly opposed to each other in their thoughts, their desires and their actions." —St John Vianney

Understanding the Cathars

It is easy to misunderstand or oversimplify the subject matter. History – the attempt to make sense of the past – prefers to make things neat. It has given the Cathars their name and tries to foist on them a single identity in order to establish a coherent narrative.

What is always missing from history is the mess of the time, the inconvenient details that go against the storyline.

Even if we try to be objective, there is a danger that we see in the Cathars what we want to see. When we sum people up in terms of their religion, it is because we want them to fit a pattern for our convenience – and we always lose them in the process.

In a way, there were no such people as the Cathars and no such thing as Catharism. Catharism did not appear fully formed out of nowhere and the people we call the Cathars did not all hold the same beliefs with equal strength.

"The Cathars" were not so much a united religious bloc as a heterogeneous segment of Languedoc society. Catharism was a disposition, tendency or component of life rather than a distinct lifestyle. The Cathars were people similar to other people except in that they ascribed, more or less strongly, to certain shared ideas. Religion was just an aspect of certain peoples' lives and it was often vague and in the background rather than the foreground. Individuals embraced its tenets with varying degrees of enthusiasm and understanding.

It is an accepted truth that the winners write history. Most of what we know about the Cathars comes from the records kept by their enemies. Hardly any documents created by the Cathars themselves have survived.

To some extent, Catharism was defined not by any positive attributes but to the extent that it was not Catholicism as declared by the papacy. It failed the artificial yes/no test of its persecutors. Catharism coalesced out of a background of other heresies. In some ways, it is better to think of it as a thousand shades of heresy linked by some common themes. History has tended to try to make their belief system seem homogenous so that it is easy to attack, rather than acknowledging that their beliefs were diffuse and varied.

From Words to War

It is not clear how exactly Catharism emerged but it is certain that by the start of the 13th century there was a flourishing cult of non-conformity in the Languedoc,

The path up to Montségur

and this was tolerated by some of its feudal overlords.

At first the church tried to win the argument with words, through preaching. Both St Bernard of Clairvaux and St Dominic preached against Cathar doctrines without success. St Dominic is said to have proved his point by a miracle. He threw his books on to a fire, along with those of a Cathar bishop with whom he was in dispute; and while the latter's works were burnt as to be expected, St Dominic's books flew out of the flames unscathed.

Catharism might have continued to spread, quietly tolerated as a personal matter of conscience, had not the Church been given an excuse to move against it.

On 14 January 1208, a murder was committed near the banks of the River Rhône, on the border between Provence and the Languedoc. The victim was Peter of Castelnau, a Cistercian monk from the Abbey of Fontfroide, who had been sent as legate by Pope Innocent III to try to persuade count Raymond VI of Toulouse to suppress the Cathar heresy.

Raymond had not done what the Catholic Church had asked of him and, much to his disgust, he had been excommunicated for his failure. This created tension between the count and the monk. The situation remained dangerously unresolved and one of the count's retinue decided to do his lord a favour by ridding him of the troublesome legate. Did Raymond know about the murder plan beforehand or even condone it? We don't know. What is certain is that the murder of Peter of Castelnau became the reason – or the pretext – for the Pope to change his tactics. Up until then, he had hoped to stop the spread of heresy by preaching and putting pressure on the noblemen of the Languedoc, but this policy hadn't worked. It was time for action.

They mounted their first great siege at Béziers, in July 1209, providing an example of what they could and would do. No one within its walls was spared. The leader of the crusading army, Arnaud Amaury, is said to have been asked by one of his men how he would be able to tell the difference between a loathsome heretic (to be put to the sword) and a good Catholic (to be spared), to which the reply came, "Kill them all. God will recognize his own".

A more precise policy was formulated the following year at the capitulation of the stronghold of Minerve: recant or be burnt alive. The Cathars within its walls responded in the only way that seemed right to them and 140 faced the flames rather than give up their religion. In memory of them a simple, moving sculpture pierced through with the form of a dove stands beside the church.

At Bram, the crusader Simon de Montfort used the defeated garrison as an example. He had the eyes of all of them put out except for one man, who was left with a single eye to guide the grisly procession along the road to Cabaret.

Memorial to the Cathars, Minerve

Cathar Locations

There is barely anything left to see of the Cathars but there are several places associated with them to stimulate the imagination.

Two long-distance walking routes cross modern-day "Cathar country". They are mainly good for scenery rather than for linking up the various Cathar locations. The 250 km (155 mi.) *Sentier Cathare* (Cathar Trail, classified at the GR367) runs from Port-la-Nouvelle on the Mediterranean coast to the town of Foix in the middle of the Pyrenees in 12 stages and passes through Montségur (see p234) – the Cathar site par excellence. The Cathar Trail intersects with the GR 107, known as the *Chemin des Bonshommes* (The Way of the Good Men, after an epithet used for Cathar parfaits) that crosses the Spanish border from Foix to Berga in Catalonia. lesentiercathare.com and sentiers-pyreneens.com/bonshommes.htm

Otherwise the best places to visit are:
- **Albi.** The city which lent its name to the Cathars has a beautiful city centre and a fine cathedral.
- **Béziers.** The scene of the first Cathar massacre at the hands of the Crusaders, Béziers has a picturesque old town around the cathedral on top of the hill.
- **Carcassonne.** A magnificent walled *cité*, which owes as much to 19th century restoration as the Middle Ages. It is the de facto capital of the Cathar region. Get there early in the morning if you want the atmosphere, before the crowds arrive.
- **Minerve.** A small medieval village that has subsequently given its name to a wine region. It was besieged in June 1210 and the populace denied access to their only well. The *parfaits* of Minerve were offered the choice to abjure their faith or face death. Only three of them renounced Catharism and 140 were burnt at the stake on July 22. It is said they climbed onto the bonfires willingly. A peace memorial stands beside the church.
- **Château de Quéribus.** Now a ruined château on a high, isolated crag, Quéribus was once a powerful fortress standing in an impregnable position. It was the last Cathar castle to fall, in 1255.
- **Toulouse.** On the first floor of the city hall is an elegant salon with a large painting at one end depicting the siege of the city during the Cathar crusades.
- **Villerouge-Termenès.** A pretty, out-of-the-way town with a restored castle which makes the most of its Cathar connection. It was here that the last surviving Cathar *parfait*, Guillaume Bélibaste, was burnt at the stake in 1321.

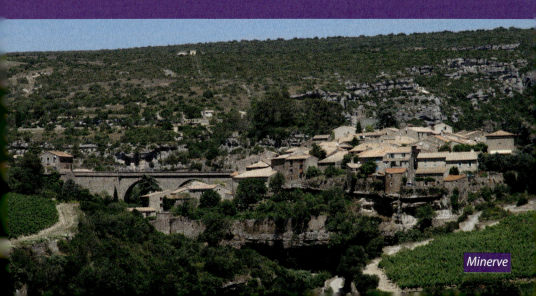

Minerve

Bilingual Occitan/French street sign in Minerve

The first Albigensian Crusade ended only after Toulouse itself had been repeatedly besieged. The crusade leader Simon de Montfort was killed in action, hit by a missile fired from a trebuchet.

Yet even the military and diplomatic victory of the northern, royalist forces, and the degradation of the southern lords, didn't eradicate the heresy and so a second and more thorough campaign against the Cathars was launched twenty years later, this time with the help of the newly established Inquisition.

The Cathars retreated to the castles of the Corbières and the Ariège, built in remote defensible sites on craggy mountain tops. The spectacular fall of **Montségur** in 1244 marked the symbolic end of Cathar resistance to the Catholic Church and the crown of France. (See p234). The castle of **Quéribus**, in the Fenouillades, clung on for another decade but was finally taken in 1255.

Mixed Motives

The crusade against the Cathars was much more than the simple opposition of one version of Christianity by another. It was also the result of a simmering north-south conflict – of political, economic and military greed. The king of France was gradually consolidating his power and expanding his territory. The nobles who served him had much to gain by going to war against the lax *seigneurs* of the south who couldn't impose order on their own people.

The Church's involvement in the Crusade requires more explanation. It could see that it wasn't winning the war with words alone but why did it collaborate in such extreme violence? Why was it willing, indeed keen, to incite Christian to wage war against Christian? Did it matter what the common people believed? Plenty of people in Christendom had confused beliefs which were not purely aligned with the teachings of the church. What, in short, was so terrible about the Cathars?

When we talk about the Cathars today, we conjure up an image of massed heretics. In reality, the Cathars need to be divided up into the great mass of sympathizers and a hard core of zealots, known as *parfaits* (perfects), or *bonhommes* (good men) who lived the Catharist philosophy to the full. It was these perfects who maintained and spread Cathar beliefs and it was they who were the true enemies of the Church.

No one knows how many there were but they must have been few in number because of the demands of their life. Catharism involved a radical attitude to Creation at odds with the official beliefs of the church.

Two Worlds

At the heart of Catharism was a perfect dualistic mysticism. Matter and spirit are not two aspects of the same God-created whole, the Cathars reasoned, but are two distinct and separate notions. God, by definition, is perfection. Nothing in the world is perfect and therefore it cannot be any-

> "God is perfect; nothing in the world is perfect ; therefore nothing in the world was made by God. The one, the good God made the invisible world, while the other, the evil god made the visible one."
> —Peter Garcia, a heretic of Toulouse

thing to do with God. It must be the work of another deity who could be thought of as the devil. All things material are necessarily evil and corrupt – including, by implication, the trappings of institutionalized religion. The only spiritual work that any of us can do is to purify ourselves and free ourselves as far as possible from the temptations of the world.

It wasn't enough to accept this intellectually or to believe it, said the Cathars: it had to be lived. *Parfaits* duly underwent a period of training in asceticism which ended with the sacrament of the *Consolamentum*, by which they freed themselves as far as possible from the attachments of the material world. Perfects dressed in black and renounced meat and sex. They were seen as teachers more than priests, and taught mostly by example. Ordinary Cathars only took the *Consolamentum* on their death beds, enabling them to live normal lives in the world but to detach themselves from its corruption before they departed life.

It wasn't the dispersed population of followers who lived loosely according to Cathar principles that so disturbed the church, nor was its outright heretical teachings. It was the behaviour of the perfects which explicitly defied the Church and everyone who held a position within it. The Cathar perfects challenged the idea that any organization could have a monopoly of the truth, especially one that aimed to administer religion by operating a hierarchy with a career structure and a bureaucracy.

The Cathar perfects were too perfect for their own safety. A would-be holy institution like the Church doesn't know what to do with a genuinely holy individual who is conspicuously ethical. No one is more intimidating to an organization that wants to

The Siege Stone, Carcassonne

dictate the rules of virtue than the individual who won't be intimated by it. The person who takes virtuous behaviour to an extreme and expects everyone else to do likewise; the person who shows by example that it is possible, even necessary, to live without fear of worldly authority – such a person has the power to shake organized religion to its core.

An individual like this, existing outside the organization, represents a threat to every individual within the organization. He places no value on power, wealth or prestige and those who value these things above all else become scared of losing them. He inevitably makes everyone who has progressed up the career structure of orthodoxy seem tainted and lacking in real virtue, no matter how high their position. He is implicitly a critic of their fine clothes and adulation.

Even worse for the church, Catharism offered a supernatural solution to the perennial problem of the existence of evil. Religious people wrestle with the same question today: if God is perfect, loving and good, how can he allow bad things to happen? Why is the world full of injustice, cruelty and pain? The Church could answer this in part by saying that God had given human beings freewill to do good or bad as they chose. Unfortunately this explanation couldn't explain famine, drought, storms, plague and all the other undesirable experiences beyond man's control. The dualism of the Cathars had it all sown up in a way that made sense even to the illiterate and that defied the Church to come up with a better explanation.

For these reasons, the Church could not

Château de Peyrepertuse

allow Catharism to grow in strength. It did not regard it as merely a form of dissent but as a competing force. The Crusade was effectively a conflict between opposite world views. For the Church's part, there could be no half measures or compromises; it could only be a fight to the death.

The Relevance of Lost Civilizations

Why does all this matter today? Why is there such a strong interest in the Cathars? It goes far beyond touring beautiful landscapes, visiting atmospheric towns, and reading history books. Something about the story of the Cathars speaks to who we are now.

In part this is because we are suckers for lost civilizations. We can make of a dead culture anything we want. We can paint its people as being "ahead of their time" and living through a golden age that we will never know. Simultaneously, it supplies us material to play the game of "what might have happened if…" in which we list all the horrors that could have been avoided had the Cathars been left in peace. A lost civilization is also a fertile source of mystery since it can't answer any of our questions.

The Cathars may be gone, but they are anything but historical. While the story of the Cathars has all the ingredients of a medieval saga – fanaticism, chivalry, brutal warfare, cruel suppression of heresy – there is also something starkly modern (if not universal) about it. It resonates with our own democratic, pluralistic and, hopefully, tolerant times in which justice, peace and human rights are to the fore.

In the 13th century everyone had to take sides. It was a matter of life and death. Today, we feel we have to follow suit but there is no doubt or ambiguity involved – few people would say that right was on the side of the Church and the Crusaders. We instinctively support the victimized minority.

Statue of a knight, Avignonet-Lauragais

The Cathar crusade was clearly a moral struggle between an oppressed, peaceful minority trying to live virtuously, and overwhelming violence meted out for sordid reasons. It is a textbook example of the need for human rights – even though the notion of a "right" was only invented long after the last Cathar had been killed. All the great 21st century themes are played out in medieval Languedoc: justice, fairness, respect, tolerance and freedom of conscience.

This last item should make us stop and reflect for a moment, since it provokes a number of important questions. Is it possible to live in a world in which everyone can think, believe and behave as he chooses? Does there have to be some agreed notion of "normality", a common definition of truth and falsity? Should there be a prevailing orthodoxy in which learned specialists deliver their expert judgement to the rest

> "No one may be disturbed on account of his opinions, even religious ones, as long as the manifestation of such opinions does not interfere with the established Law and Order."
> —Declaration of the Rights of Man and of the citizen of 1789, Article 10

of us and expect us to fall into line for their own good? Every community, from the smallest to the largest, needs a degree of unity to hold it together. Persecution is never excusable, but is non-conformity always a virtue? Are we capable of extending freedom of conscience to those who we believe to be wrong or with whom we strongly disagree? Can we distinguish between freedom of conscience and the application of the law?

The largest question that hangs over all this is this: are we so sure that, in extreme circumstances, we will do the right thing, stick doggedly to our truth against injustice and cruelty? The Cathars were nothing if not tenacious. They didn't equivocate. How could they? To them the choice was starkly clear. They were already living in an earthly hell and to come to an accommodation with it would have achieved nothing. Their attention was not on the sufferings of the body but on the eternal life of the spirit. They faced the ultimate mystical challenge at the hands of invading Barbarians. All we can do today is roam around the modern Languedoc and meditate on the collision between personal truth and any force that wants to eradicate it.

Plaque in Villerouge-Termenès depicting the last Cathar perfect, Bélibaste, and a companion

Béziers

Angels and Fairies

Is incarnation the only way to exist? Are we alone or are we in the company of invisible beings that only let us see them when they want to? In churches all over France, there are signs of the passing of unearthly beings known as angels. Fécamp abbey in Normandy has what it claims to be the footprint of an angel that passed through in the year 943. Many French people and many communes are named after angels and many days are dedicated to angels, which are seen as important figures along with saints.

Hendaye church

Folktales, meanwhile, report the doings of fairies and other sprites who are somewhat similar to angels, but differ from them in important ways. Are all these supernatural beings the product of the human imagination or is there some reality to them?

The only disembodied beings that the church recognizes are angels, the messengers and agents of God. They are mentioned in the Bible but the information given about them is vague. They do not have any precise form. Their appearance has evolved over the centuries and is largely the work of theologians and artists.

The characteristics of angels are thought to have been much influenced by Zoarastrianism and Egyptian iconography. To begin with, they were seen as young men without halos or the power of flight.

An obscure 6th century writer known as *Pseudo-Dionysus the Aeropagite* attempted to bring some order to the celestial host. Based on a reading of the New Testament, and freely speculating, he concluded that there were nine orders of angels arranged into three choirs:

> Seraphim
> Cherubim
> Thrones
>
> Dominions
> Virtues
> Powers
>
> Principalities
> Archangels
> Angels

Only the lower two choirs have a mission to humanity, particularly serving as guardian angels to mortals. Many named angels are also saints. Three archangels, in particular, stand out for particular veneration. Michael is often seen in statues dressed in armour, standing astride a dragon or Satan, and about to deliver a death blow with his sword. Gabriel appears to the Virgin Mary in the Annunciation and also appeared to Mohammed in his first revelation. Raphael is associated with healing.

In the Middle Ages, the nature of angels was much argued over. Did they have any form or substance? Could there be such a thing as a being without a physical body or is it a contradiction in terms?

Rodez

Mosaic, Lourdes

Human imagination was freely applied to the subject and the angel took on a reality in the hands of the stone sculptor and stained glass artist. Sometime around the 13th century, the angel changed from a stocky man to a feminine or androgynous woman. The angel became what we wanted him or her to be: beautiful and kind. They also served as a reassuring vision of the afterlife: to die without sins was to be guaranteed a place among the angels.

Fairies are somewhat different although they too have wings and defy the laws of physics. They have nothing to do with God or religion and there are no representations of them before the inception of the "fairy tale" – a term coined by Madame d'Aulnoy in the 17th century for a new form of fiction drawing on oral stories popularized by her predecessor Charles Perrault.

Fairies go by a variety of local names and descriptions of them are equally varied. The best known fairy in France is Melusine, a freshwater sprite who is a serpent from the waist down.

In general, the fairies seem to be a gregarious race that lives in a parallel dimension to ours, overlapping in places known as "fairy portals". They are not normally visible but are sometimes caught by chance dancing, or else are encountered in dreamlike circumstances. It has been suggested that alien abductions are merely encounters with fairies as perceived by minds brought up on 20th and 21st century technology.

In legends, fairies have their own concerns and do not normally interact with human beings. Where they do, it can be for good or malicious motives. Fairies do not care for human duplicity but they, in their turn, are capable of some cunning behaviour. A promise of help from a fairy almost always has conditions attached and fairies were often suspected of trickery, such as the switching of a human baby for a fairy changeling.

In modern times, fairies and angels have been made comfortingly cute. They have become the preserve of childhood and of people who believe in presences and energies that can, if one attunes to them with respect, make the processes of life easier to bear and to learn from.

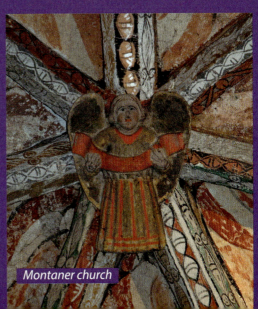
Montaner church

The Devil

The Devil (aka Satan or Lucifer) was the nightmare visitor of the middle ages, often felt or smelt but never seen, and he lingers on in Romanesque stone carvings and frescoes of the Last Judgement. He also pops up in some surprising places such as the holy water stoup at the entrance to **Rennes-le-Château** church (see p226), and appears in stories and place names, such as the *Vallée du Diable* in **Ternois** (Nord-Pas-de-Calais), and the *Grotte du Diable* and les *Roches du Diable* in Brittany.

He is easy to recognize in art by his familiar appearance – horns, tail, fangs, cloven hoof, trident and the smell of sulphur – but these are, of course, all the product of human imaginings and owe more to pagan rather than Christian iconography. The devil is not as fixed and as clear as we believe him to be. He is an ambiguous and changeable figure.

The Bible has little to say about him and most of what it does seem to say is warped by the nuances of a translation – there is a lot of difference, for instance, between "a devil" and "The Devil". He has no clear origin although one version of his story is that he is a fallen angel who was tempted away from God by the sin of pride. He may even be multiple Biblical characters rolled into one.

Much of his identity is the result of later Christian scholarship, commentary and interpretation.

What is certain is that he is the archenemy of God and all goodness. He is a professional dedicated to spreading evil in the world. Put like this, it is easy to see why the medieval mind was so obsessed with keeping him at as great a distance as possible. In the 17th century, he was held responsible for an apparent outbreak of witchcraft (see p172), which threatened (in the mind of the witch hunters) to undermine the authority of the Catholic Church.

The devil, though, is not all bad if we look at him psychologically and symbolically. He is actually useful, serving an important purpose. He personifies selfishness, vice, injustice, subterfuge and corruption, giving us a clear way of thinking about the undesirable, "negative" aspects of human existence. In Christian terms, his existence explains why a good and just God would let unspeakable things happen in the world. Either it is the work of the devil or it is the work of man himself, and therein lies the subtlety of the devil.

The devil is usually considered to be the opposite of self-awareness and conscience. He is a convenient exterior force that can be blamed for evil doing, a monster whose existence explains all our sins. The alternative is for each of us to look in-

The Last Judgement, Montaner church

side of ourselves and take responsibility for our own thoughts and actions.

However, the devil is really the bringer of awareness with the danger that it entails. He tempts, but another word for temptation is choice or freewill: to ignore the word of God in the Bible as presented in the teachings of the church and do what you want for your own reasons. The devil could be said to be the voice of intuition rather than obedience; of dissent rather than orthodoxy. Lucifer means "the carrier of light" although this can be taken to mean the light of night that reveals hidden knowledge.

Perhaps this is why the devil faded from view so rapidly after the witch hunting craze subsided. The Enlightenment and Protestantism turned each person into an individual rather than a component of a religion. Human behaviour, it was realized, was far more complex than a straight choice between vice and virtue, and there were many ways to explain it without referring to a diabolical controller.

By the time of the French Revolution – which some people saw as the work of Satan – the devil was fading out of existence leaving only his shadow behind, in art. For centuries, he had served as a coalescence of all our personal darknesses and, when we were willing to confront them ourselves, we no longer had a need for him.

Devil's bridges

The devil is not just evil and destructive; he is ingenious and he can do the impossible. In particular, he is good at building bridges. There are thought to be around fifty *ponts du diable* (devil's bridges) around France, even if they are officially called something else. Sometimes the reason for the name is obvious: the bridge looks as if defies gravity and only some supernatural charm could keep it in place. Usually there is a legend attached to the building of the bridge following a standard narrative pattern. The devil agrees to build a bridge in a single night on condition that he can have the first soul to cross it. The people of the village, who have agreed to this pact, fool the devil out of his reward: either they make a cock crow before daybreak or they drive a mule across the bridge before any person crosses it. Among the visually appealing "devil's bridges" are **Gensac-sur-Garonne** in Haute-Garonne, southwest of **Toulouse**, and **Montoulieu**, south of **Foix** in the Ariège.

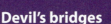

Devil above the door, Église Saint Merri, Paris

The Devil's Bridge, Gensac-sur-Garonne

Tomb, Chapelle de Caubin, Arthez-de-Béarn

IX

Custodians of Ancient Knowledge
The Knights Templar and their Heirs

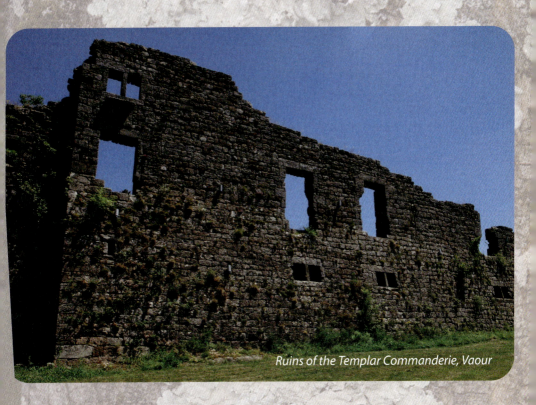

Ruins of the Templar Commanderie, Vaour

When the prosperous order of Knights Templar was suppressed by the king of France in league with the Pope at the beginning of the 14th century, it was the start of history's longest running mystery story. Did the Templars possess a great secret? Did they die with it or pass it on? What relevance do the Templars and their successor secret societies have for us today?

Mystical France

On 21 January 1793, king Louis XVI of France was taken from the Temple prison to be guillotined in front of an excited crowd in the Place de la Concorde in Paris. As soon as the blade had fallen, an anonymous Freemason is said to have leaped on the scaffold, plunged his hand in the blood and cried, "Jacques de Molay, you have been avenged!"

He was referring to another execution four centuries earlier, as if it were still living memory. Not far away, on an island in the Seine, Jacques de Molay, last grand master of the Knights Templar, had been burned to death in 1314, charged with assorted crimes that he denied.

Molay's execution was the culmination of a sordid chain of events that are much argued over today. If it was the end of the history of the Templars, it was only the start of their legend, a story filled with paradox, mystery and irony that today provides a living for novelists, mystery hunters and conspiracy theorists.

While historians sift through the scant data that has survived, it has become common in the popular imagination to believe that there must have been more to the Templars than prosaic facts and figures. It is as if we have gone beyond the question, was there anything out of the ordinary about the Templars? to what secrets did the Templars possess? Beyond that are the even bigger questions posed by conspiracy theorists: what is there that we do not know or that is being kept from us?

From a mystical approach, the questions stemming from the Knights Templar and their successor secret societies are slightly different: "what is there that we do not know that we could know, that would be useful for us to know?" and "which individuals or organizations possessed or possesses this information now?"

The answers to these questions seem to lead back to the Knights Templar and it is with them that we must start.

From Foundation to Crisis

The order of the *Poor Fellow-Soldiers of Christ and of the Temple of Solomon* came into being in the Holy Land in either 1119 or 1120, but it had close associations with France. It was created by two French knights, Hugues de Payns (from a village near Troyes) and Godfrey de Saint-Omer (from French Flanders). Its first eight Grand Masters were from France and it was under the orders of the King of France that it met its end.

The initial purpose of the Knights Templar was to protect pilgrims making their way to the city of Jerusalem, which had been captured for Christendom in 1099 during the First Crusade. The name of the order came from the knights' headquarters in the Al-Aqsa mosque, believed to be the site of the temple of Solomon. In Europe, their champion was St Bernard of Clairvaux, the great promoter of the Cistercian monastic order, and he was instrumental in getting the Templars an endorsement from the Pope at the Council of Troyes in 1129.

From the start, the Knights Templar were a paradox. They purported to be both monastic and military at the same time – warrior monks dressed in white mantles adorned with a red pattée cross. As monks, they took a vow of chastity and obedience to their grand master. They also swore themselves to poverty, but this led them into a bind which led to their undoing.

Because they were a fighting force that continually sustained casualties, the Templars were constantly in need of new recruits and the resources to keep them in the field. They proved to be extremely able at fund-raising and, while individual knights lived lives of self-denial, the order

Knight carved over the door, Bassoues church

itself grew rich. An international logistics organisation grew up in Europe to sustain the warriors in the Holy Land. This was based on the commandery or preceptory, a semi-autonomous communal Templar domain. It is estimated that at their height they had 9000 estates from Syria to Scotland. The order also controlled ports and had a vast financial complex just outside the walls of Paris.

The knights earned a reputation as brave fighters even though they lost many battles but, in the 13th century, they were faced with a crisis. Jerusalem was lost and the Christians were driven out of the Holy Land. The Templars became desperate to persuade the political and religious rulers of Europe to launch a new crusade so that the knights could regain their raison d'être, but there was little appetite for distant military campaigns.

The Templars entered the 14th century as a wealthy organisation in limbo. No one expected the resolution of their situation to be so violent and complete.

Arrests and Trials

The mass arrest of the Templars was worthy of a modern police sting operation. In preparation for it, the king consulted Pope Clement V and the Papal inquisitor in Paris and a month before the appointed time sent out secret instructions to his agents all over the country along with a summary of the charges to be brought.

On the morning of Friday 13th 1307, Europe was taken by surprise. All members of the order in France were arrested simultaneously. Altogether, 1000 Templars were arrested, of whom only a hundred were actual knights, although almost all of them were past fighting age. Included in the haul was Jacques de Molay, 23rd and last grand master who was in Paris for a state funeral. It is thought that a dozen Templars escaped the net and tried to flee to England or another country. Most were recaptured.

The captured Templars were imprisoned and interrogated, sometimes with torture. Only four of them resisted the pressure to confess to crimes, although some of those who did confess later retracted their statements.

The charge sheet drawn up by prosecutors consisted of 127 articles. The Templars were accused of:
• denying Christ, the Virgin Mary, the saints and the sacraments;
• worshipping idols – including one called Baphomet;
• treating their grand master, a lay man, as if he were a priest;
• lewd kissing during initiation ceremonies and engaging in homosexuality;
• enriching themselves in whatever ways they could;
• keeping secrets from the outside world on pain of death.

The show trials got underway and the first Templars were burned to death in May 1310. The Pope felt obliged to officially suppress the order in 1312 but there is some evidence that he had by this time absolved the Templar leaders of their supposed crimes.

Whatever the Pope's feelings, Philip proceeded with his plans to exterminate the order. Last to face the flames were Jacques de Molay and Geoffroi de Charney, preceptor of Normandy, who were burnt on the Ile des Juifs in front of Notre-Dame. It is said, almost certainly unreliably, that as he died, Molay cursed the king and the Pope, telling

Templar cross, Montsaunès

La Commanderie de Coulommiers

The Hospitallers

When the Templars disappeared, their property was confiscated and mostly handed over to another order that had been founded before the Templars and even before the First Crusade. The new owners were the *Knights Hospitallers*, also known as the *Knights of St John of Jerusalem* and the *Knights of Malta*. Many so-called Templar sites in France owe their appearance as much to the work of the Hospitallers, who took them over and adapted them to their own use, as to their original owners. Often it is impossible to say which part of any *commanderie* or castle was built by which order.

Although the Knights Hospitallers had a strong presence in France in the late middle ages, their main operations were in the eastern Mediterranean. When the Latin Kingdom of Jerusalem was lost in 1291, they moved their headquarters to Cyprus, then Rhodes and finally to Malta in 1530, which they governed until Napoleon took the island in 1798.

The order survived thereafter as a charitable institution and in 1961 became known formally as the *Sovereign Military Hospitaller Order of St John of Jerusalem, of Rhodes and of Malta*. The current organization has 13,500 "professed friars" and other Knights and Dames active in 120 countries. It describes itself as a "lay religious Order, traditionally of military, chivalrous, noble nature" dedicated to the exercise of virtue and charity.

them that they would soon have to answer for their own crimes to God. Within a year of Molay's execution, both his persecutors were also dead.

What's so Wrong with Keeping Secrets?

At the time, plenty of questions were asked about the fate of the Templars but not the ones we ask today. Why was Philip so determined to destroy the Templars? Did he really believe the charges against them? Was he jealous of their economic power over him, or was he simply after their wealth? The prosecution of the Templars, although something of a shock at first, was not inexplicable. It was probably due to a variety of factors, including misunderstanding and the difficulty of stopping a process once momentum had got going.

Whatever Philip believed, were any of the charges true? The Templars were a secret society, obedient to a rule and they must have carried out initiation ceremonies. As with any large organization, there must have been weak and corrupt members; some might, by the law of averages, have been homosexual. But it is unlikely that the Templars were institutionally riddled with vice or that they were in any way anti-religious. Here is where the matter should have ended, but the Templars proved to have an unexpected afterlife that continues to generate interesting questions.

It could be that the Templars' most serious crime was what gives them such cachet today: they hoarded information about what they were up to so that outsiders wouldn't find out and break the spell of being part of a special brotherhood engaged in a special task. They were a "secret society", the kind of organization that excites our envy and resentment in equal measure. This alliterative phrase sums up a fundamental aspect of the human condition and touches something very deep and emotional: our need to belong to a group of our own kind and to be able to say who is and who is not in that group. With a secret society, one is either a member and therefore in the know, or one is not. Those who are not members don't know what they are missing out on, or even how to get accepted by those who do. It is easy for anyone – even a king – to feel left out of what looks like the best game in the playground, one that is conducted through whispers, agreed signals and sideways glances. Anyone on the outside, by choice or by rejection, finds that secrecy excites the imagination. If we don't know, we can imagine what we want; if we are resentful, we can come to believe our imaginings; and if we are ruthless as well, we can repeat what we think is true until it becomes accepted as fact.

Rediscovery of the Templars

No one would still be talking about the Templars today if their myth hadn't been invented in the 18th century. By then, the events of the 14th century were a distant history. If anyone thought about the Templars at all, it was assumed that they had made themselves too prominent, politically and economically, and at the same time outgrown their own raison d'etre. Philip had pursued them out of greed for their wealth. There was nothing more to the matter.

In around the 1730s, however, the theory began to spread that the Templars had possessed some ancient secret that had been suppressed by the Establishment. Chevalier Ramsay, a Scottish baronet and Freemason living in France, gave encouragement to this idea in 1736, when he tried to link masonry with the Crusades and the Knights Hospitaliers. It was left to other people to draw the conclusion that the Freemasons had inherited the secret of the Templars.

Compagnons du Tour de France

Compagnonnage is a peculiarly French system of apprenticeship, concerned with encouraging the highest standards in certain industries, especially those to do with construction. Craft skills, knowledge and philosophy are passed on from master to pupil. To become a compagnon du Tour de France is to be initiated into a brotherhood and given a new "secret name" made up of the compagnon's region of origin and a quality he possesses, for example, "Bordeaux Jacques the Strong." The compagnon must travel around France as part of the learning process and finally prove his skills by completing a masterwork.

Compagnons trace their recorded history back for at least eight centuries, to the epoch of cathedral building. Compagnonnage thrived from medieval times until well into the 19th century when industrialization, socialist movements and the formation of trade unions made its arcane demands on its young members seem less relevant.

In recent years, Compagnonnage has been enjoying something of a revival because it offers an alternative to an economic system based on what is cheap, easy and disposable. Most members of the three compagnonnage organizations in existence today see it as a way to learn the highest standards of a specific trade, and so uphold excellence in their profession. For others, it is also a means by which to preserve arcane knowledge and pass it on from the initiated elder to the young pupil.

The mythical roots of the movement go much further back. Some say it started with the first association of builders that was assembled to erect the Tower of Babel. The date for the origin of compagnonage is usually cited as 960BC, at the time of the construction of the Temple of Jersualem. The founding fathers of compagnon-

Poster, Musée du Compagnonnage

nage are said to be king Solomon (who ordered the building of the temple) and two legendary French figures, Maître Jacques and Père Soubise. Maître Jacques, according to the legend, was a stonemason and companion of Hiram, the architect of the Temple who was assassinated. Jacques was either born in Provence or the Pyrenees in around 1036 BC. Père Soubise was a carpenter and workmate of Jacques who is sometimes associated with the shrine of Sainte-Baume (see p220).

In esoteric terms, the objective of the compagnon is not just to perfect his craft and transmit his knowledge to his successors. More than that, it is to educate himself into self-knowledge and virtue and thereby experience a metaphorical death and rebirth which enables him to "cross" from this reality into another within his lifetime.

There are museums of compagnonnage in Paris, Arras, Bordeaux, Limoges, Toulouse and Tours.

This was the beginning of a new career for the Templars who would be "retrospectively recruited" as the ancestors of innumerable secret societies. It became *de rigueur* for any secret society that wanted to project an aura of legitimacy to cite the Templars in the story of their origins. For example, when Bernard Fabré-Palaprat launched the latter-day Order of the Temple, he claimed that the line of succession of Grand Masters had continued unbroken up until his day.

It was as if secret societies had suddenly appeared in response to some need of the 18th century, and they felt obliged to invent a lineage or "back story" to make themselves credible.

France in the time of the Enlightenment was a very different country to the France in which the Templars had been persecuted and the Gothic cathedrals built. The Renaissance had broken the taboo that religion meant pure doctrinal Christianity. It had indulged a passion for classical pagan mythology and humanism. This was now combined with a thirst for first-hand, provable knowledge as opposed to superstition and the dogmatic teachings of priests. With this came a desire to see how far reason could be applied for the benefit of mankind. There was a demand for freedom of thought and behaviour that would eventually erupt in revolution.

This gave rise to an argument that is still with us, an argument over the nature of the supernatural and the meaning of existence; in effect, a tussle over the soul of man. For the inquisitive non-believer, the old mysteries of religion represented a challenge for the new methods of investigation to pry into and explain; but the mystically-minded regarded these same mysteries as inaccessible to empiricism and reason. They saw them as no-go areas for what they considered to be the over-active human brain.

In the foreground of religion, the Catholic Church was now well established in France. It was wealthy, dogmatic and ritualistic, and allied with political power. It had seen off Catharism, Protestantism and the Devil.

In the shadows behind it, however, was an enduring metaphysical current of alternative or popular wisdom that the church had at first tried to incorporate, then tried to eradicate through their pursuit of heretics and witches.

Arguably, absolute, dictatorial power – the collusion of monarchy, nobility and church (the first three estates) – always provokes an opposite reaction. While a majority of people are cowed by force, rebel cells inevitably spring up and associations of like-minded, disaffected individuals tend to grow. These are the groups that will keep secrets out of self-preservation – and as a way of cementing their union.

The idea of secret societies was nothing new. It almost certainly goes back to Ancient Egypt and it filtered into France by way of the Eleusian mysteries of Ancient Greece and the covert Roman religion of Mithraism. Early Christianity was itself a kind of secret society: a persecuted religion whose followers lived underground and

> "The Templar myths have proved extremely durable and their contribution to the modern image of the real Templars arguably as powerful as that of their documented history between 1119 and 1314. The Longevity of these myths…perhaps relates to their flexibility, for they have been used by both conservatives and radical proponents of the conspiracy theory of history, by romantics imbued with a nostalgia for a lost medieval past, by Freemasons seeking a colourful history to justify their penchant for quasi-religious ritual and play-acting, and by charlatans who seek profit in exploiting the gullible.
> —Malcolm Barber: *The New Knighthood: A History of the Order of the Temple*

Commanderie templière d'Arville

Templar Sites

Many of the Templars' properties in France were handed over to the Hospitallers and it can be difficult to distinguish between the work of the two orders.

- **Arville:** *Commanderie d'Arville* (northwest of Vendôme, Loir-et-Cher). The best preserved commanderie in France, now a museum of Templar history. commanderie-arville.com
- **Chinon** (Loire Valley). Templar dignitaries were held in the *Forteresse Royale* in 1308 before they were moved to Paris for their trial and execution. The graffiti on the walls is said to have been made by them. forteressechinon.fr
- **Coulommiers** (Seine-et-Marne, Ile de France). Well-preserved and picturesque *commanderie* in a small town near Paris.
- **La Couvertoirade** (Aveyron). The château in this well-preserved fortified complex was built by the Templars around 1200. The village developed around it and the ramparts were added in the 15th century. lacouvertoirade.com
- **Cressac-Saint-Genis** (Charente). *Chapelle des Templiers du Dognon*. This small chapel contains authentic 12th century frescoes showing the knights travelling to the Holy Land by ship to fight the Saracens. blanzac-porcheresse.fr
- **Laon** (Aisne, Picardy). *Chapelle des Templiers*. The Templars established themselves here in 1123 and built this octagonal chapel in 1130. It is now in the courtyard of the Archaeological Museum. tourisme-paysdelaon.com
- **Metz** (Moselle, Lorraine). *Chapelle des Templiers*. A 12th-century octagonal Romanesque-cum-Gothic chapel decorated with murals.
- **Montsaunès** (Haute Garonne, south of Toulouse). A busy main road rushes through this village and it is possible to miss the only Templar church in France still intact. You have to fetch the key from the town hall if you want to look inside. Around the doorway are carved 52 human heads. Inside are badly damaged frescoes including red crosses on the ceiling.
- **Paris: Square du Temple.** There is nothing to see in Paris relating to the Templars except a plaque marking the site of the execution of Jacques de Molay (Place Dauphine on the Ile de la Cité) and this peaceful square near the Place de la République. A fortress stood here until Napoleon had it pulled down.
- **Payns** (near **Troyes** in the Aube, Champagne). The birthplace of Hughes de Payens, one of the founders of the Knights Templar. huguesdepayns.fr
- **Richerenches** (Vaucluse, near **Avignon**). This restored Templar house is now the tourist office. richerenches.fr
- **Sainte-Eulalie-de-Cernon** (Aveyron). This village at foot of the Larzac plateau was the Templar headquarters for the region from the 12th century until the order's demise. It is extremely well preserved, although some buildings are later additions. ste-eulalie-larzac.com

identified themselves to each other using symbols that only they knew. Baptism is a form of initiation. Later, the policy of the church towards heresy forced Gnostics and others to band together for their own protection and behave with discretion.

The emergence of secret societies was also influenced by paganism – particularly the Druids, who were themselves initiates – and by various ancestral strains of magic, witchcraft and the occult.

In the middle ages, masons and other skilled craftsmen – forerunners of the *Compagnons* (see p154) – banded together in guilds to preserve the knowledge they had inherited and pass it on to apprentices. This knowledge could not be given out freely to everyone and so an aura of professional secrecy surrounded these guilds.

All of these influences came together in Enlightenment France and there was a boom in the formation of societies with evocative names such as the *Conspiracy of Equals*, the *Order of the Happy*, the *Friends of Truth* and the *Society of Universal Harmony*. When the Revolution erupted, it looked as if France was overrun by covert brotherhoods, and many people were sure that the two things were connected.

The Revolution and Afterwards

The unprecedented, seemingly co-ordinated upheavals of the French Revolution literally spelled the end of the world for those with a vested interest in the *ancien régime*, and the only way some of them could come to terms with it was by blaming secret societies. Social and economic grievances were not sufficient forces to propel such a destructive and transformative event; it had to be the work of Freemasons, Rosicrucians, Bavarian Illuminati or the members of some other shadowy organisation that was able to exert great influence at the top levels of society without showing itself. Who else would have pursued the apparent aims of the Revolution – the downfall of the monarchy and the eradication of Christianity in favour of "reason" – with such vehemence?

One of those claiming that the Revolution was the work of secret societies was Abbé Agustin de Barruel who is credited with being one of the founders of the modern conspiracy theory.

Ironically, when the Revolution came, the castle headquarters of the Templars in Paris passed into the hands of the fragile new state and it was turned into a prison. It was here that the royal family was held captive by revolutionaries, and from where Louis XVI was taken to his execution. The monarchy that had ended the Knights Templar almost five hundred years before was now itself disempowered and put to an end.

During the 19th century, in the aftermath of the Revolution, existing secret societies continued to operate and new ones were founded. By now, there were new tendencies driving people to band together behind closed doors. They could be said to be different responses to the same malaise. People were dismayed by the demise of the sacred and spiritual, which had been replaced by a world dominated by post-revolutionary ideas, politics, economic theory, equality, human rights, rationality and, increasingly, modern science.

One response was to seek to return to the "authentic", traditional roots of Catholicism – a time when the Church invested more in its metaphysical activities than in its worldly wealth and power. The other response was to offer an alternative to superstition and blind faith in an invisible supernatural being. During the Revolution, and again in the 1850s, there were earnest attempts to create a "rational religion".

The Power of Secrets

The Templars, meanwhile, were continually evoked with more interest in what they represented rather than in what they actually were. In the late 20th century they were given an entirely new lease of life by the modern mystery industry that sees the past as one long conspiracy to keep the truth from being known. If there is a consensus of such theories, it is that the Knights Templar were not just victims of a sordid monarchical campaign against them but were, instead, protagonists in one of the great plots of history. They were seen as the bearers of ancient secrets who had to be silenced.

Sometime during the 20th century, we stopped talking so much about secret societies and started to refer to cults and sects instead, but the concept is similar. What is a cult or sect, however, except a belief-system that attracts a minority following; probably won't last forever; and has no power to impose its ideas on other people?

All closed quasi-religious organizations, past or present, seem to respond to this basic human need to club together and know something that someone else doesn't. To this end, they share the same basic characteristics. There is, fundamentally, a stark difference between members and non-members. The only way to become a member is to go through a process of ceremonial initiation that involves making a commitment of loyalty and obedience. This induction process is likely to be by invitation only. Once initiated, secrecy is demanded. Even within the organization, knowledge of certain matters is restricted according to an individual's level in the hierarchy. Jargon, code and symbolism are usually employed to facilitate this secrecy and possibly to spread disinformation.

Any such society defines itself partly in opposition to everything that it is not, such as accepted authority and mainstream culture. The information that it guards so assiduously is an alternative to that which is supplied by orthodox institutions. The secret society claims to know the truth of what is really going on, and offers its members access to these mysteries. That is its allure.

All this raises some interesting questions about our present-day attitude to secrets. Most of us are ambivalent about withholding information. In practical, democratic terms, secrets are mostly suspect; but in mystical terms, there is a strong need not to say all that can be said and not to be taken in by theatricality. For example, a fact that is obstinately concealed by a self-selected organization will tend to make those in the know feel important, and also to convince those who are excluded that there is some enormous truth that they will never be allowed to know. The judicious protection of spiritual truths for the good of all is something else. There will always be a dark corner of the temple where no one needs to trespass; where the mind is not clear, and words – and secrets – become meaningless.

Masonic symbols

Chapelle des Templiers, Metz

Mystics of France

From mythical times to the present, France has been home (birthplace or adoptive home) to a variety of mystical seers and thinkers who have explored different levels of reality and often written about their experiences. Each of them is a singular voice expressing his or her direct experiences of the metaphysical and intangible. The following is a short selection from among them:

- **Maître Jacques and Père Soubise.** The legendary founders of *compagnonnage* (see p154) who are said to have initiated an oral tradition of passing esoteric secrets down the ages from master to apprentice.

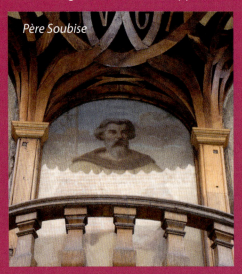
Père Soubise

- **Medieval master masons and craftsmen.** The men who built the great Romanesque and Gothic cathedrals were steeped in knowledge about astrology, the tarot, symbolism, Christian mysteries, pagan traditions and the arcane in general. Very few of them signed their work and we know next to nothing about most of them: how they acquired their knowledge and what they were trying to tell us.
- **Isaac the Blind** (Isaac Ben Abraham of Posquières). Born in Provence or the Languedoc. c1160–1235. Considered to be one of the founders of the French school of the kabbalah based in the Languedoc around Posquières (present-day Lunel), Isaac the Blind was the first scholar to give names to the ten Sephirot, the emanations through which the infinite reveals itself. It has been suggested that he was also the author of the important text, *The Book of the Bahir*.
- **Meister Eckhart** (Eckhart von Hochheim). Born in Germany. c1260–c1328. Philosopher, theologian and mystic, he taught for a time in Paris and he came to be known as the wisest of a group of men called "The Twelve Masters of Paris". He also preached in Strasbourg before being accused of heresy by the papacy in Avignon. It is not known where, when or how he died. Today he is remembered as a complex figure whose thinking went beyond Christianity and far into syncretism. Many aphorisms are attributed to him, most notably, "The Eye with which I see God is the same Eye with which God sees me".
- **Michel de Nostradamus.** Born in St-Remy-de-Provence. 1503–1566. Provencal doctor, astrologer and humanist known today for his predictions of the future. Descended from a family of converted Jews, his predictions are still cited and argued over today. He wrote predictions in rhyming quatrains, obscure and enigmatic. He lived the latter part of his life in Salon-de-Provence, where his house is now a museum.
- **Louis Claude de St Martin.** Born in Amboise. 1743–1803. Highly influential French mystical philosopher and esotericist who signed himself *le philosophe inconnu* (the unknown philosopher). His teachings, mostly inspired by Martinez de Pasqually, led to a strand of Christian mysticism known as Martinism. There are still Martinist organizations in existence today in several countries.
- **Etteilla.** The pseudonym (his surname

spelt backwards) of Jean-Baptiste Alliette. Born in Paris 1738–1791). The first man to popularize the tarot and to make his living by giving readings with the cards.
- **Eliphas Levi** (pseudonym of Alphonse Louis Constant). Born in Paris 1810–1875. "To practice magic is to be a quack; to know magic is to be a sage." So wrote Eliphas Levi of the subject to which he devoted his life. His *Dogme et ritual de la haute Magie* translated into English by Edward Arthur Waite as *Transcendental Magic, its Doctrine and Ritual*, published in 1843, was extremely influential.
- **Fulcanelli.** The pseudonym of a modern alchemist with no birthdate, birthplace or biography, and who is said not to have died. All that is known is that he wrote, or is said to have written *Le Mystère des Cathédrales* (1926) and *Demeures Philophosales* (see p170).
- **George Ivanovich Gurdjieff.** Born in Armenia, 1866, 1872 or 1877–1949. The inspiring and controversial spiritual teacher claimed to have met "remarkable men" on his travels in Asia and Egypt before establishing himself with a community of devoted followers in Fontainebleau outside Paris in 1922. His *Institute for the Harmonious Development of Man* aimed to teach the "Fourth Way" to self-development that was quicker than the normal three ways: the ways of the fakir, the monk and the yogi. Gurdjieff also made use of the Enneagram, a nine-pointed diagram used to better understand the workings of the cosmos.
- **René Guénon.** Born in Blois, 1886–1951. A metaphysician and interpreter of the sacred sciences of the East for the benefit of western audiences. He wrote particularly about symbolism which he saw as "metaphysical language at its highest". He died in Egypt, after having adopted an Egyptian name.
- **Pierre Teilhard de Chardin.** Born in the Auvergne, 1881–1955. Jesuit theologian who was also a palaeontologist of renown. His philosophical views were frowned on by the Church and had to be published posthumously. He proposed a synthesis between religion and science, proposing that the universe was in evolution towards an alignment of human consciousness with God's purpose.

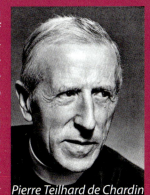
Pierre Teilhard de Chardin

- **Simone Weil.** Born in Paris, 1909-1943. Philosopher, mystic and political activist. Born Jewish, she later became a Christian. She claimed that God had found her, not vice versa. She held highly unorthodox ideas including "decreation" (a way of reversing the effects of Creation as a way of extinguishing the self) and "malheur"(the notion that to embrace suffering was a way of scourging the soul, transcending both mind and body, and driving us out of ourselves towards God. One of the objectives of life, she said, was "To see a landscape as it is when I am not there."
- **Pir Vilayat Inayat Khan.** Born in London, 1916-2004. Sufi teacher, the son of Hazrat Inayat Khan, who was sent by his master to bring Sufism to the west. The family settled in Suresnes, on the outskirts of Paris, and here Pir Vilayat Inayat Khan founded a Universal Sanctuary to facilitate meetings between the different religions.

Pir Vilayat

Ceiling of guardroom, Château du Plessis-Bourré

X

The Legendary Laboratory
Alchemists of the Past and Present

Symbols on the wall of the Château de Ménilles

The twin dreams of living forever and literally making money on demand are perennial human obsessions. These were said to be the aims of the alchemists but it is unlikely that they spent their energies on such base things. The mysterious signs carved into the walls of cathedrals and châteaux are more likely to be reminders of an ageless science dedicated to the perfection of the human soul.

In a narrow backstreet of **Paris**, half way between the *Pompidou Centre* and the *Square du Temple* (where the Knights Templar had their headquarters), there is a three-storey stone house that only those who know about it seek out. It is claimed to be the oldest auberge in Paris and is now a restaurant named after the man who built it in 1407, Nicolas Flamel, the most celebrated alchemist in France.

Born in 1330, Flamel was a scribe, notary and bookseller. One day, a stranger came into his shop and offered to sell him an intriguing book for two *florins*. It was entitled the *Manuscript of Abraham the Jew* and it purported to hold the secret to making the philosopher's stone that could render its owner rich and immortal.

After three years of unremitting hard work, Flamel managed to decipher the manuscript and learned to turn lead into gold. He and his wife *Dame Pernelle* lived well but modestly thereafter and used their wealth to build three chapels, seven churches, fourteen hospitals – and the house at 51 rue de Montmorency.

At least, that is how the story about him goes. To sceptics, Flamel was not an alchemist at all, merely a wealthy man on whom posterity stuck a label, by mistake or in a deliberate attempt at confusion.

With alchemy, nothing is ever what it seems or is said to be, and you have to be on your guard for misinformation. Few pronouncements on the subject are plain and unambiguous facts.

In popular imagination, alchemy is a synonym for magic and the alchemist is a bearded sorcerer engaged in bizarre experiments with the aim of discovering the "philosopher's stone" which will enable him to turn lead into gold and make himself immortal. Alchemy, however, is more complicated and more interesting than that.

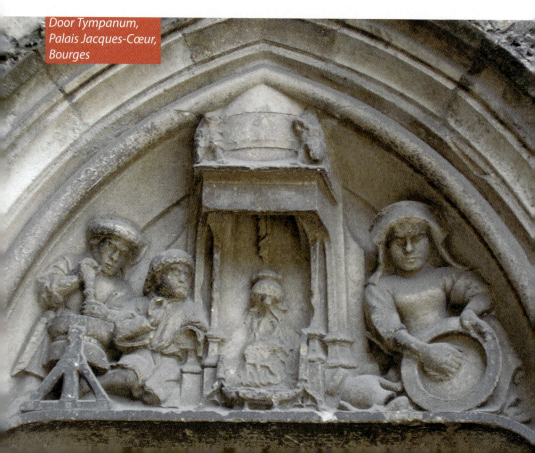

Door Tympanum, Palais Jacques-Cœur, Bourges

Who Do We Believe?

If we are to get to the truth of alchemy, the first question is: who do we believe?

Nowadays, the study of alchemy is left to experts who have not themselves put alchemical methods into practice.

Academically, alchemy is considered to be a thing of history, a blind alley in the progress of human knowledge. At best it has been described as a forerunner to modern science, but it is more often considered to be a pseudoscience, a vain delusion which cannot have yielded any useful results and was superseded by better methods of enquiry. One writer has summed it up as "failed chemistry".

This is a judgement which can only lead to misunderstanding. It is easy to think we understand the past enough to condemn its ignorance but it is a mistake to assume that things can always be divided into good or bad, true or false, fruitful or deluded.

To believe that alchemists persevered for centuries without any positive results is a naïve modern attitude. The practice of alchemy demanded dedication, expense, hard work, trial and error, discipline and self-sacrifice. It was not a career undertaken for amusement or curiosity. It is doubtful that all alchemists – following each other over many generations – were simple-minded and credulous, working away at techniques that achieved nothing.

It would be fairer to say that alchemy was early chemistry. Alchemists were scientific pioneers, hands-on researchers into the nature of things. There was in the middle ages no recognized divide between science and alchemy, only enquiry into the nature of nature. Several men who are remembered today as great scientists were also alchemists and they contributed important discoveries to the development of science. Ernest Rutherford, the nuclear physicist who won the Nobel Prize in 1908, noted the ambiguous similarity between his work and alchemy.

Corner decoration, Hotel Lallemant, Bourges

Obscuring the Truth

Historians and modern scientists can supply the dry facts about alchemy but only alchemists themselves knew – or know? – what they were up to, and there are several reasons why we should treat anything they have to say with great care.

There are among the alleged alchemists undoubtedly a number of fraudsters, gold-diggers and other unscrupulous souls. Such frivolous dabblers were known as *puffers*, after the way they pumped the bellows of their furnaces.

Added to this are the complications arising from pseudonyms. Alchemists, like internet users, liked to give themselves false names. We also have the problem of *pseudepigrapha*, the misattribution of alchemical texts and artistic creations when the named individuals had nothing to do with them as, possibly, in the case of Nicolas Flamel.

Even if we can sort out the true alchemists from the false, we still have to understand what they say. Alchemy spoke in two languages that can only be interpreted by the initiated. Plain speech was not for them. They spoke in the "green language" or "the language of the birds", that could only be understood by another *bona fide* alchemist.

The other preferred language of alchemy is that of symbolism (see p20). Alchemists were often proud that their secrets were "hidden in plain sight": symbols that anyone could see but which only spoke to the person who knew what to look for.

Alchemy was not meant to be easy to comprehend. It was a work that demanded commitment and effort, and that began with the effort needed to interpret the evidence.

This meant that anyone seeking after deeper meanings had to be attentive to clues that had to be collected in exactly the right order if they were to build on each other, and this order was dictated also by the preparedness of the student-seeker.

The implication of all this is that whatever can be said about alchemy is never going to be the definite truth about it. Mystically, alchemy must be regarded as an open question in which facts may not be relied on but may, if used wisely, contribute to insight.

Roots and History

The origins of alchemy are obscure. Systems of alchemy are known to have developed, apparently independently, in China and India, but the alchemy practiced in France derives from a western tradition which is thought to have arisen in the Greco-Egyptian world in the second or third century BC, specifically in Alexandria.

Alchemists considered their foundation text to be *The Emerald Tablet* attributed to the legendary figure of *Hermes Trismegistus* – the name which has given us the world "hermetic". This text may have been written by various authors sometime between the 6th and 8th centuries AD. It was said by an early commentator to have been found in an underground vault in the hands of a corpse sitting on a golden throne. The alchemists' motto, "as above, so below", comes from this short text, which is said to encrypt the secrets of the alchemical art.

Alchemical texts arrived in Europe in the 12th century, via the Arabic world. The golden age of alchemy was the late middle ages and the Renaissance when hermeticism was fused with *Platonism* and other ideas. This was the time of Nicolas Flamel. Several châteaux around France were adorned with alchemical symbols and it is said that many Gothic cathedrals similarly transmit secrets to those who can

The Athanor (oven) in Cénevières' alchemy laboratory

read them. The enigmatic *Count of St Germain*, nicknamed "the deathless", who fascinated the court society of Paris around 1750, was rumoured to be an alchemist who had been able to extend his life span.

Fulcanelli and the Latter-Day Alchemists

It was widely thought that alchemy had been finished off by the Enlightenment and the appearance of modern science in the 18th century – until an intriguing pseudonymous book appeared in **Paris** in 1926. *The Mystery of the Cathedrals* was written by one "Fulcanelli", who described himself as a practising alchemist. He claimed that the great Gothic cathedrals of northern France are not what they appear. They are only superficially about Christian worship. Really, we should seem them as giant "books in stone". If we read them correctly we can learn about the secret craft of alchemy. A building is better than a book. It lasts for generations: it cannot be lost like a book and is not easily burned.

We don't know who Fulcanelli was but it is clear from the amount of detail he uses and the references he draws on that he knows what he is talking about. The preface to *The Mystery of the Cathedrals* by one of his students hints that he had completed the Great Work and found the key to immortality. He lived on in anonymity without having the need for a name or an identity.

> "The alchemist's researches were coloured by moral and religious preoccupations, whereas modern physics was created in the eighteenth century for their amusement by a few aristocrats and wealthy libertines. Science without a conscience…"
> —a man believed to be Fulcanelli, quoted by Jacques Bergier

The book reawakened an interest in alchemy and the debate continues today as to whether it is the route to wisdom or an elaborate pretence. One book in the 1960s claimed that alchemists of old knew the principles of atomic physics and the threat to humanity they posed.

The scientist and writer Jacques Bergier claims in a book called *The Morning of the Magicians* that he was visited by Fulcanelli himself in a laboratory of the Gas Board in Paris in June 1937. Fulcanelli, he says, wanted to tell him that the alchemists had known for a very long time about certain discoveries in atomic physics that were about to be made, and that humanity should take great care with the technologies it was about to unleash.

The co-author of *The Morning of the Magicians*, Louis Pauwels, also claims to have met a latter-day alchemist, this time in the *Café Procope* in Paris in March 1953. In the same year, Fulcanelli's pupil Eugene Canseliet says he met his master in Seville, looking in good health even though he would have to have been 113 years old. Canseliet himself lived on, giving the occasional interview (but never clearing up the mystery of Fulcanelli's identity) until his death in 1982. Since the 1960s, the subject of alchemy has taken on a new vigour but whether or not there are still authentic alchemists around, rather than pretenders and dabblers, it is impossible to say.

Prima Materia

What, then was – or is – alchemy? Alchemists have always been insistent that theirs is a practical, not theoretical, work. It is concerned with the manipulation of matter. They do not, however, see matter only at its face value, as immutable. Matter is instead conceived as dynamic, in evolution.

Alchemy postulates the existence of a *prima materia* or primal matter that is formless and propertyless in itself. It is self-contained and self-replicating; and it contains the potential of all qualities. It is a powerful catalyst:

"That there abides in nature a certain pure matter, which, being discovered and brought by art to perfection, converts to itself proportionally all imperfect bodies that it touches," explains a Catalan author.

If it is difficult to describe, it is impossible to name and is referred to by many different epithets, including *Permanent Water*, *Spiritual Blood*, *Spittle of the Moon*, *the Bride*, *the Dragon* and *Dissolved Refuse*.

Paracelsus referred to it as *Yliaster*, "a clod which contained all the chaos, all the waters, all minerals, all herbs, all stones, all gems. Only the supreme Master could release them and form them with tender solicitude, so that other things could be created from the rest."

Prima materia is closely related to the concept of *quintessence* or *aether*, the divine substance supposed to make up the heavenly bodies and to have been present at the Creation. Quintessence is rare on earth, hence the pull that celestial bodies have on us. If quintessence can be isolated by distillation of certain substances, it can rid any matter (including the human body) of impurities, cure illness and extend life.

One way of looking at this process is that the alchemists were trying to discover the works of God and to emulate them at a faster speed than allowed by nature.

It is this concern with things natural that distinguishes Alchemy from magic. It is a way of looking at the world in order to understand the secrets of nature, in order to work with them, not to go against them. Alchemy is not the selfish pursuit of riches and eternal life for the sake of having these things. There is an intimation that it has to do with spiritual knowledge as much as material knowledge and that one has to lose oneself in order to succeed at it.

The alchemists did not merely observe nature like mystics or contemplatives. They wanted to participate in it actively, to intervene, but they did so with a sense of purpose and responsibility.

Organization of Matter and Methodology

All matter, according to alchemy, is organized under the medieval system of the four elements of earth, air, fire, and water,

Château de Chailly

Châteaux of the Alchemists

- **Château de Cénevières,** Cénevières (Lot). This beautiful Renaissance château beside the River Lot has its own preserved alchemy laboratory, although without any equipment, dating from around 1600. A series of polychrome frescoes ostensibly depicts scenes from Ovid's Metamorphosis but are said to have esoteric significance. On one side of the room is an althanor, an alchemical oven. chateau-cenevieres.com
- **Château de Chailly,** Chailly-sur-Armançon (Côte-d'Or). Now a luxury hotel-restaurant, this old château west of Dijon carries a collection of mythological beasts and allegorical figures on its façade, especially on the frieze beneath the roofline. The seven windows on each floor represent the seven metals employed by alchemists. chailly.com
- **Château de Chastenay,** Arcy-sur-Cure (Yonne). This manor house was the home of Jean de Lys, an initiate in the 14th century. The late father of the present owner wrote a book explaining how even the site of the building was chosen for esoteric reasons, benefiting from favourable lines of earth energy. At present it is only open for group visits. grottes-arcy.net *****
- **Château de Dampierre,** Dampierre-sur-Boutonne (Charente-Maritime). Two galleries look over the courtyard of this handsome château. The upper one is a masterpiece of French alchemical art. The coffered ceiling, installed in 1545-50, is divided into 93 sculptures on an extraordinary variety of esoteric themes, each bearing a caption or motto in Latin, French or Spanish. chateau-dampierre.com
- **Manoir de la Salamandre,** Étretat (Normandy). If the Manoir de la Salamandre in the town centre looks out of place in the distinctly unmedieval seaside resort of Étretat, that's because it is. This medieval mansion was built in Lisieux in the 14th century, dismantled in the early 20th century and re-erected here where it now serves as a hotel-restaurant. The decorations show a variety of mythological and alchemical symbols, not the least of which is the eponymous salamander. hotelsetretat.com
- **Château de Terreneuve,** Fontenay-le-Comte (Vendée). The focus in this Renaissance château is the fireplace in the grand salon, which represents the three stages of creating the philosopher´s stone. Fulcanelli devotes several pages to it in his second book, *The Dwellings of the Philosophers*. chateau-terreneuve.com
- **Maison Jayet,** Paray-le-Monial (Saône-et-Loire). This town is famous as the focus of a Christian pilgrimage and its main sight is a Romanesque church. The town hall occupies the Hôtel Jayet, a mansion which has one of the finest Renaissance facades in France. The conventional story is that the sculptures glorify a merchant who paid for it all and whose name it bears, but lovers of things esoteric say that its ornamentation is really a coded message alluding to alchemy. tourisme-paraylemonial.fr

- **Château du Plessis-Bourré,** Écuillé, (Maine-et-Loire). Jean Bourré (1424-1506) lived a double life. As well as being a respected aide of Louis XI and Charles VIII, he was also an alchemist. The paintings on the 24 coffers of the ceiling in the guardroom in his château testify to his occult pastime. They depict "The Great Work" and provide advice for aspiring alchemists to follow. plessis-bourre.com

and as seven principle metals, each governed by a "wandering star" in the sky:

>   Gold – the sun
>   Silver – the moon
>   Quicksilver – Mercury
>   Copper – Venus
>   Iron – Mars
>   Tin – Jupiter
>   Lead – Saturn

Alchemists had a special regard for mercury (known as *quicksilver* or *hydrargyrum*), the only metal to be liquid at standard temperatures, which was considered a fluid connection between above and below. Other substances were classed as "mundane elements" but one of these, sulphur (brimstone), represented the spirit of life because of its strong colour and smell.

An alchemist worked in a laboratory in which he combined ingredients according to his level of knowledge and put them through a series of processes which involved a lengthy supply of heat from a constantly burning furnace or *athanor*.

The nature of these processes depends on which author you read. They have been divided into up to fourteen stages with evocative names such as *Exuberation* and *Multiplication by Virtue*, but alchemy is normally discussed as taking place in just three stages, in which the concoction changes colour from black to white to red.

The number three (along with the number seven for the planetary metals) crops up often in alchemical architecture and decoration. Each of the alchemical colours is said to be represented by a cathedral, respectively Chartres, Tours and Bourges.

The three stages are also said to be represented by the three rose windows in any other Gothic cathedral marking the passage of the sun. The north rose is the darkness before day; the southern rose is the white light of the midday sun; the western rose meanwhile looks towards the reddening setting sun.

Some alchemists also report an intermediate step called the *peacock's tail* in which a variety of colours appeared.

Another description of the operation to make the Philosopher's Stone calls it the "Philosophical Egg", named after the shape of the vessel used. The material was placed in this flask, hermetically sealed and subjected to a process of rebirth.

In search of Fulcanelli

Who was or is Fulcanelli and was he right in claiming that alchemical lore is encoded in the structure of gothic cathedrals, and that alchemy is still practised today? We don't know the answers. Fulcanelli was an erudite man (or woman) who studied the buildings he writes about *in situ* and in detail. Even if his interpretation is wrong, he makes a compelling case for it and puts forward some interesting ideas.

Fulcanelli, it is surmised, was born in the early part of the 19th century. Whether or not he died is a matter of conjecture. He disappeared before the publication of his book but there were reports that he was still alive and well in the 1950s when he would have been over 110 years old.

The pseudonym is probably a combination of Vulcan, the god of fire, volcanoes, forges and metals (which alchemists were particularly interested in) and the name of Eli, the Old Testament prophet. At least thirteen candidates have been put forward for the identity of Fulcanelli but none has yet been proven correct. They include Eugene Cansielet (who wrote the preface to Fulcanelli's book); Julien Champagne (who supplied the photographs for it); the physicist Jules Violle; and the elusive Count de Saint Germain – who may or may not have died in the 18th century.

The gallery, Château de Dampierre

Magic and Witchcraft

Until at least the 18th century, everyone in Europe believed in magic and witchcraft, although few people would have been able to agree on a definition of either. They are complicated and controversial words. Whereas alchemy seeks to discover the laws of nature so as to work with them, magic seeks to override them or distort them. The aim of magic is to manipulate hidden supernatural forces to the practitioner's intended ends, whether benign or malevolent.

For ordinary people, the sorcerer and his or her arts were part of superstitious rural life, and it is likely that witches supplied a range of services that we would now class as healing, psychology, intuition, meteorology, veterinary medicine and plant lore.

For the Church, however, witchcraft was an uncontrollable force that was at best beyond its control and at worst the instrument of the devil (see p146). Fear of it peaked during the Reformation and from approximately 1450 to the end of the 17th century the witches of France were persecuted.

Alsace had particular fame as a haunt of witches and there are still *tours de sorcière* in **Rouffach**, **Thann**, **Ribeauvillé**, **Châtenois**, **Cernay** and **Selestat**. Berry is another region that seems to have had more than its share of enchantresses.

Where there was an accusation of witchcraft, the authorities moved swiftly lest it should spread. Exorcism was the first approach used, but trial, torture and punishment were resorted to in extreme cases. An outbreak mass diabolic possession in **Aix-en-Provence** in 1611 only ended with the burning at the stake of a local priest. This was echoed by the most famous trial for possession, which took place at **Loudun** (Vienne, Poitou-Charentes) in 1634. An entire convent of nuns was accused of being in league with demons. A local parish priest, Urban Grandier, was burned alive for his part in the episode. The story was written up by Aldous Huxley as *The Devils of Loudun* and filmed by the British director Ken Russell.

The belief in and fear of witchcraft waned as the rationalism of the Enlightenment spread. Witch-hunting also died out because it strained the legal system to breaking point. What exactly could constitute proof positive of black magic?

There are two museums of magic in France, the *Musée de la Sorcellerie* in **Concressault** and the *Maison des Sorcières* in **Bergheim**, Alsace.

It is a mistake, however to see alchemy as working in one dimension. The transmutation of metals was only one aim and perhaps received – and receives – so much attention because of the universal desire for acquiring riches apparently without effort.

Alchemists simultaneously sought the transmutation of organic things, including the human body, and it is likely that they made a contribution to the art of healing and medicine. It has been said that the tradition of homeopathy grew out of alchemy.

On a higher level, alchemists were striving towards the transmutation of the soul. Part of the Great Work - perhaps the essential part of it – was the purification and perfection of the experimenter himself.

All the indications are that the alchemist's work was never for personal aggrandisement and wealth but the opposite. Ego could only get in the way of the quest for true wisdom and the ultimate ambition to become a self-effacing master. The object of the alchemist is to become an awakened man.

Something or Nothing?

There are several ways we can try to make sense of all this. We could take it lightly, casting the alchemist as either a deluded misfit or charlatan. In that case, his science is seen as useless, fantastical thinking that somehow grew into a convincing body of knowledge with an air of authority. We can take delight in trying to unravel its symbols and secrets even if they have nothing useful to tell us.

Conversely, we could assume there is wisdom in the walls and the texts, even if we can't understand it immediately. It is possible that all of alchemy is true, in both the promise and the detail, and that it constitutes a covert knowledge that came before science and now, although deeply hidden, runs parallel to it.

There is, however, a third way to decipher what we see. Given that alchemy guards its secrets in metaphors, we may have to approach it as a metaphor to understand its essence.

It could be that the mechanics of alchemy – laboratory, retorts, furnaces – were only a way to occupy the brain and hands of the inexperienced apprentice, or to engage the imagination of foolish outsiders. Such images may be challenging us not to get stuck on them, not to be taken in by colourful distractions and misinformation of all kinds, and instead to ask ourselves questions about what we can and cannot know.

The Great Work, therefore, takes place not in what we call reality but within the individual mind and soul. Alchemy does tackle some of the same subject matter as science but in a different way.

It addresses the great problem of science and the human being: how to connect the world of things with the world of thoughts, the measurable with the intangible, the mundane with the divine. Its aim is not to transform matter beyond the possibilities of physical science but to comprehend the interface between the material and immaterial realms. Science is our guide to materialism; alchemy our guide to everything else.

"Too late known, too soon left", Château de Dampierre

The Virtues of the Alchemist

Alchemy can therefore be best seen not as a question of success or failure in manipulating matter and following a particular formula but as a process of manipulating ourselves.

The philosopher's stone was meant to remain beyond reach. The important task was striving to attain it.

"As above, so below" can be read as a comparison between the high ideals of alchemy and the practicalities of living a human life. Alchemy is then an inscrutable guide to wise living.

It required, or at least advised, the adept to develop certain qualities or virtues.

First, alchemy demanded a special kind of faith. This was not gullibility but rather the instinct to listen, obey and follow, to learn to choose the right path by intuition, to proceed sometimes with the benefit of guidance and sometimes by trial and error. Unpleasant and frustrating experiences are not failures to regret, but necessary parts of the procedure.

Once embarked upon, the Great Work – be it alchemy or life – demands dedication, commitment and perseverance from the participant.

The work, too, required an ethical motivation. The right path could be found only by the denial of selfish gain and the feeling of being part of something larger than an individual human life. The adept was required to refine and purify the metals within himself.

More subtly, the apprentice alchemist had to learn a sense of timing. Understandings come in a particular order and at the right moment: each can only be assimilated when the soul is ready, and each new insight can only be achieved when its predecessor has been integrated. It may take years or even a lifetime to learn one lesson and this precludes impatience and demands a sense of pace. Go too fast and our personal furnace will overheat and your enterprise will not work. Steps in the process cannot be skipped out of preference. Life on the spiritual path involves both risks and moments of discomfort

In pursuing the work, flexibility and broadmindedness are also required. The language of symbolism and metaphor precludes rigidity and dogmatism. Alchemy demands that the practicant be ever vigilant and ready to change approach if necessary, freeing himself from assumptions about what should work. Symbols demand more than attention; they require perceptive and penetrative thinking on different levels.

Alchemy also teaches discretion, circumspection and caution. Not everything can be discussed with everyone in the same terms. Not every truth should be made simple and easy to get to for others. Communication seems like a simple art but it can be very difficult to convey an exact message from one human mind to another.

Finally, alchemy reminds us of a paradox that our clever minds often refuse to grasp. Some phenomena of the universe are beyond knowing, beyond fact and truth. Wisdom and knowledge also involve mystery and an acceptance of not knowing.

When Eugene Canseliet, the chief disciple of Fulcanelli, was asked in a filmed interview towards the end of his life what alchemy could contribute to the know-all modern word, he replied "a balance that it lacks". Alchemy may seem quaint and misguided but it warns us not to be taken in by the notion of eternal progress. We shouldn't do everything we can just because we can. There are scientific advances that we can and should do without. Some secrets are better not discussed openly, let alone applied in reality. Alchemy may be defined in the popular imagination by its preposterous goals – eternal wealth and eternal life – but true alchemy has more to do with wisdom and understanding limits.

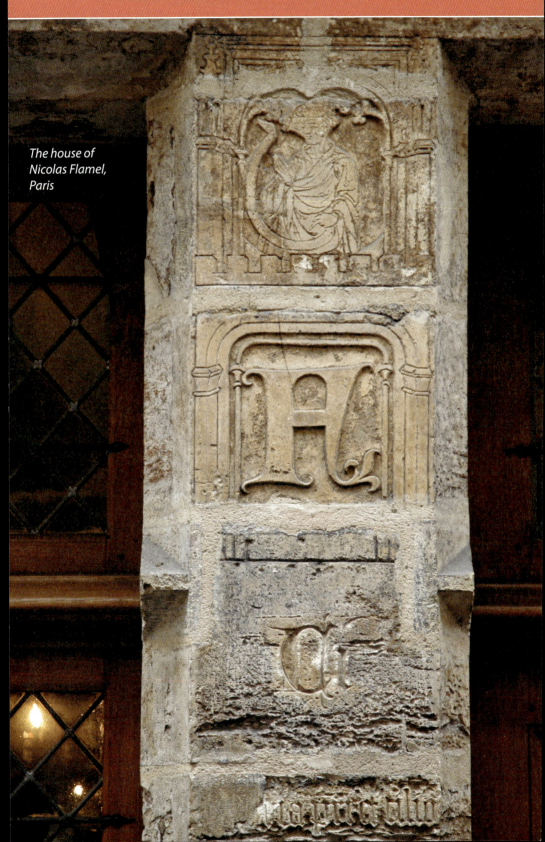

The house of Nicolas Flamel, Paris

The Tarot, Key to the Hidden Mechanisms of the Universe

The Tarot is a set of symbolic cards that are thought to encode great esoteric wisdom. No one knows their origin. The cards seem to have appeared in Europe between 1420 and 1425 but they may be much older. The traditional decks in use today date from the 17th and 18th centuries. Many of them originated in France and are referred to as the "Marseille" tarot, although this term can be confusing since very few decks were produced in that city. It is more accurate, says J-M David in *Reading the Marseille Tarot*, to speak of "Marseille-type" tarot decks. Everyday recreational playing cards derive from the Tarot with several important alterations and omissions.

Tarot cards are most often used as a form of divination although this should not be taken to mean predicting the future. Tarot practitioners prefer to see the cards as a way to gain insight into the working of the laws of nature and to access the subconscious of the individual.

On its simplest level it is a portable reminder that we can access what we already know.

Images from the tarot pop up in a variety of contexts, including alchemy and the stained glass windows of Gothic cathedrals.

There are 78 cards in a Tarot pack, the 22 most interesting ones being known as the major arcana. Every element of a tarot card contributes towards to its meaning: the number and name, the colours used, relationship of a card to its predecessor and successor in the sequence, the age, sex, posture and gesture of any characters shown and any objects they are associated with.

The major arcana are as follows:
Le Mat – The Fool (unnumbered)
I *Le Bateleur* – The Magician
II *La Papesse* – The Popess or High Priestess
III *L'Imperatrice* – The Empress
IV *L'Empereur* – The Emperor
V *Le Pape* – The Pope or Hierophant
VI *L'Amoureux* – The Lover
VII *Le Chariot* – The Chariot
VIII *La Justice* – Justice
VIIII *L'Ermite* – The Hermit
X *La Roue de Fortune* – The Wheel of Fortune
XI *La Force* – Strength
XII *Le Pendu* – The Hanged Man
XIII *La Mort* – Death
XIIII *La Tempérance* – Temperance
XV *Le Diable* – The Devil
XVI *La Maison-Dieu* – The House of God, or Tower
XVII *L'Etoile* – The Star
XVIII *La Lune* – The Moon
XVIIII *Le Soleil* – The Sun
XX *Le Jugement* – Judgement
XXI *Le Monde* – The World.

There are a great many ways of interpreting the cards. The late Jean-Claude Flornoy*, who restored several historic tarots, proposed that the cards be divided into groups to reveal the "journey of the soul" through life. Each group of five cards is introduced by a portal or gateway.

Childhood

I (The Magician) opens the door leading to incarnation and infancy. Cards II, III, IV, and V stand for the four stages of childhood represented by grandmother, mother, father and grandfather. During this period, we build the physical body and learn the meaning of "we".

Apprenticeship

VI (The Lover) is the key to youth's first passion and apprenticeship. During our progress through cards VII, VIII, VIIII, X, we are led by an opening heart to construct the mental body. This is the time in which we develop a sense of individualization or self, and learn the meaning of "I".

The Journeyman (Compagnon)

XI (Strength) represents reconstruction in the material world, through matter. This phase sees the transformation of the emotional body. The individual learns to focus his energy and to work with, rather than for, other people. Cards XII, XIII, XIIII and XV lead us through this process.

Mastery

XVI (The House of God or Tower) introduces a new phase in which we "die" before experiencing physical death. This process results in the creation of the energetic body. With this experience behind us we can now leave fear behind and attain Mastery. The next sequence of cards, XVII, XVIII, XVIIII, XX, deals with our masterwork on earth, profound learning and the transmission of knowledge.

Wisdom

XXI (The World) indicates that we have reached the centre of existence, a state of synthesis and a time of wisdom. We have built the "body glorious" and attained consciousness in order to participate in the soul of the world, the anima mundi.

The Fool

One card stands apart from the rest. The Fool, a card without a number, is not part of this or any sequence. The Fool claims the right to absolute liberty. He is best seen as a reminder of the consequences of choosing not to act in the world, of not being involved and not seeking to evolve. There is folly in thinking that living purely in the moment is an act of wisdom in itself. "He excuses himself and is irreverent," explained Flornoy. "He sits astride the moment. He detaches himself from the world and lives in the here and now." He is unaware of past and future, but in living without them he shuns the possibility of wisdom and the evolution of the soul.

*For details of how to obtain Jean-Claude Flornoy's tarot cards, go to tarot-history.com.

Millau Viaduct

XI

Spirit in our Times
Finding Meaning in Modern France

Medicine wheel in a private garden

Modern France grew out of the Enlightenment and the Revolution, shrugging off superstition as it embraced reason and secularism. Yet, today the country is a rich mix of all the traditions that have shaped it and there is mysticism all around it if you look for it.

It is not always easy to find the esoteric in contemporary France. To get to sites offering peace, contemplation and transcendental experience, it is necessary to get past the ugly, functional, prefabricated installations of the modern world that can easily deaden the spirit.

Every great cathedral is hemmed in on all sides by commerce and suburban peripheral development. The mundane obscures the mystical. France is more conspicuously a place of highways, industrial estates and shopping centres than a country of spiritual resources.

Often it feels as if mystical France is a series of islands separated by vast stretches of alienating *no man's land*. It is easy to get the impression that all things mysterious and inspirational belong to the past not the present – remnants from a lost age when such things were valued; anachronisms of interest to the minority of travellers. Either that, or mystical France is a parallel reality which uncomfortably overlaps a modern country built on uniformity, conformity, rationality and regulation.

This is one way to see things but there is another. Mysticism is never an obsolete force stuck in the past; it is an eternal human need. The enigma of death has never gone away; the relationship between the invisible individual (the mind) and the body has not been resolved; and the definitive meaning of life has not yet been discovered.

If mysticism seems in danger of being corralled or driven to extinction by the modern world, it may be because we are looking at it in a particular way. Mysticism is an unstoppable force and it sprouts anew in different ways to suit the times, if only we can adjust our vision to see this.

It is a mistake to push the division between the mystical and the non-mystical too far. The difference between the two is only ever a subjective judgement. There is something misguided in choosing to see only those parts of the modern world that are comforting and reassuring in either direction.

In one sense, France has inherited a four-fold legacy of intellectual awareness. First is Cartesian thinking, and this was followed by the Enlightenment and Humanism. Next came the Revolutionary notion that society can be re-made and gods reinvented along rational lines. Finally, 20th-century despair and disillusion led to existentialism, deconstruction and materialism. This is a country defined by politics, economics and sociology. There is no place in it for mysticism if it doesn't create jobs, provide food or ease the lives of the poor.

France, though, is more than this. The whole is indivisible. While the sobering and pragmatic consensus of reality must be accepted, so must its counterpart – an unconventional reality that enables the spirit to soar.

Marianne

Where Modern Mysticism Lurks

There are several areas of modern life in France in which it is possible to track down a sense of contemporary mysticism, even if this is not the word most people would use.

Mysticism used to be the monopoly of religion, particularly Catholicism and religion is still the first resort of the mystically inclined. While Christianity has been in slow retreat since the Revolution, it hasn't gone away. Despite the attempted dechristianization by the Revolutionaries (see p184) and the separation of Church and State, Christianity still exerts a hold on French culture and provides the most obvious places for a moment of quiet inner reflection, even for the agnostic or atheist. You don't have to be a devout Christian to find subtle and interesting qualities in the average church. There are still many monasteries and convents (see p130) which offer retreats from the world.

Other religions (see p188), meanwhile, are growing steadily, creating new opportunities for mystical experiences. Buddhism is particularly well established. Practitioners of Sufism offer a mystical strand of Islam and Judaism's mystical tradition, the kabbalah, has its modern adherents.

Curiously, many people have replaced religion with a veneration of the state, the *République seule et indivisible* which is the primary marker of French identity. Republican values have a quasi-mystical feel to them as seen in the symbols that represent them. The young Marianne in her Phrygian cap is the maternal goddess of the nation and an embodiment of liberty, reason, tolerance and inclusion. The national animal, the cockerel, also has abstract, allegorical associations. The Revolutionary and then Republican motto, *Liberté, Egalité, Fraternité*, seen on all town halls everywhere in France, may possibly have derived from Freemasonry but certainly had masonic influence in its formulation. The three words are, of course, all abstract nouns standing for notions that float in the universal ether and permeate the even more abstract and idealist *Rights of Man*.

For many people in France, the nation

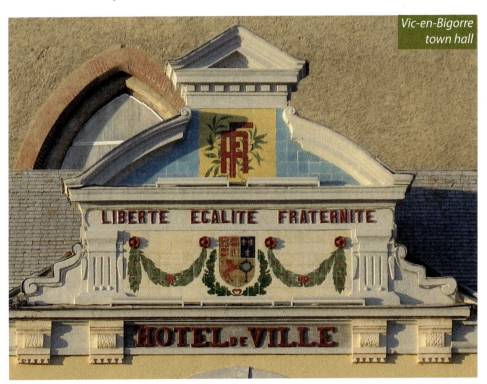

Vic-en-Bigorre town hall

Latter-Day Churches

After the era of Gothic (see p117), churches continued to be built in France, but they are of increasingly less importance in the architectural and spiritual history of the country.

The aristocrats and wealthy merchants of the Renaissance and the *Grand Siècle* of Louis XIV were more interested in erecting palaces than temples. The churches that were built speak more of sentimentality, the vanity of patronage and of a fascination with Greek and Roman mythology thanof following French religious tradition.

The Enlightenment brought the status of the church down even further, seeing it almost as an extension of human rather than supernatural power. This is perhaps best illustrated by the *Église Saint-Sulpice* in the Luxembourg quarter of **Paris** where an elaborate astronomical device called a *gnomon*, consisting of an obelisk and a straight brass line set in marble across the floor, was installed in 1743 (see p203). The emphasis is on the scientific value of the gnomon rather than the spiritual aspirations inspired by the building.

The Revolution and the 19th century reacted further against what it saw as the superstitions of the *ancien régime* and sought to make churches less dramatic and more rational. A good example of the changing attitude to religion is the church of la Madeleine, also in Paris but this time across the river in the Opera quarter. It is built in the style of a classical temple and wouldn't look out of place in Greece. During the Revolution, there was a debate as to whether it should be a bank, a theatre, a ballroom, a library or a railway station instead, as if the roles were interchangeable. For a time, it was destined to be a monument to the glory of Napoleon's armies. Clearly, any notion of creating a sacred structure to suit a sacred site had, by then, been lost.

The later part of the twentieth century saw new churches being built using modern materials and methods. Two of the most interesting examples are the chapel of *Notre-Dame-du-Haut* at **Ronchamp** (in Franc-Comté) by Le Corbusier and the *Chapelle du Rosaire* de **Vence**, decorated by Henri Matisse. Other outstanding modern churches – not to all tastes – are the *Église Saint-Joseph* in the port city of **Le Havre** (Normandy), Notre-Dame in the resort of **Royan** (on the Gironde estuary north of **Bordeaux**) and France's most recent cathedral in **Créteil** (Ile de France).

Obelisk, Saint-Sulpice

Créteil cathedral

First World War altar painting, Larreule

gion. The implication is that there is something of value in the old that we cannot find in the new or reproduce.

History is patrimoine *per se* and it often has its very non-materialistic component. France's national heroine and saint is Joan of Arc, who is celebrated for her clarity and bravery leading to political and military achievements. In reality she was resolutely mystical, being guided by Saints Gabriel, Michael, Marguerite and Catherine.

The patrimoine is not necessarily old. Every year, thousands of tourists make the trek to see the graceful **Millau** viaduct. The creation and appreciation of beauty, especially when it is married to the landscape, is very much a form of mysticism.

Art, in its many different forms, is another route to things ethereal. If mysticism is the experience of being transported to some mysterious "elsewhere", art is certainly a trigger or a catalyst.

In some ways, the art gallery has taken over some of the functions of the church and we approach it with reverence and receptivity. Exhibitions and concerts are often held in churches, cathedrals and monasteries – some deconsecrated, others not – and this reinforces the transcendental nature of art.

There is a close connection between art and spirituality, whether or not the artist is a believer. The *Chapelle du Rosaire* in **Vence** (Provence) is considered to be Matisse's masterpiece, and Chagall created a magnificent series of stained glass windows for **Metz** cathedral.

Music is especially associated with the

is not the first call on their sense of loyalty. They identify with a much more nebulous entity, the *pays*, or local area. The *pays* is a combination of the natural qualities of the land, how it is used and how the people live on it.

The French countryside comes close to being held sacred by rural people and city dwellers alike, and the food it produces, processed by Michelin-starred restaurants. Cooking is recognized as an element of the intangible cultural heritage of humanity. French cuisine is talked of in terms of reverence and mystical appreciation. The production and appreciation of wine, meanwhile, is a cult and mystique of its own.

France's national heritage (*patrimoine*) also has a quasi-mystical aura. The preservation of what has been left over from the past, having survived wars and official demolition policies, is almost a new reli-

The Dechristianization of France

The French Revolution was more than a political and economic upheaval. The more extreme of its perpetrators sought to remake the entire *ancien régime* in more fair and logical ways. They found it comparatively easy to pass laws to change the physical living conditions of people, but it was more difficult to dictate changes to the life of the spirit. In trying to do so they came up against the perennial problems of how far an individual should be permitted to follow his or her own faith and how much any religion should be allowed to establish itself on earth.

Before the Revolution, the Catholic Church had enjoyed a near-monopoly on religious practice and it had enormous influence. As the largest landowner in the country with the ability to raise taxes, it was a wealthy institution with many peasants subservient to it. The clergy comprised the First Estate and enjoyed a position of privilege and power in alliance with the aristocracy and the monarchy.

To anyone brought up on the rationalist ideas of the Enlightenment and the materiality of urban living, the Church stood in the way of social reform. It was, they thought, oppressive and reactionary. Its concentration of worldly wealth was at odds with its Christian message and any notion of spirituality.

Yet, for the majority of ordinary people, Catholicism was the only faith they had ever known or wanted and they saw no reason for change.

Some revolutionaries believed that they had to "dechristianize" France if the country was to modernize itself. Thus began an *ad hoc* process involving both legislation and direct militant action. In 1789, the Church's property was confiscated. Many great artistic treasures were plundered, damaged or destroyed in the ensuing years. Churches were attacked by radicals and some clergy killed.

Extreme dechristianizers, including many atheists, thought that France would be better off without any religion. Most people, however, thought that some sort of faith was needed and a first response to this was to create a *Cult of Reason* and to extol Republican values. Robespierre considered this to be lacking in ethical structure and in May 1794 he announced a new state religion, the *Cult of the Supreme Being*. Less than three months later, Robespierre was executed, and his religion died with him.

The Catholic Church survived the Revolution and Napoleon finally brought the process of dechristianization to an end in 1801. However, the tussle between religious reformers and reactionaries went on through the 19th century. The state gradually took on many key functions formerly exercised by the church, notably education and the registration of births and deaths. A law passed in 1905 enshrined the principle of secularity (*laïcité*): the permanent separation of church from state.

Abbaye de Bonnefont

pure and divine. Some of the best classical music was written on religious subjects for religious settings. It is hard for a secular choir to sing a sacred song without evoking the sacred.

Another item of intangible heritage is the French language – although we should really talk about French languages to take in Breton, Occitan, Basque and other tongues. Any language is more than a grammar and a lexicon; it facilitates thinking, identifies feeling and gives form to the abstract. French is revered by its native speakers especially for its "non-English" qualities: its glorious illogicality. The language is watched over by the *Académie Française*, a body made up of forty distinguished men and women who are called, without irony, *les Immortels* (the Immortals) as if they were gods.

Where there is language there is the written word, and France has a rich literature that may often be prosaic and naturalistic, but is also an idealist, romantic quest for the human spirit.

Writers are still held in high esteem in France. It is the same with philosophers and intellectuals who are so admired that they often become talking head celebrities on television. France likes discussing ideas and it is impossible to philosophize far without coming up against the big questions of life, death, meaning and the nature of reality. Too often, very clever, very cerebral French intellectuals steer around the very idea of mysticism by assuming that the human being is merely material, but this is a sleight of hand that seeks to ignore the un-ignorable.

Some renowned French thinkers come close to addressing mysticism from a conventional scholarly direction. One of them is Pierre Nora who invented the term *lieu de memoire* (memory space), which he used in his 1992 book, *Lieux de Memoires*.

Sign on a Paris street

In it, Nora and his contributors attempt to sum up the "material, symbolic and functional" nature of Frenchness.

Another influential commentator on French culture was Roland Barthes who looked for the meaning behind the ordinary in his *Mythologies* (1957).

All of the above could be said to be part of the mainstream of French society, but just out of sight exists a rich variety of subcultures put together, for want of a better phrase, under the title of Mind, Body and Spirit.

This category could be divided into old and new. Traditional skills such as water divining and alternative techniques of healing are direct links to France's ancestral mysticism. Some *coupeurs de feu* (burn healers) work in hospitals alongside conventional medical personnel and *magnétiseurs* are often sought out when GPs are unable to offer effective treatment.

> "Everything begins in mysticism and ends in politics, said Charles Peguy. Not any more, it doesn't. In this part of the Midi, what starts in mysticism ends in tourism."
> —Christopher Hope, The Guardian.

Mystical France

Palais Idéal du Facteur Cheval

The old trades are now complemented by a burgeoning sector of alternative healing techniques and lifestyles, both home-grown and based on imported influences. You don't have to go far in France to find someone who dissents from the materialist, consumerist orthodoxy and whose outlook in life is entirely mystical.

All over France, mostly on private land, there are meditation huts, medicine wheels, statues of the Buddha, labyrinths and gardens designed for quiet contemplation. To give just one example, the *Palais du Facteur Cheval* at Hauterives in the Drôme is an extraordinary folly built by one dedicated man who defied conformity.

These places are the haunts of a huge cast of mystery hunters, misfits, eccentrics, neo-Druids, herbalists, yoga-teachers, therapists, ecologists, and biodynamic farmers. They are not considered as part of French culture but they still make a great contribution to the immaterial, that is mystical, life of France.

Modernity 187

Statue by the roadside in the Saintonge

Faiths of France

There are no official statistics for religious practice in France. The state takes no direct interest in the matter out of respect for the private right of belief, and so as not to encourage faith groups to see themselves as minorities and thereby undermine the principal of equality. It could be said that there is a fourth value of the Republic (along with "liberty, fraternity and equality"). This is *laicité*, or secularity. The absolute separation of church and state was legally codified in 1905 and this particularly affects schools, where religion is not taught.

France has been a predominantly Christian country for at least the last 1600 years and, de facto, it continues to be one. For most people, Catholicism is still part of the background of French culture even if most people don't go to church. Many communes are named after saints; and several public holidays coincide with Christian feast days. Protestantism accounts for just 2% of the population. Meanwhile other religions are growing in importance.

Islam

Numerically, the second religion of France is Islam, accounting for 6-7% of the population or 4.5 million people – the largest proportion of any EU country. Islam is especially the religion of immigrants who arrived in France during the process of decolonization, and of their descendants.

There are over 90 mosques in France but many more are planned. They are, inevitably, sited in areas of high concentrations of Muslims: cities and suburbs rather than the French countryside. Often they are inspired by oriental or African architecture. The *Missir mosque*, in **Fréjus**, for example, built in the 1930s, was inspired by the *Djenné mosque* in Mali. Several have elegant minarets, such as that of **St Denis**.

The largest mosque in France is that of **Marseille** with a capacity of 7,000, followed by **Évry**. **Paris** also has a large mosque, the oldest in metropolitan France, with a 33m (36 ft) tall minaret.

As in other modern countries, there is a tension between the vast majority or peaceful practicants and a small but energized group of extremists who challenge the norms of society with respect to religion. This had tragic consequences on 7 January 2015 when two gunmen belonging to an Islamist terrorist group stormed into the offices of the satirical magazine *Charlie Hebdo* and killed 11 people. The killers were motivated, it seems, by a belief that freedom of expression should not allow what they considered to be blasphemy against their religion.

There are various Sufi groups present in France that practise a more mystical, less doctrinaire variety of Islam.

Buddhism

The third religion of France, if it can be considered thus, is believed to be Buddhism (including Zen Buddhism). There are estimated to be upwards of 600,000 practising Buddhists and 200 Buddhist monasteries or centres for meditation retreats. The umbrella organisation, *Union Bouddhiste de France* with its headquarters in the *Pagode de Vincennes*, just outside **Paris**, claims that there are a million Buddhists in France and around 5 million sympathizers.

Buddhism in France is nothing if not diverse, with a range of different traditions followed, several of them born out of links with France's ex-colonies in Indochina.

Buddhist monasteries, temples, pagodas, stupas and wats are spread out across the country. Although there are some in Paris and the Ile de France, most are to be found in the countryside.

Dhagpo Keundreul Ling at **Biollet**, 50 km (30 mi) northwest of **Clermont-**

Ferrand in the Auvergne, is thought to be the biggest Buddhist monastery outside Asia. It was founded in 1984 by Lama Guendune Rinpoche and forms part of the Karma Kagyu lineage of Buddhism. Another well-known Buddhist community of monks and nuns is *Plum Village* in the Dordogne, set up by the Vietnamese monk Thich Nhât Hanh.

The best-known French Buddhist monk is Matthieu Ricard, author of a number of books including one in which he discusses the meaning of life with his father, a philosopher.

Judaism

France has Europe's largest Jewish community, a population of just under half a million or 0.75% of the population (3.4% of the world total). The figure, however, is declining due to emigration to Israel.

Judaism in France has a long and sometimes troubled history. In the Middle Ages, the Languedoc was a centre of kabbalistic thought. During the Revolution, in 1791, Jews were given their emancipation on condition that they did not think of themselves as part of a separate community but as individual citizens of French society, in the same way as all other citizens.

In the 19th century, the Jewish population was swelled by the arrival of Askanazi Jews from Eastern Europe. Sadly, a current of anti-Semitism ran through the 19th and 20th centuries. It erupted first in the *Dreyfus Affair*, in which a Jewish army officer was unfairly accused of espionage, and later during World War II, when the Vichy regime collaborated with the Nazi's persecution of the Jews. After the war, there was an influx of Sephardic Jews from North Africa.

Other Religions and Denominations

Around a quarter of the population say they have no religion at all. The remaining 2–3% of French people adhere to a variety of small faith groups, sometimes numbering their followers in the hundreds only. There are a sizeable number of Jehovah's Witnesses. Other religious groups include the Mormons, the Sikhs and the Baha'is. There are also a number of "new religious movements". The most interesting of France's home-grown religions is contemporary Druidism which is practised in Brittany by around a dozen groups (see p88).

Buddhist Centre in the Dordogne

This section of the book is a guide to selected places in France of mystical interest. There isn't space to cover everywhere that deserves to be included, or to give more than brief details. I have divided France into the following 14 areas (which do not always correspond to the official regions of France):

1. **Brittany** The Celtic-influenced western peninsula extending into the Atlantic.

2. **Normandy** The ancient Duchy on the coast around the mouth of the Seine.

3. **The North** The area between Paris and the Belgian frontier.

4. **Paris and Ile de France** The capital and the cluster of small departments that surround it.

5. **Champagne, Lorraine & Alsace** The three regions that make up the northeast of the country.

6. **Burgundy** The historic region in eastern France, now consisting of seven departments.

7. **Loire Valley** A broad swathe of land following the river from the centre to the Atlantic.

8. **Massif Central** The uplands in the middle of France are defined by topography, out of the way.

9. **Rhône Valley & Alps** The great broad valley of the River Rhone and to the east the Alps.

10. **Provence** The southeast of France, extending inland from Marseille and the Riviera.

11. **Languedoc** The belt of land inland from the Mediterranean coast as far as Toulouse.

12. **Dordogne, Lot, Tarn & Aveyron** The valleys (and departments) of Dordogne, Lot, Tarn and Aveyron.

13. **Western France** The west of France including Poitou, Charentes, Gironde and Gascony.

14. **The Pyrenees** The east-west chain of mountains across southwest France forming the border with Spain.

Travel Guide

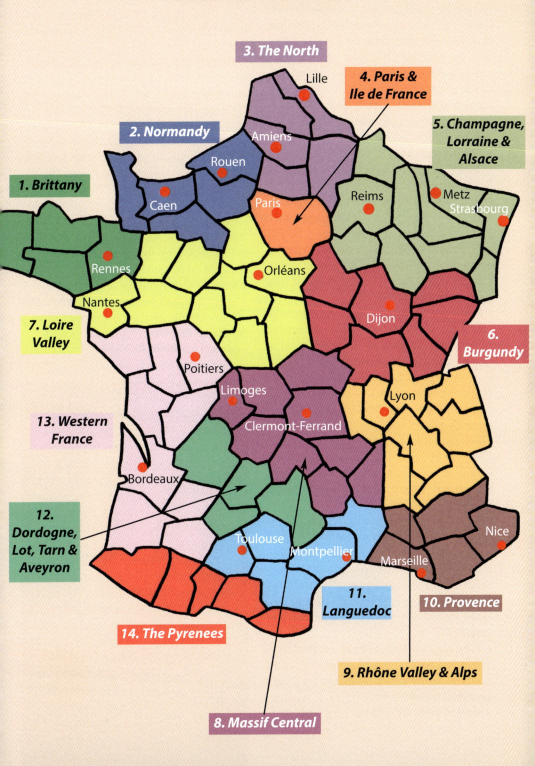

1. Brittany

The peninsula of Brittany – *Armorica* to the Gauls – has the heavily indented Atlantic coastline on three sides and is characterized by its Celtic heritage. Its Christian monuments and traditions have a vestige of paganism about them. Brittany has numerous local saints and its own distinctive religious festivals, *pardons*. It also has the greatest concentration and variety of megaliths in France.

• **Auray** (west of Vannes). The shrine of Sainte Anne d'Auray is dedicated to the patron saint of Brittany, the grandmother of Jesus. Several *pardons* (pilgrimages) take place here during the year.

• **Barnenez** (Plouezoch, Kernelehen peninsula). A massive tumulus constructed around 4000–3500 BC and dubbed "the Megalithic Parthenon."

• **Baud** (north of Carnac). The Venus of Quinilipy, which stands over a monumental fountain in a garden, is a granite statue of a goddess of unknown origin, possibly Roman or even Egyptian. The subject of pagan veneration, it used to stand on a nearby hillside until the Church discouraged its cult.

• **Bieuzy** (north of Carnac). The picturesque Chapelle St Gildas incorporates the living rock in its construction. Inside it is a "ringing stone" which emits a noise when struck.

• **Etorn Valley** (near Morlaix). This valley is renowned for its parish closes (*enclos paroisseux*), enclosures of religious buildings – usually consisting of church, cemetery, entrance arch, charnel house and calvary – that are typical of Brittany. Notable among them are St Thegonnec and Guimilliau.

• **Finistère** (extreme west of Brittany). There is a natural mystical symbolism to the "End of the Earth" (matched by Land's End in England and Fisterra in Galicia, Spain). There are plenty of good spots where you can stand on top of a cliff or on a headland, or even a rock, and look at the vast, untameable ocean of swelling and breaking waves beyond which is the New World.

• **Islands:** Brittany has almost 800 islands and islets around its shores. The smaller and remote ones are good places to seek solitude, shrink your horizons, sit with nature – particularly colonies of seabirds – and concentrate the mind. The *Ile de Sein* is extremely small, low, flat and treeless. Ushant or Ouessant, far out into the Atlantic, includes France's most westerly point.

• **Plouarzel** (west of Brest). The *Kerloas menhir* is the tallest dolmen still standing in France at 9.5m (originally 12m) high. It is situated on private land but access is unrestricted. tourismeplouarzel.fr

• **Langon** (Ile-et-Vilaine). The *Demoiselles de Langon* are 29 standing stones mainly small and low, the largest up to 1.63m.

• **Lanleff** (south of Paimpol). A mysterious, ruined round church (see p225).

The Lost City of Ys

It is said that, when the sea is calm, the sound of bells can be heard on the coast of Finistère coming from a lost city beneath the waves. Ys (or Is or Ker-Is) is usually said to lie in Douarnenez Bay. Legends about it vary but they agree that it was built below sea level by Gradlon, king of Cornouaille. The city was protected by a dike with a single gate set into it, to let ships in at low tide, to which the king kept the only key. Gradlon had a daughter, Dahut, on whom he doted but one day she stole the key, opened the city gate and let the sea flood in. Gradlon was able to escape on horseback but the city behind him was lost. A statue of him stands on the roof of Quimper cathedral looking forlornly out to sea.

A church in Finistère

- **Locronan** (northwest of Quimper). Known for its religious procession, the *Troménie* (see p38).
- **Monteneuf** (between Vannes and Rennes). The *Domaine des Pierres Droites* is an assembly of prehistoric stones that once formed a second, if smaller, Carnac inland. Only 40 stones are left out of an original 400.
- **Notre-Dame de Tronoën** (southwest of Quimper on Audieren Bay). This is the oldest example of a particularly Breton monument, a granite cavalry sculpted with scenes of the Passion.
- **Ploumilliau** (southwest of Lannion). The church here contains a unique carved wooden statue of *L'Ankou*, the Breton personification of Death: a skeleton holding a scythe.
- **Le-Vieux-Marché** (south of Lannion). The *Chapelle des Sept-Saints* is dedicated to the Seven Sleepers of Ephesus, after a story which forms part of Christian tradition and also appears in the Koran. This chapel has therefore been proposed as a place of Islamo-Christian pilgrimage. Beside the chapel is a pagan-venerated spring, with a dolmen in the crypt.

King Arthur of France

The first stories about King Arthur emerged in England or Wales during the Dark Ages and it was a British historian, Geoffrey of Monmouth, who first gave them cogent form. He insisted that Arthur was a historical character and king of the Britons. In 1191, the monks of Glastonbury abbey claimed to have found the graves of Arthur and Guinevere, thus locating the site of the island of Avalon and making the story unequivocally British.

There may or may not be any historical truth to any of this. What is certain is that the King Arthur we know today owes as much – or more – to French tradition and imagination as to his British roots.

The Arthurian legends as they have reached us are romances and full of symbolism. That is such an important part of the tales, and was contributed by French writers, especially the late 12th-century Chrétien de Troyes, a retainer at the court of Champagne. He is responsible for adding several key ingredients to the tale

Street sign, Île Grande

that have become indispensable. He presents the figure of *Lancelot du Lac* and mentions Camelot in passing.

Chrétien also initiated the story of the Holy Grail, which is first glimpsed by the knight Percival when he is staying in the castle of the Fisher King, the wounded ruler of an ailing land. Percival neglects to ask the right question at the right moment – "Who does the Grail Serve?" to heal both king and kingdom. Various locations have been suggested for the Grail castle, some in France, including the Pyrenees and near the former Gorze abbey in Lorraine.

Two other French poets added to the accumulating tales of Arthur and his knights. The Norman poet Wace (c1110–c1174) was the writer first to mention the Round Table and King Arthur's sword, Excalibur. Robert de Boron (late 12th/early 13th centuries) gave an all important twist by associating the Arthurian legends with Christianity. He offered an explanation of what the Grail was and how it came to be in Europe. All of these writers may well have been drawing on local Celtic sources to enrich the crude tale that they had inherited. They kept the basic story and the original location of Britain, but the great themes and many of the characters were continental.

Brittany is the region of France most associated with the Arthurian legends. Before France was unified, Britain *(la Grande Bretagne)* and Brittany *(la Petite Bretagne)* had close ties and were not thought of as foreign countries to each other. There was even some confusion in the histories of the time as to which territory was being referred to.

Lancelot is the son of King Ban of Bénoïc, a country on the edges of Armorica. Several episodes of the saga take place in the magical *Bois de Brocéliande*, which is now generally accepted to be the Fôret de Paimpont, southwest of Rennes in Brittany. In it are such locations as the *Valley of No Return*, the *Fontaine de Barenton* and the *Tomb of Merlin*.

To the west of Paimpont is another Arthurian landmark, although one that is very much of the 20th century. The Église Sainte-Onenne at Tréhorenteuc is known as the "Grail Chapel" for its beautiful symbolic decoration created after the Second World War.

Another recent addition to the theme is the Centre Arthurien in the Château de Comper, north of Paimpont. Another

Arthurian location in Brittany is the city of Nantes, where Wolfram sites Arthur's court.

Not everyone accepts the Breton connection with the legends. In the 1960s the French author, René Bansart, argued that Brocéliande wasn't in Brittany but was based on the Andaines forest, near the ruined castle of Domfront, in the Orne (Normandy).

Even further away from Celtic Brittany is Burgundy, which also may also have played a role in the development of the Arthurian world. Whereas Glastonbury is often identified as the mythical isle of Avalon, there is another candidate town that is still called Avallon, near Vézelay.

Legends, of course, do not have precise locations; some may be based on fact but others may be entirely invented. Any search for genuine Arthurian sites must always end in teasing speculation.

The futile quest to find legendary places is, however, an opportunity to return to the stories and read them as an exploration of universal themes. They work on several levels of our psyche simultaneously.

Camelot, on the surface, is a world of black and white; of good and evil; and of heroes and villains. The tales of Arthur's knights tell us to suppress ego in the pursuit of just and noble causes; and that only by co-operation, chivalry, loyalty and nobility can we live spiritually pure lives.

On a second level, nothing is clear. Even the good and brave wrestle with their inner demons and no amount of magic can save them from themselves. Lancelot is considered the most pure, valiant and spiritual of the *Knights of the Round Table* but he is torn inside by an irreconcilable dilemma: he has sworn allegiance to Arthur, his king, but he betrays him through his love for Guinevere.

We cannot help looking at the Arthurian age with modern eyes and we always find in it what we want to see. The more we dig into the stories, the more we are reminded that worldly acclaim is hollow if we are not at peace with ourselves; that heroes are not always happy; that strength is not always physical; and that dramatic action can easily be used an excuse for not looking closely at ourselves.

Window in the so-called "Grail Chapel", Tréhorenteuc, Brittany

Carnac, Locmariaquer and Gavrinis

Three of France's most important prehistoric sites stand close together on the heavily indented coastline of Morbihan department, in the southwest of Brittany. There are over 750 megalithic monuments in the department of Morbihan alone.

Carnac features regularly on lists of the world's most sacred sites even if we don't know exactly what it was created for. Anywhere else in Europe, three menhirs in a row would be remarkable; here the number of stones – 2,800 large stones densely gathered onto a 4 km (2.5 mi) long site covering 40 hectares (100 acres) – is overwhelming. The scale is far grander than any cathedral or palace and yet there is nothing recognizable or familiar to get a modern mind around. All we can do is look and speculate.

There are three main groups of parallel alignments of standing stones, from west to east, *Le Ménec* (the closest to Carnac town), *Kermario* and *Kerlescan*. Le Ménec is the largest with 1,099 stones up to 4 m (13 ft) high set out in 11 rows. Beside it is a visitors' centre, the *Maison des Mégalithes*.

Many theories have been put forward for the purpose of erecting so many megaliths close together but none of them has completely accounted for the evidence. It has often been supposed that the alignments had some religious or ritualistic function. Perhaps Carnac was a pilgrimage centre of the ancient world.

Chief among questions to ask is: why here exactly? The proximity of the Atlantic coast must have had something to do with the choice of location. Dowsers have reported magnetic forces around the stones suggesting that the stones stand on a favourable point for tapping into "earth energy".

The Scottish engineer Alexander Thom, who made meticulous surveys of over 500 megalithic sites, proposed that Neolithic people were anything but primitive. They

Alignments of Carnac

had a sophisticated grasp of astronomy and geometry. Carnac was an instrument used to keep track of the calendar. They lived by a "megalithic solar year" that was punctuated by midsummer, midwinter and the two equinoxes. The alignments were thus used as a kind of "megalithic graph paper".

The alignments are not the only prehistoric monuments around Carnac. Most notably, between the alignments and Carnac town is an artificial mound 125 m (410 ft) x 60 m (200 ft) at the base, the *Tumulus Saint-Michel*, crowned with a chapel dedicated to St Michael (see p53). Although it is only 12 m (40 ft) high, it is an extremely impressive tumulus and makes a good viewpoint from which to get your bearings.

Carnac also forms part of a larger concentration of megaliths, a "conurbation" of dolmens, tumuli and gallery graves forming a loose arc of placed stones that extends west almost as far as Erdeven, north to Ploemel and east to Crac'h.

Locmariaquer, 7km (4.5 mi) to the east of Carnac, is another hub of megaliths and it may well have been connected to the alignments. Just outside the town there is a large dolmen named the *Table des Marchands* (Merchants' Table), which is assumed to be a funerary chamber. Its two great slabs are decorated with engraved marks. Near it are the remains of the Great Menhir that now lies on the ground in four pieces. An estimated 4,500 years ago, this gigantic stone, still in one piece, was dragged, rolled or floated for 12 km (7.5 mi) and shaped with stone chisels before being erected in this precise spot. It was then the tallest menhir in the world at 20.3 m (66 ft). How and why it came to fall is unknown. It may have been because of an earthquake but another theory is that it was brought down deliberately. It is now known that it formed part of a larger construction of other 18 stones, which have since vanished. There is a third megalithic monument on the same site at Locmariaquer, but less well preserved: the *Tumulus d'er Grah*.

The *Table des Marchands* is unusual because most megalithic monuments are unadorned. At the opposite extreme is the Cairn of Gavrinis, unique in France and comparable only to sites in Ireland and Spain. It stands on an island of the same name in the Gulf of Morbihan, 10 km (6 mi) east of Carnac and can only be reached by boat from Larmor-Baden.

Built around 6,000 years ago, it is older than Stonehenge and the pyramids of Egypt. It consists of a passageway that leads to a single chamber.

Of the 29 slabs that make up the dolmen, 23 of them are decorated, particularly in the passage. What the dolmen was built and used for, and what the decorations mean, is not known. It is likely that, with such detailed decoration, it was not "just" a tomb. It has been suggested that the corridor was a processional way for a candidate for initiation, who moved symbolically from life to death to rebirth. In this interpretation, the carvings of arcs, spirals and what have been called shields (the most frequent motif in Gavrinis), axes and croziers represent the stages of initiation. There is only one true spiral. The other similar forms are double knotworks.

For information see:
- ot-carnac.fr
- carnac.monuments-nationaux.fr
- megalithes-morbihan.com
- locmariaquer.monuments-nationaux.fr
- gavrinis.info.

The site:
culture.gouv.fr/culture/arcnat/megalithes/en/mega/megagav_en.htm
has excellent detailed information about Gavrinis in English.

Mont Saint-Michel

With its elegant spire pointing skyward from the top of an ancient abbey, which looks seamlessly joined to the conical granite rock beneath it, Mont Saint-Michel is one of the iconic silhouettes of France and, along with Lourdes, the country's best-known sacred site. Victor Hugo remarked that it was France's equivalent of the Great Pyramid.

The setting itself is irresistible. Mont Saint-Michel stands just offshore in a vast bay whose appearance changes dramatically according to the push and pull of the moon. The bay experiences the most extreme tidal movements in Europe. At an exceptional low tide, the sea withdraws 15 km (9 mi) and the difference between the high and low water marks can be 15 m (50 ft). The most spectacular movements of water occur with the spring tides, 36 to 48 hours after full and new moons, when the sun, earth and moon are in *syzygy* (alignment). When the tide is out, Mont Saint-Michel is stranded in a landscape of glistening sand. Another, much smaller islet in the bay, *Tombelaine*, is a bird reserve.

Geographically, there is a curious resonance between Mont Saint-Michel and Carnac, on either sides of the Brittany peninsula and between Mont Saint-Michel and the very similar-looking St Michael's Mount across the English Channel on the coast of Cornwall. Mont Saint-Michel also has affinities with other sacred hills and mountains across the world, including *Skellig's Mickael* in Ireland, *St Miguel de Aralar* in northern Spain, *Monte Gargano* in Italy, *Mt Sinai, Mt Arafat, Lalibela* in Ethiopia, *Nashik, Hampi* and *Ajanta* in India, *Huang Shan* in China and *Uluru* in Australia.

Even when the place is crowded at the height of summer, it resonates with 1300 years of its eventful history. In 708, St. Aubert, Bishop of Avranches, was inspired by repeated visions of the archangel Michael to build a modest chapel on the

79 m (260 ft) granite *Mont Tombe* (so named because it was believed to be an ancient graveyard). There was almost certainly a pagan sanctuary on the rock before the Christians arrived.

Benedictine monks settled here in 966 at the invitation of the Duke of Normandy and a village soon formed around them. A Romanesque church was constructed in the 11th century and work continued on other buildings over the following centuries. For centuries, Mont Saint-Michel was an important place of pilgrimage.

In the 13th century, the finest Gothic buildings, an ensemble known as *La Merveille* (the Marvel), were added to the abbey.

John James notes that Mont Saint-Michel is a version of the holy mountain in exquisite, microcosmic miniature. "The mountain has been hollowed into crypts and crowned with high ramparts and towers; piled upon one another are lilac-tinted halls, chambers, shrines, and cloisters. Here is quite clearly expressed the hierarchy of the mediaeval abbey. It was a large household, in a sense like a royal palace with a church at the centre."

Mont Saint-Michel grew to be a famous place of medieval pilgrimage with pilgrims following roads called the "paths to paradise". The Mount subsequently fell into decline and was transformed into a prison after the Revolution. In 1874 it was declared a national monument.

Three years later Emmanuel Frémlet's gilded statue of St. Michael was placed on top of a new steeple, 157 m (515 ft) high. The archangel (see p53) is the protector of the world, watching over humanity from the heights with his wings outstretched and a sword raised above his head,

The Mount is divided into two parts: the village down below, wrapped around the south and east of the rock, and the abbey above. The former is dedicated to commerce and, for any sense of the spirituality of the place, it is necessary to ascend to the next level.

The abbey is state property and, while it is a visitor attraction, it is also a working monastery. A monastic community returned to the site in 1966, the 1000th anniversary of the installation of the original abbey, and today 7 sisters and 4 brothers of the order of the *Fraternités Monastiques de Jerusalem* continue to provide a spiritual counterbalance to what might otherwise be merely a hub of commercialism and tourism. They welcome visitors for prayer retreats of up to 5 days.

The layout of the abbey, on three levels, is somewhat confusing. The lowest parts, the crypts, are generally older and Romanesque in style. Together they form a platform on which stands the church, which is mainly Flamboyant Gothic in style. Also delightful is the Gothic cloister, part of *La Merveille*.

Behind the abbey, lower down the slope, is a humble chapel dedicated to St Aubert, founder of Mont Saint-Michel.

To visit Mont Saint-Michel, it is advisable to park in one of the designated car parks and cross the bridge by foot or by shuttle bus to the island. If you're planning to visit during the peak summer months it's worth arriving very early (around 8am) or late in the day (after 5pm) to get a sense of the atmosphere of the place. Another option is to stay overnight in one of the four hotels in the village. Before visiting, consult the tide tables and choose high or low water, as preferred.

For general information on Mont St Michel see:

ot-montsaintmichel.com

If you are interested in staying in the abbey see:

abbaye-montsaintmichel.com

Grisaille window, Mont Saint-Michel

2. Normandy

Normandy, with its white cliffs to the north, and D-Day beaches to the west, is centred on the lower valley of the Seine and is easily accessible from Paris. It has many ancient abbeys, the most famous being that of Mont Saint-Michel.

- **Abbeys.** Normandy's most important abbeys are grouped together in an association (abbayes-normandes.com). Six of them are still occupied by active monastic communities. Some of the more interesting are:
  - **Bec-Hellouin** (southeast of Pont-Audemer). Now owned by the state but housing an active community. abbayedubec.com
  - **Fecamp: Abbaye de la Trinité** (on the coast north of Le Havre). Its relics include a "pas de l'ange", the footprint of an angel in stone (next to the dormition of the virgin in the south transept).
  - **Jumièges** (Seine valley, west of Rouen). A very early abbey founded in the 7th century by St Philibert and now in ruins. www.abbayedejumieges.fr
  - **Saint-Wandrille Abbey** (near Caudebec-en-Caux in the Seine Valley, south of Yvetot). An early abbey which is still functioning and offers retreats for men, women and couples. st-wandrille.com
  - **Allouville-Bellefosse** (southeast of Yvetot). Venerated oak tree. (See p45.)
- **Mémorial de Caen**. The beaches of northern Normandy were used for the D-Day landings of World War II which led to the liberation of France but caused a huge loss of life. Three quarters of Caen were destroyed. Elsewhere there are war memorials but the Mémorial takes a different approach. It is dedicated to promoting reconciliation, peace and human rights. normandy.memorial-caen.com.
- **Château du Champ de Bataille** (outside Le Neubourg, southwest of Rouen). The house may be a grandiose aristocratic monument called "the château of the battlefield" but the gardens are an exploration of things cosmic. The main axis follows existence in stages: vegetable, animal, human, consciousness, light, spirit. The transverse axis represents the finite and the infinite with the interior world to the right and the exterior world to the left. chateauduchampdebataille.fr
- **Étretat** (On the coast, north of Le Havre). The town is famous for its extraordinary white cliffs, reached by steps and footpaths. The *Manoir de la Salamandre* in town, now a hotel, is decorated with alchemical symbols. (See p169. Photo p40.)
- **La Haye-de-Routot** (northeast of Pont-Audemer on the edge of the *Forêt de Brotonne*). Two venerated yew trees, see p45.
- **Lisieux** (south of Le Havre). France's second most popular pilgrimage destination after Lourdes. (See p38.)
- **Louviers** (southeast of Rouen). The *Cloître des Pénitents* is the only cloister in France to be built beside a river. (See p131.)
- **Ménilles** (east of Évreux). The outer wall of the château is decorated with cryptograms or cabalistic signs in brick set into the wall of the chateau.

Carvings on a house in Caen

Wayside Crosses and Shrines

No one notices them any more and yet they are almost everywhere in France. Creeping secularism in the 19th century reduced their importance in the spiritual life of the people; 20th century maps and high speed car travel meant they became less visible and less useful for navigation; now consumerism and GPS technology has made them even more anachronistic and redundant.

Yet thousands of crosses and statues of the Virgin Mary still stand beside French roads, in town or country, or else preside over road forks and crossroads, relics of a bygone, pious time when they served as a reminder of the difference between right and wrong and as valuable landmarks of more use than road signs.

No two of these roadside ornaments are the same. They are made of iron or stone or even concrete; rarely of wood because it decays. Some are coloured, most monochrome.

Crosses come in a surprising variety of shapes for such a simple graphic form. There are Latin, Celtic and Basque crosses; crosses of Lorraine and Jerusalem; and crosses that only a semiotician might be able to identify – moline, fleury, pommé, formé, calvary, crosslet and so on. Usually the basic shape is ornamented with scrolls and other decorations.

Each cross, statue or oratory was placed where it was for a precise need, even if this need has now been forgotten. Some mark historical parish boundaries and sought to ward off evil from the village – even if now they have been swallowed up by spreading suburbs. Others are memorials, including to recent wars; still others record the site where a holy man once preached. A cross may hover over a sacred spring or stand on a spot associated with a saint.

The most ancient crosses, replaced over the centuries, are a reminder of the evangelization of France: either they stand on sites of pagan superstition or they indicate territory conquered for the faith and remind new converts not to lapse.

3. The North

The main sights scattered around the flat expanses of farmlands to the northeast of Paris are the great Gothic cathedrals.

• **Amiens** (north of Paris). One of the greatest of Gothic cathedrals, with a wealth of stone carving and misericords, and a famous labyrinth.

• **Saint-Quentin** (northwest of Soissons). An octagonal labyrinth is set into the floor of the *Basilique Saint-Quentin*, near the west end of the nave. In the Middle Ages, it is said, demons and death came from the west but could only move in straight lines and so would get caught in the devious route of the labyrinth.

• **Laon** (northeast of Paris). A chapel built by the Knights Templar (see p156) stands in a garden near the cathedral and archaeological museum.

• **Soissons** (northeast of Paris). The Gothic church of *Saint-Jean-des-Vignes* was dismantled after the Revolution leaving the ghostly remains of its façade and two spires, with empty holes where the doors and windows once were.

• **Mont des Cats** (adjacent to Godewaersvelde). The abbey on this low hill is an active monastic community which welcomes visitors. abbaye-montdescats.fr

The Wheel of Fortune at Beauvais

The cathedral of **Beauvais** (northwest of **Paris**) is a masterpiece of Gothic architecture, but the older church of Saint-Étienne is of interest for a particular reason. The north rose is known as the "Wheel of Fortune" window because it is thought to represent the medieval notion of human life (also seen on tarot card number 10). Four hapless figures climb in fortune on the right rim of the wheel, which turns in an anticlockwise direction, and four prone figures descend on the left. They are separated by "Dame Fortune", at the top. Three other figures make up a total of twelve. One (difficult to make out) lies at the bottom as if asleep or uninvolved in the cycle and another stands at the point where the wheel starts to ascend, although he isn't in motion. These two are ambiguous but at least they are aligned with the direction of travel. Another standing figure, on the left, defies the logic of the composition with his head pointing against the flow.

The message of the Wheel of Fortune may seem to be, "it doesn't matter who you are or what you do, if you are on the way up now, you'll be going down before long" – but in the Middle Ages this fatalistic myth was not seen as discouraging. The window is set into the north wall for a reason: this is the cold side of the church that hasn't yet received the light. Material life may be a treadmill but the life of the spirit is a linear progression driven by hope. The unfortunates depicted on the Wheel are on its circumference: they have invested in the outer world and not the luminous inner world and so they are far from reaching the still point at its centre.

4a. Paris

Like every capital, Paris speaks more of worldy power and prestige than things esoteric but it has some semi-concealed treasures if you look for them. The suburbs of the city shade into the Ile de France which is made up of eight departements all served by public transport. The names in brackets indicate the closest metro station.

• **Cemeteries.** The city's most visited cemeteries are *Père Lachaise* (Metro: Père Lachaise) and *Montparnasse* (Edgar Quinet) but *Montmartre* is quieter and more atmospheric. The Catacombs are also much visited.

• **Colonne Médicis** (Les Halles). A freestanding, orphan column adjacent to the commodities exchange which is said to have been built by *Catherine de' Medici* so that her astrologer could climb the steps inside to the platform at the top and take readings of the stars.

• **Crypte du Martyrium de Saint Denis** (11 rue Yvonne-le-Tac, Montmartre. Metro: Pigalle). A peaceful subterranean chapel on the site of the martyrdom of Paris's St Denis. Nearby is the Art Nouveau church of **Saint-Jean-de-Montmartre**.

• **Église Saint-Merri** (Châtelet). You can make what you will of the devil figure who squats at the apex of the arch over the main door of this church, a place usually reserved for some holy person. It has been suggested that this horned hermaphrodite is the Baphomet that the Knights Templar are said to have worshipped but it was carved long after their demise.

• **Église Saint-Sulpice** (St-Sulpice). This church south of Saint-Germain-des-Prés has an unusual feature: a gnomon, an astronomical device installed by an 18th century priest who wanted to determine the exact date of the spring equinox and thus Easter. A hole in the window in the south transept lets the sun fall on the elements of the gnomon: a brass line forming a meridian across the church floor running between an obelisk and a marble plaque.

• **Fontaine Saint-Michel** (Metro: St-Michel). The archangel St Michael (see p53) is seen subduing the devil over a fountain into the basin of which two chimera spew water. On the columns above, four figures represent the cardinal virtues.

• **Grande Mosquée de Paris** (Monge). A *Neo-Mudéjar* building in the *Jardin des Plantes* quarter.

• **Grande Synagogue de la Victoire** (Notre-Dame de Lorette). The largest synagogue in France.

• **Musée de Cluny** (Cluny La Sorbonne). A Gothic mansion on the edge of the Latin Quarter that is a museum of all things medieval. Notable among the exhibits are the stained glass and *The Lady and the Unicorn* tapestry.

Eglise Saint-Jean-de-Montmartre

Mystical France

The pyramid of the Louvre Museum

the last Knights Templar Jacques de Molay, was burnt at the stake in 1314. The only other hint of the Templars' presence in Paris is the Square des Templiers, a pleasant but ordinary garden.

• **51 Rue Montmorency** (Arts et Metiers). One of the oldest houses in the city and the former residence of alchemist Nicolas Flamel. It is now a restaurant.
auberge-nicolas-flamel.fr/histoire.php

• **Sacré-Coeur** (Abbesses, then Funicular). Famous viewpoint over Paris, spendidly sited at the top of the hill of Montmartre.

• **Sainte-Chapelle** (Cité). A 13th-century masterpiece famous for the quantity and quality of the stained glass in the upper chapel.

• Tour Saint-Jacques (Châtelet). A remnant of a church of the same name and the traditional starting point of the pilgrimage route to Santiago de Compostela.

• **Musée du Louvre** (Palais Royal). Art is not necessarily mystical but it can be a good route to the mystical. The modern glass pyramid in the courtyard has given rise to much esoteric speculation as to its site and symbolic meaning. The museum's collection is also said to be a treasure trove for mystery hunters.

• **La Grande Pagode** (Porte Dorée). Headquarters of the French association of Buddhists, the Union bouddhiste de France. It is not always open. Check the calendar before visiting. bouddhisme-france.org

• **Place Dauphine, Ile de la Cité** (Cité). A sign announces that this is the spot where

Window in Montmartre

Notre-Dame de Paris Cathedral

According to Fulcanelli (see p170), the best way to get to know about alchemy is to stand in front of the west façade of Notre-Dame Cathedral. To the left and the right of the central door (the Portal of the Last Judgement), 31 panels are arranged in two rows along the base of the façade at convenient viewing height. It would be easy to dismiss them as additional decorations on a building already overflowing with ornate stonework but, says Fulcanelli, they depict alchemical scenes.

A bas relief near the bottom of the column separating the two doors of the Portal of the Last Judgement shows "Cybele" or "Lady Philosophy". She has her feet on the earth but her head in the clouds. A ladder placed against her symbolizes the connection between the two. In her right hand she holds two books. One is open indicating exoteric worldly knowledge, the other half hidden behind it, pointing to esoteric wisdom, or wisdom gained through interior means.

There are many other points of interest in the cathedral. On the rooftops of the building, among chimera and gargoyles, there is a figure said to be an alchemist leaning over the balcony and scratching his beard.

The apse of Notre-Dame

4b. Ile de France

- **Abbeys.** There are several around Paris. Notable among them are *Chaalis* (northeast, chaalis.fr), *Lieu-Restauré* (northwest) *Port-Royal-des-Champs* at Meaux (east, port-royal-des-champs.eu) and *Royaumont* (north, royaumont.com).
- **Clamart** (southwest of Paris). An unusual modern sculpture, the *Colonne Zodiacale*, stands in the cemetery. It shows the signs of the zodiac of four civilizations: Western, Aztec, Cambodian and African.
- **Coulommiers** (east of Paris near Meaux) The last Templar commandery north of the Loire was saved from demolition by a local association and can be visited Wed, Fri, Sat and Sun. (Photo p152.) coulommiers.fr
- **Évry** (southeast of Paris). A modern cathedral built to a circular plan. (See p225.)
- **Basilique Saint-Denis** (northern suburbs of Paris). This church, a royal mausoleum, is considered to be the place where Gothic architecture (see p117) was born.
- **Saint-Germain-en-Laye** (west of Paris). The *Musée National d'Archéologie* is the place to go to study neglected religions from the old Stone Age to the Middle Ages. musee-archeologienationale.fr

Joan of Arc

Even in her lifetime, Joan of Arc was treated more as a symbol than a person. Ever since, history has emphasized that what she did is more important than anything she experienced. Nowadays she is lauded as a national icon and few people today want to face the essential truth: Joan of Arc was not primarily a soldier but rather a mystic motivated by encounters with disembodied beings.

She had her first vision in 1425, at the age of 13, in her father's garden. On that and subsequent occasions she claimed to have interacted with St Michael, St Catherine and St Margaret and, if we are to believe the stories, these celestial characters gave her political and military instructions.

She was tried as a witch in Rouen, convicted and burnt at the stake on 30 May 1431, still only 19 years old. Even the Pope accepted that she was a witch rather than a religious visionary. The sentence was revoked only in 1456 and thereafter Joan became a paragon of piety and a focus of French national identity. She was canonized in 1922.

At her trial, she refused to answer questions about her visions and there has been much debate about them ever since. It has been suggested by modern psychiatrists that she suffered from a mental disorder, such as schizophrenia but, even if this is true, it is another way of restating the problem without doing much to explain it.

In *The Witch Cult in Western Europe* (1921), Margaret Murray argued that we really should see Joan as a witch, but not in the derogatory sense. She formed part of the lingering pagan tradition that was in permanent competition with the medieval Catholic Church. Her birthplace, *Domrémy-la-Pucelle* has become a shrine to her memory. domremy.fr

5. Champagne, Lorraine & Alsace

These three regions form the northeast corner of France, along the German border. Champagne can claim to be the birthplace of the Templars as the order was officially announced in the Council of Troyes. Lorraine produced the mystic-warrior Joan of Arc. Alsace has a strong association with symbolism, legends and sorcerers.

- **Avioth** (north of Montmédy). The church of *Notre-Dame d'Avioth* is a pilgrimage destination. Beside it stands an unusual ornate structure, *La Recevresse*, of uncertain purpose. avioth.fr
- **Half-Timbered Churches** (between Troyes and Brienne-le-Château). Scattered around the *Parc Naturel Regional de la Foret d'Orient* are nine quaint churches and one chapel built between the late 15th and 18th centuries using the locally available materials of oak, clay and straw. The finest of them is the *Église Saint-Jacques-et-Saint-Philippe* at Lentilles.
- **Massif du Donon** (southwest of Strasbourg). A 1009m (3310 ft) mountain venerated in ancient times because it stands out conspicuously in the landscape. The Romans consecrated it to Mercury. It now has an imitation classical temple on the summit.
- **Metz.** The capital of Lorraine has a Templar chapel (see p156) and one of the oldest churches in Europe, *Saint-Pierre-aux-Nonnains*. The cathedral has a mythological animal (see p126) as its mascot, the *Graoully*, a species of dragon. (Photo p159.)
- **Mont Sainte-Odile** (southwest of Obernai). Mountain with a basilica church on top of it (see p52).
- **Sion-Vaudemont** (southwest of Nancy). Sacred hill (see p53).
- **Strasbourg.** The Gothic cathedral has a number of points of interest. The legendary King Solomon, associated with *compagnonnage* (see p154) is represented

The Symbolism of Alsace's Half-Timbered Houses

Alsace has many half-timbered houses that are not just beautiful buildings. They tell stories in symbols – if you know how to "read" them. The earliest surviving examples date from the 15th century and are identified by their long corner posts stretching from ground to eaves. The symbols are either carved into the wood or can be seen in the arrangement of the timber themselves.

Some are there to attract happiness and prosperity to the inhabitants; others are meant to keep malevolent forces away. Almost always they combine layers of ancestral meaning derived from both pagan and Christian tradition.

Sometimes the exposed timbers are arranged to represent a tree of life; a lozenge or a St Andrew's cross (both of which are invocations of fertility); or a circle with a cross through it (the sun combined with a crucifix). Sometimes the timbers suggest a stylized man with legs apart and arms outstretched as if holding the house together. Other shapes include a *curcule* chair – the folding stool of a magistrate in ancient Rome, perhaps indicating the prestige of the house's owner.

Other symbols carved into the timbers, engraved on stone door posts or painted on to the limewash of the walls include five-pointed stars (signifying the elements of earth, air, fire, water and spirit), hearts (happiness), swastikas (the sun), and the recumbent figure 8 (∞), which represents infinity.

Half-timbered houses can be seen in **Strasbourg's** *Petite France* quarter, *Petite Venise* in **Colmar** and in the towns of **Eguisheim** and **Riquewihr**.

Cornerpost of a house in Riquewihr

six times in the building, in four stained glass windows and two statues. People go to the cathedral each equinox to see the curious phenomenon of "the green ray", a beam of light that passes through the foot of Judah in a stained glass window and strikes the pulpit in a particular place.
cathedrale-strasbourg.fr

6. Burgundy

Prosperous, independent and on an important route of transit between southern and northern Europe, Burgundy has had a disproportionate influence on the development of France. It was a crucible for the development of Romanesque architecture and sculpture, and the birthplace of medieval monasticism. Burgundy may also, according to one theory, be a key location of the mythical Avalon from the Arthurian legends.

- **Abbaye de Fontenay** (near Montbard, northwest of Dijon). In a small valley stands Burgundy's most complete surviving medieval monastery. The church and cloister show the Cistercian ideal of simplicity, without ornamentation to distract from piety and contemplation. Various functional buildings form part of the complex, including an infirmary, bakery and, strangely, the oldest ironworks in Europe. abbayedefontenay.com
- **Autun** (southwest of Beaune). As well as a handsome cathedral, this ancient town has three other places of interest. The *Couhard* pyramid is thought to be a 1st century AD funerary monument, although what the form represents no one knows. The *Temple of Janus* is a misnamed ruin which is, in fact, a "fanum", a temple built by the Gauls to an unknown deity. There is also just outside town an alignment of standing stones, at the *Champs de la Justice*.
- **Avallon** (northeast of Vézelay). An historic town which has been suggested as a possible location of the Avalon in the Arthurian legends (see p194).
- **Bibracte** (west of Autun). The walled town built by the Gauls on top of Mount Beuvray is now an archaeological site. It includes a most unusual monument, an 11 m (36 ft) pink granite public water basin in the form of a *vesica pisces* (see p22). bibracte.fr
- **Château de Chailly** (west of Dijon). The façade of this château (now a hotel) is decorated with alchemical motifs. (See p169.)
- **Citeaux** (northeast of Beaune). The Cistercian monastic order was founded in 1098 at Citeaux in the valley of the Saône by monks from Cluny who aspired to a more simple and self-sufficient life. The monastery was partially destroyed in the wake of the French Revolution, but has since become home to a small community of monks. citeaux-abbaye.com
- **Clairvaux** (west of Chaumont). The fourth house founded by the Cistercian order was presided over by St Bernard (1090–1153), an early champion of the Knights Templar. abbayedeclairvaux.com
- **Cluny** (northwest of Mâcon). The name has become synonymous with the medieval monastic empire – of 1400 religious houses occupied by 10,000 monks – to which this monastery gave birth. Today, there is not much left of its days of political and spiritual greatness but perhaps just enough to get an idea of how much influence Cluny had. Its great church, begun in 1088, was the largest structure erected in the Middle Ages. Only a group of chapels and spires, the cloister, and five of the original fifteen towers survive from the demolition after the Revolution. (See p130.) cluny.monuments-nationaux.fr

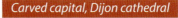
Carved capital, Dijon cathedral

• **Paray-le-Monial** (northwest of Mâcon) The basilica church attracts pilgrims (see p39). The town hall is a Renaissance mansion decorated with alchemical carvings (see p169).

• **Ronchamp chapel** (northwest of Belfort). "I haven't done anything religious but when I saw myself faced by those four horizons, I didn't hesitate", announced the architect Le Corbusier when asked about the avant-garde chapel of Notre-Dame-du-Haut that he had designed. The roof was inspired by the shell of a crab. The interior is illuminated naturally by different shaped "wells" of light piercing the walls.

• **Source-Seine** (northwest of Dijon). In 1864 the city of Paris bought the land in which the river Seine rises because it symbolized the source of its wealth and importance, but it was a late arrival. The cave had been venerated two thousands years ago by the Gaulish tribe of the *Lingons* who built a sanctuary to the nymph Sequana on the spot and left behind them innumerable exvotos. The statue of *Sequana* at the mouth of the cave is of the 19th century. It is marked on older maps as Saint-Germain-Source-Seine. source-seine.fr

• **Taizé Community** (southwest of Tournus). An ecumenical monastic community founded by the Swiss Protestant pioneer, *Brother Roger* (Roger Schütz). He chose Taizé as a place to live and work in 1940 because it was just outside the Occupied Zone of France. Forced to flee, he returned to establish the community in 1944. Brother Roger was murdered during evening prayers in 2005 by a deranged woman. Visitors coming to Taizé are asked to register beforehand. taize.fr

• **Vézelay** (northwest of Dijon). The hilltop church overshadowing this village is a masterpiece of Romanesque art (see p101) and one of the rallying points of the pilgrimage to Santiago de Compostela. (See p35. Photo p28.)

Vézelay nave

Ley Lines of France

Many of the places we see on the map of France are explained by history: we know why certain features of the landscapes are where they are, how they got there and how they relate to the whole.

There are, however, many other features without obvious explanation. Sometimes it is hard to see why an ancient road takes the route it does and it's impossible to know why a standing stone was placed on one spot and not another. This begs the question: are such things random or is there some scheme behind them?

Several curious people have looked at both the landscape and the map and asked whether there isn't some hidden organization that history does not talk about.

The notion that ancient buildings and monuments are "aligned" in relation to each other along "ley lines" was first proposed by the Englishman, Alfred E. Watkins, in the 1920s.

Without knowing about Watkins' work, a Frenchman came up with a similar idea at about the same time. Xavier Guichard (1870–1947) was a director of police and the model for Maigret's superior officer in the Georges Simenon detective novels. He published the results of his research in a book, *Eleusis Alesia: An Enquiry into the Origins of European Civilization*.

Guichard began his research around 1910 with toponyms, noticing that the name Alésia or variations of it occurred frequently across mainland France. It might, he suggested, tentatively, have something to do with Eleusis, site of the Eleusinian mysteries in ancient Greece.

He came to the conclusion that lines through the various "Alésias" converged on a point in eastern France. This, he hypothesized, was the hub of a system of routes for the use of the prehistoric traveller punctuated by hills overlooking rivers and sources of salt or freshwater.

Since Guichard, other authors have proposed landscape lines of their own by joining up certain place names, churches, menhirs and dolmens, wells and sites that show the vestiges of pagan religion.

Recently, researchers have identified or imagined sacred geometric shapes in **Paris** (centred, for instance, on the Egyptian obelisk in the Place de la Concorde), ley lines running through **Mont Saint-Michel**, a "Mary Magdalene triangle" in Provence, and the spokes of a Zodiac wheel radiating out from Toulouse.

If they are right and these lines really do exist, it implies that the prehistoric inhabitants of France had a sophisticated grasp of earth geometry.

All such "ley-lines" are always speculative rather than proven and there is always the possibility that they exist only in the human mind, which likes to identify patterns. If they are real, there are far fewer ley-lines in France than in the British Isles. Either there aren't very many in France, for some reason yet to be explained, or they haven't been discovered yet.

Luxor Obelisk on the Place de la Concorde in Paris

7. Loire Valley

The broad corridor created by the Loire Valley and its tributaries is best known for its Renaissance pleasure palaces. This area also takes in the great Gothic cathedrals of Chartres and Bourges, subterranean structures and a host of other interesting sights.

• **Abbaye de Fontevraud** (southeast of **Saumur**). The gardens and cloisters in this royal monastic "city" are still imbued with spiritual peace but most interesting of all is the circular Romanesque kitchen building (see p225), a pleasing piece of sacred architecture even if its use was prosaic. abbayedefontevraud.com

• **Abbaye de Solesmes** (Sable-sur-Sarthe, southeast of **Le Mans**). Large, active and influential monastery (see p131). www.solesmes.com

• **Arville** (northwest of **Vendôme**). A Templar commandery, now a museum of the Templars (see p156).

• **Bourges.** The city of Bourges styles itself as the "capital of alchemy". The city walls are said to form the shape of a "philosophical egg" (a vessel used in alchemy), the cathedral to represent the red phase of the Great Work and the *Palais Jacques-Cœur* to be the work of a rich adept. But it is a Renaissance mansion, the *Hotel Lallement* (now a museum of decorative arts), that is most interesting. The coffered ceiling of the chapel consists of 30 carved panels representing various hermetic objects or angels performing unusual tasks. Thirteen of the panels have flames in them, alluding to the importance of fire in alchemical processes. bourges-tourisme.com

• **Congressault** (near Blancafort, southeast of **Orléans**): *Musée de la Sorcellerie*. A semi-serious museum of witchcraft (see p172). musee-sorcellerie.fr

• **La Celle-Condé** (east of **Châteauroux**, Cher). The Saint-Denis-de-Condé church features two tunnels from nave to crypt, with five moons on the south side of the nave. Said to be a central meeting point/sanctuary of the Druids for their annual general meeting. *Association des Amis de Condé* on Facebook. Pagan monument preceeded the church. stands in square pagan enclosure. lacelleconde.free.fr

• **Lac de Grand-Lieu** (southwest of **Nantes**). The largest lake in France is home in winter to a naturalized population of the bird venerated by the ancient Egyptians, the sacred ibis.

• **Maulevier** (southeast of **Cholet**). The Parc Oriental is in the style of the Japanese Edo period and has various symbolic aspects. At the centre is a lake with two isles named *Island of the Crane* and *Island of the Tortoise*, representing yin and yang and the harmony between them. The colour red of the bridge indicates that this is a sacred space. parc-oriental.com

• **Nantes.** The tomb of François II de Bretagne in the cathedral has curious sculptures at its four corners. There is a spiral spire above the building at 48 Quai Malakoff (see p212).

• **Neuvy-Saint-Sépulchre** (south of **Châteauroux**, Indre). A round church, (see p225).

• **Château du Plessis-Bourré** (Écuillé, north of **Angers**). Château associated with alchemy. (See p169.) plessis-bourre.com/en/

• **Dénezé-sous-Doué** (west of **Saumur**). La cave aux sculptures: an enigmatic group of underground sculptures (see p69).

• **Le Mans.** A 4.5 m (15 ft) menhir, known as the *Pierre Saint-Julien*, stands at the north-

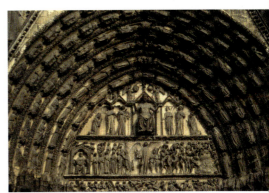

Portico of Bourges cathedral

west corner of the cathedral on Place Saint-Michel, testifying to the site's sanctity in pagan times. The cathedral itself has 47 angel-musicians painted on the vault of the *Chapelle de la Vierge*. Also worth seeking out in Le Mans is the Renaissance-style *Maison d'Adam et Ève* on the Grande Rue: although it is called "the house of Adam and Eve", the two people featured on the bas-relief carving are probably pagan gods.

Spiralling Spires

Almost every church spire is straight and true, pointing directly from the Earth to heaven in smooth symmetry. Over 100 spires in Europe, however, defy the norm and are twisted. Some of these are the unfortunate result of internal weaknesses coupled with external forces; but many of them are deliberate masterpieces of craftsmanship.

There are 65 such spires in France with a distinct concentration in the Anjou in the Loire Valley, particularly around Baugé. There is another little cluster in the Cher and the Loiret. The other examples are scattered around the rest of France, including Saint-Come-d'Olt in the Lot valley and Barran in the Gers. A magnificent example can be seen in Nantes, not above a church but over the headquarters of the *Maison des Compagnons du Devoir*.

Almost all twisted spires spring from an octagonal base and most of them turn left to right (anti-clockwise) and move through about 1/16th of a turn – but every one is different in structure and in appearance.

These spires were made to be contemplated from different angles, to intrigue and tease the eye. Beyond aesthetics, the spiral is an interesting and symbolic form with many associations. In it, there are echoes of spirals etched in prehistoric rocks, the minaret of the mosque in Samarra (Iraq), the entwined snakes of the caduceus symbol, the brushstrokes of Van Gogh, and in Dante's *Purgatory* - imagined as a conical peak with seven ascending levels.

The church spire which turns on its way to its vanishing point challenges the rational mind to make sense of it. It is visually unpredictable and, with its plays of light and shade, slightly disorientating, surprising the viewer and forcing him or her out of complacency. Each side, or plane, of the spire begins at one compass point and shifts to another.

The eye is led upwards by a deliberately indirect and less steep route, and this suggests human spiritual evolution towards higher things. A spiral is often used as an image for a human life in which "outer" time is clearly cyclical but inner time experienced as a sense of linear movement from birth to death, growing in awareness as we age.

The spiral church spire offers us a slow track to heaven, a path that is within our means to manage. Those of us who are not saints are not equipped to take the steep straight route. Instead, we meander as we climb, making what progress we can.

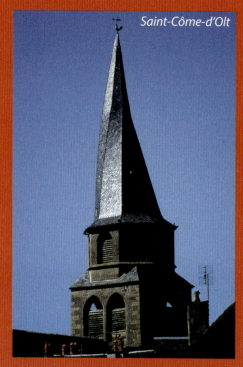

Saint-Côme-d'Olt

The Apocalypse Tapestries, Angers

The six large panels of tapestries displayed in the castle at Angers total 103 m (338 ft) in length and portray the events in the *Book of Revelations*, the last and most mystical book of the Bible. The tapestry, finished in 1380, is read left to right and top to bottom, just like a book, .

Many attempts have been made to decipher the complex, layered, dream-like imagery of Revelations, which predicts the dramatic and violent end of the world known as the *Apocalypse*.

The narrative is couched in symbolism, particularly numerology (see p23). Seven is a constant theme: there are seven seals on a scroll which must be broken, seven angels who blow seven trumpets and so on.

The tapestry also depicts disasters visited upon humanity, the four horsemen of the Apocalypse, war in heaven, St Michael's fight against the dragon (Satan), the whore of Babylon and the Beast whose number is 666.

For more information: angers.monuments-nationaux.fr

The Ark of the Covenant

Mosaic, Germigny-des-Prés

Along with the Holy Grail, the other most searched for lost sacred object is the *Ark of the Covenant*, the chest containing the tablets of the *Ten Commandments*, as described in the book of Exodus and as shown in the mosaic on the east apse of the church of **Germigny-des-Prés** (east of **Orléans**). The only evidence for it ever having existed is the Bible and even then its fate is not clear. It could have been requisitioned by the Babylonians or hidden to prevent this from happening. Various modern theories have tried to locate the Ark in the Holy Land, Ethiopia – or France. The Knights Templar, it is reasoned, set up their headquarters on the Temple Mound in Jerusalem for a reason. In a tunnel underneath the Mound, they found the Ark which they brought back to Europe and either secreted it to near **Rennes-le-Château** or in the cathedral of **Chartres** (100 km/60 mi northwest of **Germigny-des-Prés**).

Chartres Cathedral

Chartres cathedral stands out in both literal and metaphysical senses and it excels even among Gothic cathedrals. It was built to be visible from a long distance and, even today, it can be seen rising above the city from 20 km (12 mi) away across the farmland of the Beauce plain.

Because it was completed in a relatively short and continuous spurt of building, and spared by the Revolution and the world wars, it is a near-perfectly preserved 13th-century Gothic cathedral.

While it can be approached as a magnificent piece of architecture, or as a testament to the piety and penance of the Middle Ages, it is also replete with symbolism, for which it is regarded as one of the archetypal mystical sites of the world. A great many people have speculated on the nature and meaning of Chartres, even associating it with the Templars and the Holy Grail.

Professor Keith Critchlow has suggested that Chartres represents a fusion of Christian, Jewish (kabbalistic) and Arab thought under the umbrella of the Virgin Mary, standing for Sophia or wisdom. He also says that it sums up the Seven Liberal Arts and owes a lot to Platonism.

It is possible to wander around it and not have a transcendental experience, but with a little knowledge of particular points to look for, a visit becomes deeper and more moving. There is said to be a proper way of experiencing the building.

Sir Ronald Fraser suggests that Chartres " is an instrument of high initiation… crucible for the transmutation of mankind… that raises its towers into aerial currents, and is rooted in terrestrial influences." The orientation of the apse, he says, probably shows the direction of the telluric current (stream of earth energy). Chartres is, in effect, a menhir. To activate this instrument, he says it is necessary to face it "upright, with bare feet, hands raised. To turn the back on it is to reject the gift". A probable "correct" route through the cathedral is to enter by the north door into what Jacques Charpentier calls the "transept of the initiated" and to leave by the south door.

This route of discovery can be traced on a plan of the cathedral that reveals the building to be based on the elements of sacred geometry (see p22): mystical shapes, numbers and proportions. The *vesica piscis*, the lozenge, the kabbalistic tree of life and a complex geometric form called the flower of life have all been read into the

The zodiac window, Chartres cathedral

The Royal Portal

plan of the building. A recurring number in Chartres is seven.

Certain features of the cathedral are worth special attention. Outside, the three portals are astonishing compositions of sculpture. The signs of the Zodiac, along with their corresponding labours of the year, are carved into the archivolts of the Ascension doorway (the left part of the royal Portal on the west façade).

These zodiac signs appear again inside the cathedral, in a stained glass window in the south ambulatory that is read from bottom to top. Note the man with three faces (see p232) – probably representing past present and future – standing next to the figure of Aquarius. Chartres has the largest collection of medieval stained glass in the world (covering 2,500 sq m/27,000 sq ft). Its finest features are the very old *Belle Verrière* window and the three rose windows corresponding to the three facades. These are conceived in order of time: the north rose represents the past, the south rose the present and the west rose the future.

On the floor of the nave, meanwhile, is the famous labyrinth (see p120), the largest "decorative" item in the building that has given rise to a literature by itself. "The pattern and location must therefore have some meaning," concludes John James, "Yet no one has told us what it is." There are records of it being used for Christian ceremonies as a route for pilgrimage or penance, but it is possible that it harks back to an earlier pagan tradition. The labyrinth is not a maze; it has a single path to the centre. This starts near the western door and makes 11 snaking revolutions, doubling back on itself at regular intervals. At the centre is a six-petalled flower. Six is a perfect number and the centre of the labyrinth may represent heaven, to which men and women are admitted if they diligently follow the prescribed route. Eleven revolutions plus one (the centre) makes twelve, the number of perfection.

Below the floor, and built before all the above in chronological terms, is the atmospheric crypt, the largest in France. It is thought that the church stands on the site of a pagan sanctuary to the mother goddess and that this ancient cult was carried over into the worship of the Black Virgin of *Notre-Dame-sous-Terre* (Our Lady of the Underworld). The original statue was destroyed in the Revolution but a copy stands in the north gallery. The Gallo-Roman Well of the *Saints Forts* (literally, "the strong saints"), whose water is said to have curative properties, is further evidence of a pre-Christian cult on the site. There are three chapels in the crypt and a number of wall paintings.

For further information on the esoteric aspects of the building see *The Mysteries of Chartres Cathedral* by Louis Charpentier; *Chartres Sacred Geometry, Sacred Space* by Gordon Strachan; and the various books by John James. There is also a good documentary featuring Professor Keith Critchlow available online: *Chartres Cathedral: A Sacred Geometry*. cathedrale-chartres.org

8. Massif Central

The mountainous, volcanic interior of France has perhaps guarded its traditions and superstitions longer than elsewhere because of its relative inaccessibility. Romanesque churches (such as *Saint-Nectaire*) and Black Virgins abound.

- **Dhagpo Keundreul Ling** (northwest of Clermont-Ferrand). Thought to be the largest Buddhist monastery outside Asia, this Centre for spiritual retreats was founded in 1984 by Lama Guendune Rinpoche and forms part of the Karma Kagyu lineage of Buddhism. It has two sites. The main one, *Le Bost*, is for men; nearby *Laussedat* is for women. There is a guided visit at 3pm every Sunday. One of the lamas speaks English. dhagpo-kundreul.org
- **Le Puy-en-Velay.** A quite extraordinary city that is both a pilgrimage destination and is itself the point of departure for the *Via Podiensis*, one the main routes of the pilgrimage to Santiago de Compostela (see p35). The cathedral (cathedraledupuy.org) stands on a mound and is approached by a slope. Inside is a black virgin on the altar and, set into the floor, a slab of stone taken from a dolmen that is said to have healing powers. The city is looked down on by two monuments. One is the iron statue *Statue of Notre-Dame de France* standing on a pinnacle, the *Rocher Corneille*. The other aerial monument is the 10th-century *Chapelle de Saint-Michel-d'Aiguilhe* which crowns an exposed volcanic plug. rochersaintmichel.fr
- **Souvigny** (north of Vichy, southwest of Moulins). The museum, housed in the barns of a former monastery, has a unique exhibit. The "calendar stone" dating from the 12th century is an octagonal column carved on two sides with the signs of the Zodiac, the labours of the year, and on the other sides strange people and fabulous beasts. ville-souvigny.com

The Writers of Glozel

In 1924 a grandfather and grandson crawled into a hole near the hamlet of Glozel to rescue a lost cow. They discovered an immense horde of prehistoric objects that have been argued over ever since. It has proved hard to fit them into the conventional story of prehistory. In particular, the horde included over 100 rectangular tablets of baked clay inscribed with what appears to be an early form of writing consisting of at least 111 characters. Are they genuine? And how old are they? No definite answers have yet emerged. Despite many attempts to decipher the tablets, no progress has been made and the arguments over what to make of Glozel finds continue. Glozel is part of the commune of Ferrières-sur-Sichon in the Allier, southeast of Vichy. Many of the finds are on display in the *Musée d'Emile Fradin*. museedeglozel.com

The chevet, Saint-Nectaire

Detail of the zodiac window, Chartres

Astrology

In the 4th century, the nascent Christian church condemned astrology, a body of interpretative knowledge dating from at least Babylonian times, as the work of demons. It undermined the notion of free will – the individual's power to choose to be good or turn away from God.

By the 12th century, however, signs of the zodiac were appearing in stained glass and stone as if they were an integral part of the Christian tradition. They can be seen in carvings at Chartres and Amiens cathedrals, and on an octagonal 12th-century pillar of unknown provenance in the museum of Souvigny in the Auvergne. The signs were not seen as part of a pagan system of superstition but as a way of illuminating the meaning of Christianity.

Until the Renaissance, astrology and astronomy were two aspects of the same discipline and it was felt that knowledge of both was essential to wisdom. It was obvious to any educated mind that everything in the universe was connected to everything else, from which it follows that the heavenly bodies must influence affairs on earth. The only remaining questions was "how?" and that was left to skilled interpreters of the art to explain. Astrology was used to identify auspicious or inauspicious days and to determine the likely success of medical interventions.

The symbols of astrology made sense not just to the learned who could read them, but also to the mass of people when they came across shortcomings in Christian teachings. If God was beneficent and merciful, how could disaster fall upon the good man or woman? And why couldn't the local priest predict or prevent hail storms and disease? Such things seemed to be beyond the control of God, or at least beyond human powers of intelligibility; and astrology was evoked as a way of filling the gap in religious teachings.

In the 16th century, Catherine de' Medici had a handsome classical column erected in the middle of Paris so that her astrologer could climb it and make observations of the heavens.

Astrology continued to be popular until the Enlightenment brought doubts about its efficacy.

In recent decades there has been a revival in interest in astrology in France, with an emphasis put on understanding the psychological aspects of the human condition rather than predicting future events. Everyone and everything has its sign of the zodiac and ruling planet – including the Fifth Republic, which is Libra.

Three of the most important modern French astrologers are Dane Rudhyar, Michel Gauquelin and André Barbault.

In the cemetery of Clamart, outside Paris, there is a modern astrological column showing the signs of the zodiac according to four different world civilizations (see p205).

9. The Rhône and the Alps

The valley of the river Rhône has always been a conduit of people and ideas between northern and southern France via Lyon, France's third largest city and once capital of Gaul. To the east rises the great chains of mountains of the Alps, merging into Italy and Switzerland.

- **Ars-sur-Formans** (north of **Lyon**). A locally-renowned pilgrimage destination (see p38).
- **Grenoble.** The Archaeological Museum is built over the very early, 6th century Saint-Laurent crypt.

musee-archeologique-grenoble.fr

- **Palais Idéal du Facteur Cheval** (**Hauterives**, southeast of **Vienne**). The dream building of a postman, a work of great singularity and originality, completed in 1912 after 33 years work. He was partly inspired by the first illustrated magazines he had to distribute and it was to be called the *Temple of Nature*. It is "inhabited" by an incredible and unclassifiable stone bestiary. (Photo p186.) facteurcheval.com
- **Sainte-Croix-en-Jarez** (northeast of **Saint-Étienne**). A Carthusian monastery in the Pilat massif which was turned into a village after the Revolution. The various parts of the monastery are used by the present-day lay community. They are made up of the *Brothers' Court* (dedicated to the monks' material life) and the *Fathers' Court* (for spiritual contemplation) with the communal "cenobite" facilities between then, including the kitchen.
- **La Salette** (southeast of **Grenoble**). Shrine to the Virgin (see p38).

Aristotle as Beast

Aristotle is one of the towering figures of philosophy but, on the west front of Lyon's *Cathedrale Saint-Jean*, he is unflatteringly depicted in an apocryphal story current in to the Middle Ages. One of the 280 bas relief panels – that are mostly to do with Biblical stories and hagiographies – shows Aristotle on his hands and knees with a woman sitting on his back raising a riding crop in the air. The philosopher is said to have advised his patron, Alexander the Great, to abstain from sex in order to concentrate on the more important activities of philosophy and empire building. His consort, Phyllis, took her revenge by seducing the philosopher. She tested his devotion to her by asking him to come to her chamber on all fours so she could ride him like a horse. Like those of Notre-Dame in Paris, the carvings are said to conceal truths about alchemy. If that is true, what would be the lesson to be learned from this one? Perhaps that the female principle (symbolizing innate wisdom) should be encouraged to literally override the animal passions?

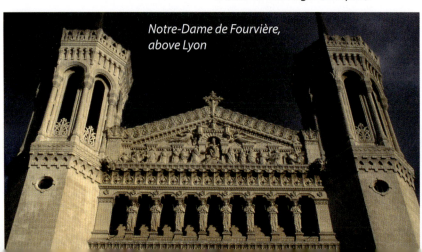

Notre-Dame de Fourvière, above Lyon

10. Provence

Provence was one of the first places in Gaul to be Christianized and some of the earliest baptisteries in France are found here. In the Middle Ages, there was a significant Jewish community; more recently it has acquired a Muslim population. Both of these have added to the variety of Provencal religious buildings. The region also has several megalithic sites and many vestiges of paganism dating from Roman times.

- **Arles.** Among the major sights of Arles are two particularly worth seeing: the Romanesque cathedral of *Saint-Trophime*, with its cloister and carved portal, and *Les Alyscamps* Roman necropolis. (See p82).
- **Carpentras** (northeast of **Avignon**). The oldest synagogue in France – still a functioning place of worship – was founded in the 14th century when Carpentras was under the protection of the Pope. The actual building dates from the 18th century. Closed to visitors at weekends and on Jewish holidays (synagoguedecarpentras.com). There is another old synagogue to visit at **Carvaillon** (due south of Carpentras, cavaillon.com).

Natural arch in the Dentelles de Montmirail

- **Cistercian abbeys.** Provence has a trio of great medieval abbeys built by the Cistercian order: *Silvacane* (northwest of **Aix-en-Provence**; abbaye-silvacane.com), *Sénanque* (East of **Avignon**; senanque.fr) *Thoronet* (southwest of **Draguignan**; thoronet.monuments-nationaux.fr).
- **Draguigan** (northwest of **Saint-Tropez**). The *Dolmen de la Pierre de la Fée* is a megalithic monument thought to be a collective sepulchre dating from 2500/2000 BC.
- **Jardin de l'Alchimiste, Eygalières** (northwest of **Salon-de-Provence**). The garden of the *Mas de la Brune* is a modern creation in three parts: labyrinth, magical garden and alchemical garden. The latter is divided into the three stages of alchemy: *the Black Work* (birth and materiality); *the White Work* (emotions and intellect) and *the Red Work* (the culmination of the alchemical art). jardin-alchimiste.com.
- **Fréjus.** This garrison and port town on the Mediterranean has several interesting monuments. Curiously, two of them – the *Sudanese mosque*, a replica of the mosque at Djenné (only viewable from the outside) and the *Hong Hien pagoda* – derive from the town's military history. The cathedral complex includes the remains of one of the

Clock tower, Salon-de-Provence

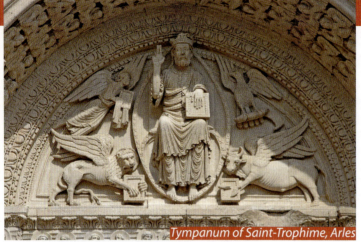
Tympanum of Saint-Trophime, Arles

first baptisteries in Gaul and has a medieval cloister, the ceiling of which is painted with fantastical animals. The chapel of *Notre-Dame de Jerusalem*, meanwhile, is decorated with the vivid designs of Jean Cocteau. The symbol of the town is a classical bust of a two-faced (see p232) rural divinity on display in the archaeological museum. frejus.fr

• **Laus** (near Saint-Étienne-le-Laus, southeast of **Gap**). Shrine dedicated to the Virgin Mary (see p38).

• **Marseille.** The Neo-Byzantine *Notre-Dame de la Garde* crowned by a statue of the Virgin overlooks the city. (See p53 & p97.)

• **Saint-Maximin-la-Sainte-Baume** (east of **Aix-en-Provence**). The relics of Mary Magdalene, including the skull (sometimes on display, sometimes paraded in a golden mask), are housed in this Gothic basilica which is considered to be one of the holiest sites in Christendom (mariemadeleine.fr). For the nearby cave that Mary Magdalene is said to have lived in for the last years of her life see saintebaume.org.

• **Saintes-Maries-de-la-Mer** (southwest of **Arles**). A church on the coast dedicated to two female saints who are said to have accompanied Mary Magdalene when she arrived in France.

• **Salon-de-Provence** (between **Avignon** and **Marseille**). *Michel de Nostradamus*, famous for his prophecies, lived here from when he was 44 until his death in 1566. His house is now a museum in his memory.

• **Vaison-la-Romaine** (northwest of **Orange**). Carved into the lintel of the cloister is the curious portrait of a man who seems to have horns, a halo and a handlebar moustache. Is it a strange Byzantine portrait of Christ, a devil, or perhaps a pagan god?

• **Chapelle du Rosaire, Vence** (inland from **Nice** on the Riviera). Henri Matisse spent four years (1948–51) creating this sacred building at the request of a nurse who served as his model and later became a nun. Everything is to his design: the plan, the architecture and all the decoration. "It is the result of my life's activity and despite its imperfections, I consider it my masterwork". The chapel is interesting as an exploration of the interface between art and religion, especially as Matisse was a convinced atheist. vence.fr

Vallée des Merveilles

The *Vallée des Merveilles* beneath Mount Bego (2872 m/9423 ft) in the Mercantour National Park contains Europe's largest collection of open-air prehistoric petroglyphs (engravings in rocks). It takes a long walk to get to the valley from Saint-Dalmas-de-Tende but there is a hostel if you want to stay overnight. If you can't manage the trek, there is always the museum at Tende. The engravings are spread out over an area of 17km at altitudes ranging from 1900 m (6233 ft) to 2700 m (8858 ft). They date from the late Copper Age to the early Bronze Age (2500-500BC). Many of the engravings are figurative but their purpose is not known. Suggestions range from idle doodles by shepherds to processional markers pointing the way to a sacred mountain. See: mercantour.eu and museedesmerveilles.com.

Mary Magdalene in France

According to a legend much told in Provence from at least the early Middle Ages, the Biblical character Mary Magdalene, disciple of Jesus, lived the latter part of her life in southern Gaul.

There are various versions of the story of how she came to be here but the essence of them is the same. Around the year AD40, the Jews of Palestine were being persecuted. Mary Magdalene was forced to board a boat with at least five companions: Mary Salome (mother of James the Greater, venerated in Santiago de Compostela), Mary Jacob (mother of James the Less), Lazarus (who Jesus had raised from the dead) and his sister Martha, and another disciple, Maximinus. The boat they were in had no oars or sail, no helm or rudder and, when it was set adrift in the Mediterranean, those on board seemed sure to perish.

Miraculously, the vessel landed on the shore of the Camargue at what is now **Saintes-Maries-de-la-Mer**. Mary Salome and Mary Jacob stayed where they had arrived and a cult of the "Saintes Maries" developed around a church built on the site.

The other people from the boat went off to convert Gaul. Maximinus became the first bishop of **Aix-en-Provence** and Lazarus the first bishop of **Marseille**. Martha is famed for taming a monster in the town of **Tarascon** with the cross, holy water and a sash from around her neck.

Mary Magdalene went first to Marseille and then to **La Sainte-Baume** where she lived in a cave in the hills for the last thirty-three years of her life. On the day she knew she was to die, she went down to plain so that Maximinus could give her communion and arrange her burial.

The shrine of Saintes-Maries-de-la-Mer

Her remains were discovered in the 13th century. They were moved to **Vézelay**, in Burgundy, for safekeeping but finally returned to La Saint-Baume where they are now displayed for the faithful in the *Basilique Sainte-Marie-Madeleine de Saint-Maximin-la-Sainte-Baume*. The cave where she lived is a sanctuary tended by Dominicans.

According to another legend, she went the other way, to **Rennes-le-Château**, where the church is dedicated to her.

The Bible gives scant information about Mary Magdalene and most of her "biography" has been added by tradition – particularly from Jacobus de Voragine's medieval bestseller, *The Golden Legend*.

For a long time – and this is still in the popular interpretations of the Bible – Mary was considered to be a prostitute, sinful until she meets Jesus. This reputation was almost certainly imposed on her by the early church, which promoted celibacy and chastity as spiritual virtues, and allotted women a subservient role.

11. Languedoc

Less well defined and less visited than Provence, the Languedoc is the "other south of France", a belt of land north of the Pyrenean foothills, with a climate influenced by the Mediterranean. The southern route of pilgrimage to Santiago de Compostela (see p36) passes through it. It is best known for its Cathar history (see p133) centred on Carcassonne and, among mystery hunters, for the out-of-the-way hilltop village of Rennes-le-Château.

• **Alet-les-Bains** (south of Limoux). A small town off the main road up the Aude valley with the atmospheric ruins of a medieval abbey at its centre. The windows of the adjoining church have tracery forming the Star of David.

• **Cathar sites.** Most of the sites related to the Cathar crusades (some by reputation more than fact) are in the Languedoc with Carcassonne as a hub. The castles of *Quéribus*, *Peyrepertus* and *Termes*, and the village of *Villerouge-Termenès* are in the Corbières region southeast of **Carcassonne**. **Minerve** is due north of Lézignan-Corbières. (See p137.)

• **Dolmen des Combes** (north of Florac). This dolmen is included in a 5-km (3 mile) footpath called *Balade au Pays des Menhirs* (allow 2 hours). causses-et-cevennes.com

• **Dolmen des Fades** (north of Pépieux, southwest of Minerve). An extremely large dolmen in a beautiful and peaceful setting on top of a low hill. [*Fada* is the Occitan for fairy.] (Photos p75 & p78.)

• **Montady** (near Capestang, between Béziers and Narbonne). The *Étang de Montady* is unusual for a lake in having no water. It was drained in the 13th century and what is left looks like some gigantic piece of land art, if not a permanent crop circle with thin straight lines (drainage ditches) running from the circumference to a circle in the middle. It is not natural or mysterious but is still very pleasing to gaze on. It can be seen from the *Oppidum d'Ensérune*, the remains of a Gaulish village.

• **Nimes.** The *Maison Carrée* in the city centre is the only temple from the classical world to be completely conserved. Built by

Béziers bridge

UFOs in France

France is the only country in the world with a state-funded, civil organisation tasked with collecting and investigating reports of unidentified aerial phenomena. *Geipan* was set up in 1977 as part of the French Space Agency (CNES) and has its offices in the *Toulouse Space Centre*.

The agency has two fulltime members of staff backed up by a team of 30 scientific experts. Every report is meticulously logged and analyzed with the aim of eliminating every possible explanation before classifying an incident as "unexplained".

Reports of unexplained aerial phenomena in France have a long history. In the early middle ages, Agobard, archbishop of Lyon, wrote a treatise called *On Hail and Thunder* in which he criticizes the popular belief in the cloud realm of Magonia populated by aerial sailors who would raise storms as a cover to plunder crops.

In 1608, there were bizarre resorts all along the Mediterranean coast from Marseille to Genoa in Italy describing aerial battles involving human-like creatures with scaly arms, and there were reports of blood raining from the sky.

Ufology took off in France, as elsewhere in the world, in the 1950s. On the night of 10 September 1954, a railway worker in northern France, Marius Dewilde, went outside his house to find out what his dog was barking at. He says he saw two small humanoid creatures hurriedly return to their spaceship and fly off.

France's most celebrated cases of close encounters took place in the mid 1960s. In the early hours of 1 July 1965, a farmer in Valensole (Provence) reported seeing two more extraterrestrials and their spacecraft. Two years later, on 29 August 1967, a brother and sister, aged 12 and 9, claimed to have had contact with a UFO and its occupants near the village of Cussac in the Massif Central.

UFO enthusiasts, however, are most keen to talk about the Trans-en-Provence Affair on 8 January 1981, in which a space craft looking "like two dinner plates, one turned upside down on top of the other" left physical traces which could be scientifically analyzed. The results are far from conclusive. The best that can be said is that some puzzlingly anomalous event did actually take place on the spot.

Most investigators take a cautious line. Sceptics point out that a vast amount of "evidence" has resulted in nothing conclusive. This doesn't stop enthusiastic believers congregating at hotspots said to offer the best chance of a sighting. These include the *Pic de Bugarach* in the Corbières hills of the Aude department, the Col de Vence near Nice and *Mont Mézenc*, a volcanic hill in the eastern Massif Central.

Geipan's job is not to deny anyone their belief, but just to sift through the evidence scientifically. After subjecting masses of data to rigorous checks, there remain around 230 cases of sightings in France that have not yet been explained.

For information about Geipan, or to report an observation go to cnes-geipan.fr.

---

the Romans in the first century AD, it is a *hexastyle* temple – that is, six columns form the façade. There is also a romantic but enigmatic building in the public part of the *Jardins de la Fontaine* known as the Temple of Diana, although it is not certain that it had any sacred function.

- **Pic de Bugarach** (east of Quillan). The highest summit in the Corbières, 1230 m (4,035 ft), stands out dramatically from the landscape and is visible from Rennes-le-Château. It is said to have powerful telluric properties and some ufologists (see above) believe it is a hollow, giant hangar for alien

The dry lake of the Étang de Montady

craft. In 2012 it was supposedly (according to the media) the focus of a belief that when the end of the world came (according to the Mayan calendar) Bugarach would be the only safe place to be. The police, it is said, blocked access to the mountain for fear that some cult might have been planning a mass suicide.

• **Rieux-Minervois** (northeast of **Carcassonne**). A 7-sided or round Romanesque church (see p225). In the village cemetery is the unusual tomb of a 19th century freemason.

• **Saint-Gilles-de-Gard** (west of **Arles**). This very early Benedictine Abbey (originally 7th century) is now partly ruined but preserves some carvings and a 12th century spiral staircase, considered a masterpiece of stonework.

• **Toulouse.** The modern capital of the Languedoc has a strange cathedral (Saint-Étienne) but it has a magnificent pilgrimage church, the Romanesque *Basilique Saint-Sernin*, the largest Romanesque church in France, distinguished by its five-storey octagonal belltower and carved portal, the *Porte Miègeville*. In the ambulatory are 11th-century marble bas-reliefs of God, a seraph and a cherub. Below is a hexagonal crypt containing a reliquary. The church of *Les Jacobins*, which houses the tomb of Saint Thomas Aquinas, can be less busy and therefore more peaceful

• **Vauvert** (northeast of **Montpellier**). In the Middle Ages, the French school of the kabbalah was based in this now unpresuming town which was then called *Posquières* (see p160). Nearby **Lunel** was also a centre for kabbalah studies.

• **La Ville-Dieu-du-Temple** (east of **Montauban**). There is not much left of the Templars in this town between the Tarn and Garonne rivers except for the name and a well documented history, but it does have a curious carving over the door of the church and a modern painting of a Templar knight on the water tower (behind the cemetery). The inhabitants are known as *Theopolitains*, "the citizen's of God's town".
lavilledieudutemple.fr

Chapel, Chambon-sur-Lac

Round Churches

The Christian church grew out of the Roman basilica, a broad rectangular hall with three aisles. Later it became elongated and was given two transepts to develop its distinctive cross shape, with the altar placed at the east end to indicate the direction of Jerusalem.

This became a more or less mandatory plan for Christian churches but a few churches break the mould. They are either round or polygonal, with no obvious orientation except inward, towards the centre. These churches recall the *Church of the Holy Sepulchre* (built over the supposed tomb of Christ) and the *Dome of the Rock* mosque, in Jerusalem. They almost certainly result from the influence of Constantinople and the *Basilica of San Vitale* in Ravenna. Some round churches were built by the Knights Templar, notably those at Laon and Metz.

Many early, Carolingian churches were round even if they are now buried in crypts, are in ruins or have vanished.

Circular structures recall the prehistoric stone circle – of unexplained use - and the mandala. It is the shape of concentration as it doesn't point to anywhere other than where it stands, perhaps on a sacred rock. The circle also suggests continuity and equality, making all worshippers equal rather than opposing the priesthood to the congregation as in a rectangular church.

Some of the best round churches are in France:

• **Église Saint-Étienne** in **Neuvy-Saint-Sepulchre** (Indre). A 12th century pilgrimage church to which a nave was attached in the 13th century. The eleven columns symbolize the apostles less Judas.

• **Chapel of the Templars** in **Laon** (Aisne, Picardy). An octagonal chapel built by the Knights Templar.

• **Temple de Lanleff** (Côtes-d'Amor, Brittany). A picturesque ruin of a church of unknown date, possibly 10th century. It has two rotundas separated by an ambulatory. Carvings on the stones include a man with giant hands.

• **Abbaye Sainte-Croix de Quimperlé** (Finistère, Brittany). An 11th century church with remarkable capitals.

• **Notre-Dame de la Merci** in **Planes** (Pyrénées-Orientales). Probably 13th century with a curious plan based on an equilateral triangle.

• **Église de l'Assomption** in **Rieux-Minervois** (Aude). A heptagonal church with remarkable capitals sculpted by the Master of Cabestany.

• **Chapelle des Templiers** in **Metz** (Moselle, Lorraine). Built between 1180-1220 as part of a Templar *commanderie*.

• **Église Saint-Bonnet** in **Saint-Bonnet-la-Riviere** (Corrèze). A picturesque restored church with a squat spire.

• **Abbaye de Saint-Sauveur** (**Charroux**, Vienne). A ruined abbey church out of which rises an octagonal sanctuary tower.

• **Saint-Pierre d'Yvetot** (**Yvetot**, Seine-Maritime). A modern church built in 1956.

• **Cathédrale de la Resurrection** in **Évry** (Essonne, near Paris). A modern church built in 1995.

• **Octagone de Montmorillon** (Vienne). An octagonal 11th century funerary chapel.

• **Abbaye de Fontevraud** (Maine-et-Loire). The elegant round Romanesque building which forms part of this abbey was once thought to be the chapel or lantern of the dead (see p82), but is now thought to have been the kitchens.

• **Chambon-sur-Lac** (Auvergne). A round baptistery or funerary chapel stands in the cemetery.

Rennes-le-Château: the Mystery of a Mystery

In 1969, the English writer Henry Lincoln was travelling through France on holiday when he chanced upon a paperback called *The Accursed Treasure* by Gérard de Sède. His interest was piqued by this mystery centered on the then unknown village of Rennes-le-Château in the foothills of the Pyrenees of Aude departement.

The book inspired him to make three documentary television programmes for the BBC and to co-author a bestselling book called *The Holy Blood and the Holy Grail* (1982) that purports to reveal the biggest cover-up in history.

Since then many other books and films have elaborated on the hypothesis that Rennes-le-Château is at the centre of specific secret knowledge that demonstrates that Jesus was not entirely as the Bible and subsequent Christian tradition portrays him. The theory is that he was married to Mary Magdalene and that they had one or more children who were brought to southern Gaul after the crucifixion and hidden among the Jewish community. Centuries later, one of their descendants became the ancestor of the Merovingian dynasty of French kings, which was therefore the continuation of the authentic bloodline of Christ. When the Carolingians supplanted the Merovingians, their lineage was maintained by the House of Lorraine and a secret society, the *Priory of Sion*, which was created to preserve the secret of the rightful bloodline over the centuries. Into this basic story is woven many other intriguing strands connecting Rennes-le-Château to the Cathars of Montségur, the Knights Templar, buried treasure and the Holy Grail.

All this was based on an investigation into the activities of the priest of Rennes-le-Château, *Bérenger Saunière*, who, when carrying out the reconstruction of his village church in 1885, allegedly discovered a set of hidden documents. Saunière is said to have become suddenly wealthy and this, says the theory, was because he had discovered the secret of Jesus's bloodline and was blackmailing the Church not to disclose it.

While Rennes-le-Château's fame as a site of mysteries has grown steadily over the last decades, fresh research has cast doubt on much of the evidence. The Priory of Sion turned out to be the fantasy of one man, Pierre Plantard, and the mystery an elaborate hoax perpetrated by him and his associates. Saunière had not discovered any dramatic secrets, and what wealth he did accumulate came

The Devil at the entrance to the church

Wall carving in the village

Travel Guide 227

Nave of Rennes-le-Château church

Rennes-le-Château, present or past? It is important perhaps to separate two aspects, the literal and the metaphorical. One is a historical detective story that depends on verifiable facts, and the other is a personal feeling of mystery that may or may not be engendered in the visitor.

As Mariano Tomatis, one of the co-authors of *Welcome to the Bérenger Saunière Museum*, puts it: "I consider Rennes-le-Château to be a place that functions as a shaman's tent: an archetypal site where people come to have visions and to invite profound experiences. The myths surrounding the region have contributed towards making Rennes-le-Château a place of great symbolic power. This proves the potent influence of literature and symbolism upon the human being."

Rennes-le-Château is reached by a minor road from Couiza. rennes-le-chateau.fr

Tour Magdala

from selling masses that he didn't perform.

These revelations haven't stopped Rennes-le-Château from being a place of fascination to modern visitors. High above the Aude valley, south of Limoux and reached by a winding road, the village definitely has something about it. At the very least it has atmosphere, great views and a good story to tell.

The two points of interest are the church and Saunière's "domain" next to it. The church is dedicated to Mary Magdalene. All the details in it, beginning with the grimacing devil who holds the water stoup by the door, were chosen by Saunière and many meanings have been read into them.

The domain consists of the presbytery (now a museum that provides a very detailed analysis of everything to do with Rennes-le-Château) and two buildings added by Saunière – the *Villa Bethany* and the *Tour Magdala* – which, like the church, are named after Mary Magdalene.

Is there anything mysterious about

12. Dordogne, Lot, Tarn & Aveyron

These four departements in the mid-southwest are all named after rivers flowing east to west through leafy, picturesque valleys and gorges. There are a lot of interesting places to visit, including prehistoric painted caves.

• **Albi** (northeast of Toulouse). The redbrick town which gave its alternative name to the Cathars (see p133) is built around a massive Gothic cathedral. The adjacent bishop's palace (a museum to the memory of painter Toulouse-Lautrec) has a riverside garden. (Photo p118.)

• **Brantôme** (north of Périgueux). Take the *Troglodyte Tour* to see the caves that were used by the monks of the abbey as outbuildings. One includes the *Grotte du Jugement Dernier* and has a disturbing bas relief of the *Triumph of Death* (see p82).

• **Caves.** The Dordogne department (and to a lesser extent the Lot) has one of the most important concentration of prehistoric painted caves in the world. *Lascaux* (near **Montignac**) can no longer be visited but a replica has been built. Of the caves that can be visited, *Font-de-Gaume* (outside **Les Eyzies**), *Rouffignac* (north of Les Eyzies) and *Pech-Merle* (northeast of **Cahors**) are probably the best to visit. Depictions of human beings are rare in cave art but *Grotte du Sorcier* (grottedusorcier.com) at **Saint-Cirq** (between Les Eyzies and **Le Bugue**) has three, including one known as the *sorcier* (the magician). Guided tours for all these caves must be reserved in advance, as the size of groups is strictly limited.

• **Cénevières** (east of **Cahors**). A château containing a room which was used as an alchemical laboratory. (See p169.)

• **Conques** (northwest of **Rodez**). A Romanesque abbey church dominates this beautiful hill village on the pilgrimage route to Santiago de Compostela. It has a remarkable *tympanum* showing the Last Judgement (best seen with the afternoon sun on it). On the outer edge of the archivolt are the *Curieux de Conques* – faces peeping out of the stonework.

• **La Couvertoirade** (southeast of **Millau**). Several old villages on and around the *Causse du Larzac* were Templar possessions later passed on to the Knights Hospitallers. *La Couvertoirade* and *Sainte-Eulalie-de-Cernon* are the most visited (see p156). Also worth seeing are *La Cavalerie* (northeast of Sainte-Eulalie), *Viala-du-Pas-de-Jaux* (southeast of Sainte-Eulalie-de-Cernon) and *Saint-Jean d'Alcas* (southwest of Viala-du-Pas-de-Jaux in Saint-Jean-et-Saint-Paul).

• **Moissac** (northwest of **Montauban**). It's easy to be put off by a first impression of Moissac, a nondescript town with a rail

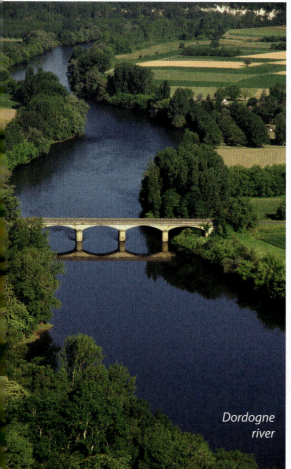

Dordogne river

line running through it on the north bank of the Tarn river but it has two remains from a once important abbey: a magnificent carved *tympanum* over its south portal and the richly carved cloisters (entered through the tourist information office). (Photo p105)

• **Monts de Lacaune** (east of **Castres**). The best preserved menhir statues (see p76) are in the museum in Rodez (see below) but some still stand in the countryside. They are linked up by a route, the *Circuit des Statues Menhirs* which begins at Murat-sur-Vèbre (where there is a museum), and passes through Moulin Mage, Lacaune and Nages. tourisme-montsdelacaune.com

• **Plum Village** (northeast of **Marmande**). A community of monks and nuns set up by the Vietnamese monk *Thich Nhât Hanh*. It

The shrine at Rocamadour

has four different sites or hamlets. Visitors are welcome to attend a *Day of Mindfulness* which takes place on almost every Thursday and Sunday of the year.
villagedespruniers.net

• **Rocamadour** (northeast of **Cahors**). One of France's most visited places of pilgrimage, spectacularly sited on the steep side of a valley. You either have to start at the bottom or, more commonly, approach it from the top, from *L'Hospitalet*. The sacred parts of Rocamadour are arranged around the *Parvis*, an enclosed square. The most important sanctuary is the *Chapelle Notre-Dame* where a Black Madonna is venerated. Above her hangs an iron bell that was believed, in the Middle Ages, to ring out by itself to announce miracles. On the facade of the chapel are the remains of a fresco of the dance of death. (Photo p39.)

• **Rodez** (northeast of **Albi**). This small city has a magnificent southern Gothic cathedral and an archaeological museum, the Musée Fenaille, with a collection of menhir statues (see p76) on the top floor.

Lascaux

The most famous of the prehistoric painted and engraved caves was only discovered in 1940. It is the most studied and discussed but just as enigmatic as all the rest. The walls and ceilings are adorned with a Magdalenian menagerie of horses, deer, ibex and aurochs (an extinct wild ox). There is also a rhinoceros, a wolf, and a bear. Theories abound. Are the animals symbolic or part of some visual mythology? Were they seen in shamanic trances? Did the cave have some ritualistic function or was it just an art gallery? Another idea is that the animal paintings are really star charts depicting patterns in the Stone Age heavens in the same way as we define constellations using the imagery of the Zodiac.

The cave has long been closed to the public who are directed to a replica, Lascaux II. This can't, of course, have the same atmosphere as the original but at least it is a way to contemplate the art and the motivation that produced it. lascaux.culture.fr
(See photos on pages 54 & 61.)

13. Western France

The Atlantic seaboard, south of the Loire valley, takes in the regions of Poitou, Charente, Bordeaux and the Gironde, and Gascony. The route of the pilgrimage to Santiago de Compostela is marked by Romanesque churches and "lanterns of the dead".

- **Aubeterre-sur-Dronne** (south of **Angoulême**). A large cave church. (See p68.)
- **Auch** (west of Toulouse). Esoteric significance has been read into the stained glass and the carvings of the choir stalls in the late Gothic-cum-Renaissance cathedral.
- **Barran** (southwest of **Auch**). An excellent example of a spiral church spire. (See p212.)
- **Bougon** (northeast of **Niort**). Six tumuli composing an impressive prehistoric complex dating from around 4700 BC.
- **Avrillé** (southeast from Les Sables-d'Olonne). The area around this town has a large number of megalithic monuments. The most impressive include the dolmens of *Cour de Breuil* and *Frébouchère* and the menhirs of *Plessis*, *Petite Pierre* and *Camp de César* – all of which once formed part of alignments. The latter is 8.70m (29 ft) high and has been called the "king of menhirs".
- **Charroux** (east of **Civray**). The *Abbaye de Saint-Sauveur* has a curious octagonal tower rising from its ruins (see p225).
- **Chauvigny** (east of **Poitiers**). The capitals in the chancel of the church show winged monsters, sphinxes, sirens and demons torturing resigned-looking human beings.
- **Cressac-Saint-Genis** (southwest of **Angoulême**). A chapel containing murals left by the Knights Templar. (See p156.)
- **Dampierre-sur-Boutonne** (northeast of Saintes). A château renowned for its alchemical carvings. (See p169. Photos p173 & 175.)
- **Fontenay-le-Comte** (northwest of **Niort**). The *Château de Terreneuve* is associated with alchemy. (See p169.)
- **Lanternes de la mort.** The exact purpose of these towers is uncertain but they seem to be concerned with lighting the way for the dead (see p82). Good examples can be seen at *Cellefrouin* (southwest of Confolens) and *Fenioux* (southwest of Saint-Jean-d'Angély, beside the A10 highway).
- **Montmorillon** (southeast of **Poitiers**). Octagonal funerary chapel. (See p225.)
- **Pons** (southeast of **Saintes**). The hospital des Pélerins, on the way out of town, is the

Talmont-sur-Gironde church

Misericords

A misericord or "mercy seat" is a shelf underneath a folding chair in a choir stall for the discreet use of a monk who is required to spend long hours of prayer standing up. Many such seats were decorated by wood carvers who were given a free reign in their choice of subject matter. While some misericords illustrate Biblical stories, others are secular or irreverent in theme, depicting mythological creatures and human figures in a variety of postures, some even lewd or scatalogical. Amiens cathedral in the north of France has the largest collection of such carvings, followed by Auch cathedral in the Gers.

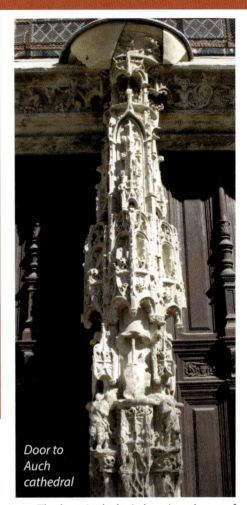

Door to Auch cathedral

only pilgrims' hospital left standing on the *Chemin de Saint-Jacques* (see p26). Medieval carved graffiti can be seen on the walls beneath the arch over the street. Inside the building there is an exhibition on the pilgrimage and, behind it, a medieval garden. (Photo p247.) pons-tourisme.com
• **Pougne-Hérisson** (west of **Parthenay**). In one sense, all mysticism comes down to storytelling and this town excels in stories. A granite rock between a chapel and the château is known as "le nombril" (the navel) and it is said to grow daily. This legend has led the town to proclaim itself as the "Navel of the world". nombril.com
• **Saint-Émilion** (east of **Libourne**). A beautiful wine town with an underground church, the *Église Monolithe*. (See p68. Photos p17 & 244.) saint-emilion-tourisme.com
• **Saintonge** (the area around **Saintes**). This area of countryside is known for its Romanesque churches, many of which have exquisite and often inscrutable stone carvings. The best include *Aulnay* (northeast of Saint-Jean-d'Angély), the *Abbaye Royale* in Saint-Jean-d'Angély, *Corme-Écluse* (southwest of Saintes), *Trizay* (southeast of Rochefort), the *Abbaye de Fontdouce* (east of Saintes) the *Abbaye de Sablonceaux* (west of Saintes), and the *Abbaye aux Dames* in Saintes itself.
monuments-saintonge.com
• **Saint-Savin-sur-Gartempe** (east of **Poitiers**). A large abbey church with exceptional paintings of Genesis, Exodus and the Apocalypse. abbaye-saint-savin.fr
• **Talmont-sur-Gironde** (southeast of **Royan**). A Romanesque church picturesquely sited on a low cliff of the Gironde estuary on the edge of a village filled with flowers.

Two and Three Faces

The Roman god Janus had two faces so that he could look both ways at once, forwards and backwards. He is the god of beginnings, change, time and transitions since he sees into the past and into the future simultaneously. There is a temple reputedly dedicated to him at Autun, in Burgundy, and a two-headed Gallo-Roman sculpture, possibly related to him, was discovered at the acropolis of Roquepertuse in Provence. It is now on display in the archaeology museum in Marseille.

A more curious derivative of Janus is the tomb of *François II de Bretagne* in Nantes cathedral, into which much esoteric significance has been read. On the corners of the tomb are four figures representing the cardinal virtues. The head Prudence has two faces looking in opposite directions. One is an old bearded man and the other a young woman.

Several Romanesque churches take this notion one step further with the "trifron". This singular form of stone carving shows three faces fused together and sharing four eyes. One face looks out of the wall to the left, another to right and the middle one straight towards the viewer. The two side faces are shown either in profile or three-quarter view.

Trifrons are found mostly in the Poitou-Charentes region, particularly in the Saintonge. Two of the best examples are at Aujac in the *Église Saint-Pallais* in Saintes and there is another not far away in *Aubeterre-sur-Dronne*. All of these are medieval. There is a later, probably 18th-century, mural of what looks to be a three-faced portrait of a Pope at *Romegoux*.

Conventionally it is held that the trifron is a representation of the Trinity of God, Christ and the enigmatic Holy Spirit, but there is no evidence for this and the idea of three joined heads predates Christianity. It is thought to date back to Egypto-Hellenic civilizations. It could be also argued that the Trinity arose as a way to assimilate similar triads of pagan deities, found in Gaul, into Christianity.

Symbolically, the three faces of the trifron could refer to the past, present and future. It could also depict the three dimensions of life – a literal interpretation of the sense of the word "face", meaning the side or surface of a three-dimensional object. Even today we talk of the face of a mountain – for example the North Face of the Eiger – or of a problem having several facets. In this way the trifron could also be a prompt to the viewer, reminding us that, although we are individuals, we have multiple points of view. To be mystical means being able to look more than one way at the same time.

Column plinth, originally from Larreule abbey

14. The Pyrenees

The Pyrenees form a physical and symbolic barrier across southwest France from Catalonia to the Basque Country. There is a dramatic and lonely grandeur to the highlands and the valleys and foothills have a great many curious sights to see. The Pyrenees also have their own rich folklore. Curiously, the name of the devil often shows up in connection with the many bridges needed to cross the rivers that flow out of the mountains For convenience, the chain can be divided up into its eastern, western and central sections.

Saint-Genis-des Fontaines lintel

Eastern Pyrenees (Pyrénées-Orientales)

• **Abbaye Saint-Martin-du-Canigou** (south of **Vernet-les-Bains**). To get to this reactivated monastery requires a stiff walk uphill from the carpark at Casteil or a ride on a jeep. It is located high in the Canigou massif that includes the *Pic du Canigou*, the sacred mountain of Catalonia (see p52). Single people and couples are welcome to take a spiritual break here but visitors are expected to join in the life and prayer of the community. stmartinducanigou.org/en Not far to the north is another monastery the Abbaye Saint-Michel-de-Cuxa (abbaye-cuxa.com).

• **Arles-sur-Tech** (southwest of **Perpignan**). This town grew up around a Benedictine abbey beside which is the *Sainte Tombe*, a sarcophagus which seems to produce water from nowhere. It is said to be free of impurities and to have miraculous curative powers. Just outside the town is a dolmen, *La Caixa de Rotlan*. ville-arles-sur-tech.fr Half an hour's drive to the southwest of Arles-sur-Tech, pressed up against the border with Spain, is the small village of *Coustouges* in which some of the streets and squares have been given teasing names to make the passer-by think: "The Way of Challenges", "Calvary of Inconfessable Dreams" and "The Square of the Unforgettable Well".

• **Céret** (southwest of **Perpignan**). Modern artists have put this town on the map but it is also known for its extraordinary bridge, the *Pont du Diable* which crosses the river Tech with a slender span.

• **Elne.** The former episcopal seat of Roussillon still has an intact 11th century cathedral to which cloisters were later attached. They are made of white marble veined with blue and exquisitely carved. ot-elne.fr

• **Planes** (southwest of **Mont-Louis**). A unique church built to a curious plan. (See p225.)

• **Prieuré de Serrabona** (north of **Amélie-les-Bains**). A former priory considered a masterpiece of Romanesque art for its carvings of flowers, angels and animals.

• **Abbaye Saint-Genis-des-Fontaines** (south of **Perpignan**). This Benedictine abbey was built in the 8th century. It has a particularly charmingly carved lintel over its door. saint-genis-des-fontaines.fr

The Fall of Montségur

The siege of Montségur that ended in March 1244 was not quite the last stand of the Cathars – the outpost of Quéribus clung on for a further eleven years – but it was the dramatic climax of the campaign against them. To many people, it stands today as a symbol of the heroic resistance of a persecuted religious minority that combined bravery, faith and dignified resignation when confronting the most awful fate.

The precipitating event occurred in May 1242. The five hundred or so Cathars gathered in the fortress sent out a band of soldiers to assassinate a group of inquisitors in session at the town of Avignonet, to the north.

This was the excuse for the French crown to finally move against this stubborn heresy that had never been completely eradicated in the Languedoc. An army of up to 100,000 was sent to surround the mountain.

Around Christmas 1242, the Cathars were able to remove their treasure for safekeeping. We don't know what it consisted of. It was never to be heard of again and some people believe it is still hidden in the region nearby.

The castle held out for almost 11 months until a *trébuchet* (siege catapult) managed to partially destroy the eastern tower, which had then to be abandoned by the garrison.

On 2 March 1244, the inhabitants of the fortress could see that there was no escape for them and they agreed to surrender. Curiously they asked for and were granted a fortnight's grace before the terms of the surrender came into force. The reason for this delay has never been explained.

On 16 May, the Inquisition gave the Cathars a last chance to recant or face the flames. Over two hundred of those who had taken refuge in Montségur refused to renounce their faith. They were taken down the mountain to the plain below in chains and burnt on a giant pyre. Most of the soldiers who had been protecting them, and who were not of the Cathar faith, were spared.

Today, the ruined castle crowded upon the 1207m (3960 ft) peak above Montségur village is an atmospheric place to visit, even if you don't know its history, although there is not much to see except stone walls. Park on the approach road from Lavelenet and Foix. Prepare for a stiff walk uphill through scrubland. The ticket booth is half way up the slope. Wear a hat and take water.

The ruined château of Montségur

Central Pyrenees (Ariège, Haute-Garonne and Hautes-Pyrénées)

• **Caves.** The central Pyrenees have several caves adorned with prehistoric art. The best caves to visit are *Niaux* (southwest of **Tarascon-sur-Ariège**) and *Gargas* (northwest of **Saint-Bertrand-de-Comminges**). (See p57.)

• **Gensac-sur-Garonne** (on the D62 towards **Cazères-sur-Garonne**). The *Pont du Diable* describes an improbable brick curve over the river Volp. Steep to ascend and descend, it looks more like a structure made to be admired than to be used. Its date of construction is uncertain. (Photo p147.)

• **Grotte du Mas d'Azil** (northeast of **Saint-Girons**). A road passes through this gigantic natural corridor. Inside, is the entrance to a prehistoric painted cave. The handrail of the pavement leading up to it is formed by a timeline of human history. The most picturesque view of the cave is from the south.

• **Mancioux** (east of **Saint-Gaudens**). Two menhirs stand together, somewhat neglected, in this small village just off the main N117 road. There is another stone planted outside the church of nearby Saint-Martory. (Photo p79.)

• **Montsaunès** (south of **Saint-Martory**). Templar church. (See p156.)

• **Montoulieu: Pont du Diable** (south of **Foix**, signposted on the mainroad, not the highway). Very different from the "devil's bridge" at Gensac, this is a romantic bridge with a broad level deck spanned by two arches and ruined buildings near one end. The name recalls a legend that the devil built it in time immemorial but the truth is it was constructed in the 19th century by a local entrepreneur. It is still a beautiful, peaceful place.

• **Saint-Bertrand-de-Comminges** (southwest of **Saint-Gaudens**). A massive, fortified church – Romanesque structure with Gothic and Renaissance additions – stands out from the rest of the town. Adjoining it is a peaceful cloister with one open side giving onto the surrounding countryside. cathedrale-saint-bertrand.org On the plain below are the ruins of the Roman town of *Lugdunum Convenarum* which had a temple and, later in its development, an early Christian basilica. Also worth seeing is the nearby church of *Saint-Just de Valcabrère* which has a curiously minute crypt or shrine beneath the altar. (Photo p100.)

• **Saint-Lizier** (outside **Saint-Girons**). History has left this small hilltop commune of 1,500 souls with a cathedral and cloister making it a charming place to escape from the main road and the city of Saint-Girons below.

• **Vals** (west of **Mirepoix**). A 10th-century semi-underground church. (See p68.)

Western Pyrenees (Pyrénées-Atlantiques)

• **Chapelle de Caubin** (southeast of **Arthez-de-Béarn**). An alcove of this small chapel on a backroad contains the tomb of an unknown knight. (Photo p148.)

• **Cromlech of Lous Couraous** (Ossau valley, south of **Pau**). (Photo p81.) Go through the village of **Bilhères** and continue upwards until you come to a chapel and a picnic area. Just after this, a track climbs gently to the right and leads after 1.5 km (1 mi.) to a small terrace on which stand the remains of several prehistoric stone circles. The site has clearly been chosen partly because it is a natural vantage point over the valley and the mountains. The village of

Fountain decoration, Fenouillèdes

Lourdes

On 11 February 1858, a fourteen-year-old girl was collecting bones and branches by a river in the foothills of the Pyrenees with her sister and a friend when she met – or so she said afterwards – a stranger by the mouth of a cave. She described her as a "little young lady" wearing a white dress, a white veil, a blue belt and a yellow rose on each foot.

Only Bernadette Soubirous could see this lady, and at first she didn't know who or what she was. She couldn't even decide whether she was good or bad and she sprinkled holy water over the apparition just to be sure.

At first the lady said nothing but at the third apparition she spoke to the girl in Occitan, the regional language. When Bernadette asked what her name was, she replied, "It is not necessary". After the 6th apparition Bernadette was asked by the police commissioner who or what she had seen and she replied "aquera" ("that one").

Bernadette's parents tried to stop her going back to the grotto but eventually relented because the phenomenon was arousing public interest. The lady appeared to Bernadette a total of 18 times over the next five months and each time more and more townspeople turned out to watch her commune with the invisible visitor and, they hoped, effect a miracle.

Disturbed by what was happening, the local priest repeatedly demanded to know the apparition's name and it was only on the 16th apparition that she revealed her identity to be "the Immaculate Conception." By that time the civil and religious authorities of Lourdes had become hostile to the idea of crowds of people gathering to witness a young girl talking to an invisible entity and they blocked access to the grotto.

It took the local bishop four years to pronounce the apparitions of *Our Lady of Lourdes* to be genuine. After that the town quickly grew to be the most important pilgrimage centre in France.

Everything about this story, and about Lourdes itself, is, of course, Christian. Or is it? It is curious that the lady took a long time to identify herself; appeared only to Bernadette; and eventually revealed herself to Bernadette not simply as Mary, the blessed virgin and mother of Christ, but as the "Immaculate Conception". This is the term given to the subject of a doctrinal debate in the late 19th century in which the Church tried to resolve a conundrum of its own making: how God could have been born of an ordinary human being.

The story can also be read psychologically or symbolically. Apparitions are often experienced by adolescents, who are in transition from childhood, in which the difference between reality and imagination is blurred and the fantastic is not extraordinary, to maturity. The cave, it should be noted, often represents the inner person, the subconscious: what comes out of it is a "realiza-

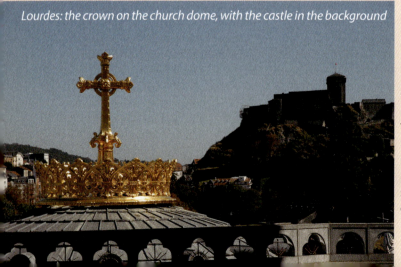
Lourdes: the crown on the church dome, with the castle in the background

Invalids queuing to get into the grotto

tion" of self. It could be that Bernadette was meeting another part of herself for the first time – or perhaps the adult self she aspired to be. This apparition or personal revelation was visualized by her imagination and became convincingly real. To those around her, however, it was inscrutable. The only way they could make sense of it was to define it using the religious terminology with which they were familiar. Changing the frame of reference, Bernadette's apparition could be considered to be a fairy or water sprite, a common figure in Pyrenean folk tales.

Modern Lourdes is, of course, quintessentially Catholic. It is built on the collective belief that Bernadette really did see the Virgin Mary and that the water issuing from the cave can effect miraculous, holy cures.

Six million visitors converge on the town each year from 140 countries, most of them for religious reasons rather than sightseeing or curiosity. In numerical terms, Lourdes is almost as popular as the Eiffel Tower and the Riviera.

The sanctuary area beside the river teems with people more or less all year round, but their numbers are swelled on feast days and when a special mass is being celebrated. Many of those drawn to Lourdes are on crutches or in wheelchairs and they are attended by teams of volunteers and nuns.

The cave, where mass is celebrated almost nonstop and the faithful line up to take the water, is now dwarfed by two churches, upper and lower, with a crypt between the two. A long line of taps is provided for those who cannot get into the cave to fill up plastic bottles with holy water. Beside the sanctuary area, tall candles burn in constant memory of innumerable prayers.

Anyone who is not devoutly Catholic can see another aspect Lourdes. What was once an old Pyrenean town overlooked by a castle is now dominated by its faith-driven tourist industry. The brash commercialism – hotels, restaurants and 220 souvenir shops that sell bottles of holy water and other keepsakes to take home – can easily overshadow the spiritual origins of the Lourdes phenomenon.

An interesting contrast to Lourdes is a visit to its precursor, the *Sanctuaires de Bétharram* (15 km/ 9.5 mi. down the valley along the road to Pau), where the Virgin Mary has been venerated since the Middle Ages. In the 17th century, the medieval oratory on the site was converted into a baroque church and in the 19th century an extraordinary series of chapels was built on the hillside above marking the stations of the cross.

For more information on the sanctuaries of Lourdes see: en.lourdes-france.org. For information on the town in general see: www.lourdes-infotourisme.com. For Bétharram, see betharram.fr.

Bielle, down below in the valley, is delightful to walk around to see the stone carvings that adorn many of its houses. One of them shows the face of a *cagot*.

• **L'Hôpital-Saint-Blaise** (northwest of **Oloron-Sainte-Marie**). This small village in a wooded valley was formerly the site of a medieval pilgrims' hospital. For centuries, the place was neglected and it is still on a road that few people take. It has a highly unusual church which displays influences of the Moorish civilization of nearby Spain. This is most evident in the stonework patterns of the windows and the eight-pointed star of the dome. (See p38.)
hopital-saint-blaise.fr

• **Lacommande** (northeast of **Oloron-Sainte-Marie**). Behind the church (which has some beautiful stone carving in it) there is an immaculate cemetery of discoidal gravestones divided into two triangles. These particular stones date only from the 17th and 18th centuries but it is thought that the form is prechristian. Their circular heads are marked with a variety of crosses. (Photo p83.)

• **La Rhune** (reached by funicular from **Col de Saint-Ignace**, south of **Ascain**). Sacred Basque hill (see p53).

• **Oloron-Sainte-Marie** (southwest of **Pau**). The *Cathédrale Sainte-Marie* has an outstanding carved portal of sacred and profane characters. Inside is a group of carved capitals with a number of inscrutable faces peering out of them. The *Église Sainte-Croix* in the district of the same name gets less visitors. In the inside of its dome is an 8-pointed Mozarabic star (Photos p112.)

• **Saint-Jean-Pied-de-Port** (southeast of **Saint-Jean-de-Luz**). Principal town on the pilgrimage route to Santiago de Compostela, always busy with pilgrims getting ready to cross the mountains into Spain. (See p35. Photos p25, p31 & p33.)

• **Sauveterre-de-Béarn** (southwest of **Orthez**). Only half of the fortified 12th century bridge, the *Pont de la Légende*, remains as if prompting us to symbolically complete its passage over the river in our imagination.

• **Stèle de Gibraltar** (north of **Ostabat**, signposted from the D933). Meeting point of three routes of pilgrimage. (See p32.)

Pyrenees view

The Mystery of the Cagots

Europe used to have its own caste of untouchables. The *cagots* (also known by a variety of other names) were a persecuted minority that lived mainly in southwestern France, but also in northern Spain.

Not much is known for certain about them because all the information we have has been filtered by their persecutors and later by historians.

We do know that they were not an ethnic, religious or linguistic group. They were only identifiable by families: a cagot was descended from cagots, born into afflicted minority status in a perpetual chain of discrimination.

They were reported to have had many distinguishing physical features – to be small of stature, swarthy, blonde with blue eyes, with puffy faces and swollen fingers – but there is considerable variation and contradiction in such descriptions.

Because they were so difficult to distinguish from other people, they were sometimes required to have an identifying mark stitched on to their clothing: a goose or duck's foot cut out of red material.

The cagots were excluded from political and social rights and confined to *cagoteries*, quarters of the village set apart from "normal" folk. Other measures were taken to ensure that the two classes of people were kept apart. Some churches have two doors, the smaller one allowing cagots to enter a segregated part of the nave and to use a secondary holy water stoup without mingling with the rest of the congregation.

They were also limited in employment. They could only engage in certain crafts, particularly those to do with wood and iron working. Although they, themselves, were discriminated against, their construction skills were highly prized.

Not much is known about their origin or why they attracted such opprobrium. There are many theories as to how the status of cagot came about. It has been suggested that they were reputed to be lepers, cretins, cannibals or heretics – perhaps the last of the Cathars (see p133) otherwise persecuted to oblivion. It has also been hypothesized that they were the descendants of the Visigoths; of the Muslim Saracens who invaded France in the 8th century; or the workmen employed by the Knights Templar (see p149) before the latter fell into spectacular disgrace. The writer Louis Charpentier suggested that they were compagnons (see p154), the remnants of an initiated brotherhood of craftsmen that had been cast out of society because of their secretive behaviour.

After the Revolution, with the spread of education and much greater mobility of labour, persecution faded and the cagots merged into the general population. There is a museum devoted to them in the Pyrenean town of **Arreau** in the Hautes-Pyrénées.

Statue of a cagot outside the museum in Arreau

Time to Come: the Cyclic Cross of Hendaye

Hendaye is a holiday resort in the Basque Country, in the extreme southwest corner of France. Most people either pass straight through it on their way across the Bidasoa river into Spain, or else they make straight for the beach. Few of them go out of their way to visit the old part of town that stands on a hill set slightly back from the coast. Fewer still seek out the rather inconspicuous cross that stands in the shadow of the south transept of the 16th-century Eglise Saint-Vincent.

No one knows how old this cross is (although it is probably no earlier than the late 17th century), who carved it, or why; but the enigmatic Fulcanelli (see p170) considered it significant enough to discuss alongside the Gothic cathedrals and alchemical palaces of northern France.

He was convinced that it encodes the greatest secret of all, that of time. In particular, he wrote in the second edition of The Mystery of the Cathedrals, that the "cyclic cross" of Hendaye foretells the end of the world. "The unknown workman who made these images," he remarks, "possessed real and profound knowledge of the universe."

The clue to the significance of the cross, explains Fulcanelli, is in the inscription written at the top. This has a literal sense to it but mistakes in the Latin suggest that it is meant to be read esoterically using the cryptic "language of the birds". Esoterically, he translates the phrase as, "It is written that life takes refuge in a single space", implying that there is somewhere safe to take refuge from the coming apocalypse, although it is up to us to find out where.

Three of the four faces of the pedestal on which the cross stands are carved with images of heavenly bodies recalling the tarot: a star, the moon and the sun (with an expressive face).

The fourth face of the cross is inscribed with a circle divided by horizontal and vertical lines. In each of the four sectors is placed the letter A, the capital alpha, standing for the four cyclical ages of the earth. This contrasts with normal practise. For example, on the facades of many medieval churches, the four ages are represented by the symbols of the evangelists who are shown as four winged creatures drawn from the vision of Ezekiel and the Book of Revelations: a man-angel (Matthew: incarnation); a lion (Mark: consciousness and courage); a bull or ox (Luke: sacrifice and service); and an eagle (John: the soaring of the soul and eternity).

Travel Guide 241

Ruined window, Château de Najac

Gatepost in Montsaunès

End Notes

Being There, Knowing More

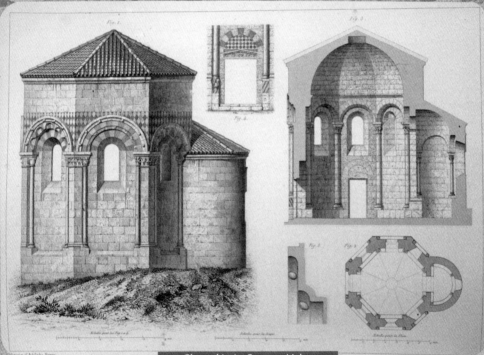

Chapel in Le Puy-en-Velay from a book by Jules Gailhabaud

Much of the practical advice needed for travelling in France – accommodation, transport, etc. – can be easily found online. This section of the book supplies some additional guidance for visiting the country mystically - especially where to find further information.

General Information

Travelling in mystical France can mean shuffling between the modern world and the mystical world. Fortunately, there are ways to ease the transition in both direction and make a deeper contact France and its people at the same time

Where to get some quiet

Most churches are kept unlocked and the larger ones have space set aside for prayer and worship. Where a church is locked, the local town hall will usually be delighted to give you the key. The main airports have basic religious facilities set aside from the crowds. These are usually religion-specific –chapel, mosque and synagogue - but sometimes there is a shared spiritual space. Paris-Charles-de-Gaulle Airport, for instance, has a meditation room (*Espace de Recueillement*) in terminal 2D.

Spiritual retreats

The majority of establishments offering spiritual retreats in France are Catholic monasteries or convents (see p130). Some of have accommodation for only men or women, but several cater for couples. Rooms may be in a modern guesthouse but they may just as well be in some antiquated monastic building. You may even be expected to stay in an original monk's cell. A retreat in a monastery is not a holiday. You will be expected to take part in the life of the institution: to observe communal meal times and perhaps do a few hours work. There is usually a set charge for a retreat but occasionally you will be invited to make a donation. spiritualite2000.com and fondationdesmonasteres.org link to most monasteries with accommodation for visitors.

The Taizé Community (see p209) is a Christian community but ecumenical.

Most Buddhist communities also welcome guests for varying lengths of time. buddhanet.info

The best way to find out about retreats in all kinds of places is the latest edition of *The Good Retreat Guide* by Stafford Whiteaker. thegoodretreatguide.com

Mystical holidays

Several companies run guided tours (in English) of the sacred, mysterious or mystical sites of France. Others organize pilgrimages to Lourdes or walks along the Way of St James. A websearch usually

Spiral handrail in Saint-Émilion

yields information about tour operators but another way to find out about such things is to contact the French tourist authority uk.rendezvousenfrance.com.

Good eating

France prides itself on its meat-rich culinary tradition and few conventional restaurants feel the need to provide a specifically vegetarian option. Restaurateurs, however, will usually try to accommodate particular dietary needs where they can. There are vegetarian and vegan restaurants in the larger cities. One way to find out about them is vegan-france.com.

Alternative medicine

An extraordinary variety of complementary medicine techniques are on offer in France), sometimes in the most unlikely places in the depths of the countryside. Some practitioners are regulated by national or international organizations but many are not. Inevitably, word of mouth is the best recommendation. Otherwise see medicines-naturelles.com or search to begin with for "medicine non conventuelle" or by the name of the technique you looking for.

Workshops

For full immersion in mystical France you may want to do a workshop or course (*stage*) in French on some subject that appeals to you, be it yoga, art therapy or herbalism. There are many available, mostly taking a weekend or a week. While you will need a basic level of comprehension, language becomes less of an issue when you are with like-minded souls engaged in something of mutual interest.

The best workshop centres are either in Paris or in some exquisite part of the countryside, typically the Dordogne or Provence. For workshops outside the big cities, board and lodging is available in situ but charged separately to the course fee.

Many websites exist to promote events around France. Among them is meditation-france.com.

Some of these workshop centres are run for the rest of the time as bed and breakfasts by practicants of yoga, meditation or some other mind, body and spirit technique. They make extremely good bases for exploring mystical France. They can usually be found by a websearch using an appropriate keyword or by asking the relevant tourist information office.

Sharing

Car sharing (*covoiturage*) can be a good way to get around France cheaply with reduced impact on the environment. Various websites put together drivers and passengers, the best known of them being *Bla Bla Car* (blablacar.fr).

Volunteering schemes such as those run by *Workaway* (workaway.info) and *World Wide Oppportunities on Organic Farms* (WWOOF: wwoof.net) provide opportunities for a cheap stay in various corners of France, often with interesting and knowledgeable hosts, in return for a few hours work.

Shops

Good places to connect with all things Mind, Body and Spirit in France are wholefood shops. The *Biocoop* network has 325 branches throughout France indicated by a prominent logo. To find the nearest one see biocoop.fr/magasins-bio/trouver-mon-magasin-Biocoop. Somewhere near the till, you are likely to find a free newspaper or magazine full of information and adverts about what is going on both nationally and locally.

A more specific way into *Mystical France* is to find the nearest esoteric bookshop by searching online for "librarie ésoterique". Most are in Paris but there are a few such shops elsewhere, noticeably in Rennes-le-Château (see p226).

Walking the Pilgrimage Routes: Practical Tips

Routes

The four main routes of the pilgrimage to Santiago de Compostela (see p35) have had several variations and extensions added to them in recent years. In addition, several other long-distance paths feed into them, especially:

- *Chemin du Piémont-Pyrénéen* (GR78), along the foothills of the Pyrenees
- *Chemin du Littoral*, down the Atlantic coast
- *Chemin du Mont Saint-Michel*, connecting Mont Saint-Michel with Saint-Jean-d'Angély

Meanwhile, an entirely independent path of pilgrimage, the *Via Francigena*, leads across northern France on its way between Canterbury and Rome.

Some of these routes are classified as *grandes randonnées* (gr-infos.com or ffrandonnee.fr). The GR65, for instance is the *Via Podiensis* from Le Puy-en-Velay to Roncesvalles in Spain.

All this adds up to an immense choice of mindful walking. You can, of course, join any route anywhere along it and walk as much of it as you want, or walk it in reverse.

Preparation and what to take

Summer – particularly the school vacations in July and August – is prime time when the pilgrimage routes and places to stay along them are at their busiest. Earlier summer is quieter. Packing for a long walk requires some thought: everything non-essential must be left behind. A 50-litre (3,000 cu in) backpack weighing little more than 10kg (22 lb) should be adequate. Essential items include a good pair of walking boots (broken-in before you start), a sleeping bag (and perhaps a mattress cover and pillow cover), a hat, a waterproof jacket, first aid kit and a water bottle.

Tour Saint-Jacques, Paris

The pilgrim's passport

The passport or *credencial* is essential in Spain and desirable in France. It is stamped at official halts along the way. It is obtained from one of the regional *Associations des Amis de Saint-Jacques*.

Accommodation en route

The longer routes are divided into recognized stages with each night's halt served by a choice of accommodation. Names of types of place to stay vary but the most common cheaper places to stay, are:

- *gîte d'étape, refuge* or *auberge du pélerin*: the standard pilgrim's hostel that may be provided by the town council or an association. It is usually looked after by a warden and has strict opening and closing times. Beds are usually in a shared dormitory and there is a communal kitchen. Preference is given to *bona fide* pilgrims bearing a "passport".
- *chambre d'hôte* or "chez l'habitant" bed and breakfast in a private house

Tourist offices are generally very good at finding alternative places to stay including bungalows and caravans on campsites. Note that "*sur la voie*" in the description of a place to stay means that it is on the pilgrimage route.

Websites and organizations
• The *Confraternity of St James* (CSJ) has a great deal of information and publishes guides to the routes. csj.org.uk
• The *Fédération Française des Associations des Chemins de Saint Jacques de Compostelle*, based in Le-Puy-en-Velay compostelle-france.fr
• *Pélerinages de France* (Pilgrimages in France). A useful site for pilgrimages in general. pelerinagesdefrance.fr
• *Villes Sanctuaires en France* is an association of the major shrines of France. www.villes-sanctuaires.com

Books (see bibliography for details)
• Edwin Mullins' *The Pilgrimage to Santiago* covers the French routes in its first chapters.
• *The Roads to Santiago* by the photographer and writer Derry Brabbs has four chapters on the French routes.
• Louis Charpentier's *Les Jacques et le mystère de Compostelle* (sadly, not translated into English) offers some highly original speculations about the esoteric nature of the pilgrimage. For practical use there are very few guides to the French routes in English but a great many in French, noticeably published by *Topo Guides* and *Rando Editions*.

Continuing through Spain
Once in Spain, the French routes turn sharply westward. They meet at *Puente La Reina* and continue to Santiago de Compostela. *A Pilgrim's Guide to the Camino de Santiago* by John Brierley (Camino Guides) gives details of the route broken down into stages.

The pilgrims' hospital in Pons

Note on Sources

There isn't the space to mention every book, article, website, radio programme or film that I consulted in the course of researching and writing this book. In addition, some subjects I have explored are so vast that they have extensive bibliographies of their own.

Here, I can only point out the key sources I made use of for the most important subjects. Each subject is listed alphabetically, not in the order it appears in the book. An author's name in capitals indicates that his work is detailed in the bibliography. Inevitably, some of my best sources are in French but there is a surprising amount of good material in English.

General sources

Conventional travel guides are a useful way to get an overview of France and find out a little about the most well-known places. The French version of Wikipedia is a mine of information on both place and subject; but it is only ever a starting point for a train of thought and it is important to follow up the sources at the food of each page .

Early good reads were **Jonathan BLACK, Graham ROBB, Claude ARZ** (both 1 and 2) and **John JAMES** who has a long and fascinating introduction that goes far beyond his brief of explaining French churches. There are several compilations of the world's best sacred and mysterious places that list the obvious sites in France but do not go into great detail. I looked at several of these but have no strong preference among them.

The web, naturally, has a mass of information if you know how to find it and which sites to trust. I particular like *Sacred Destinations* (sacred-destinations.com) and *Lieux-Sacrés* (lieux-sacres.com).

Another very useful source has been the archive of BBC Radio 4's *In Our Time* series that includes authoritative, in-depth discussions of several topics in this book.

Alchemy

The two books by **FULCANELLI** are dense but frequently illuminating. **Colin WILSON** gives a summary of the subject in chapter 11. *Le Teinturier de la Lune* by **Violette Cabesos** (Albin Michel, 2015) breathes some novelistic life into alchemy.

Cathars (including Montségur)

Most of the background is from **Jonathan SUMPTION** supplemented by *Montaillou* by **Emmanuel Le Roy Ladurie** (Peguin, 1978) and **Jean Durban**'s *Montségur* (Harriet, 1982). Some of my information about the Cathars comes from an interview with James Macdonald of Cathar Tours.

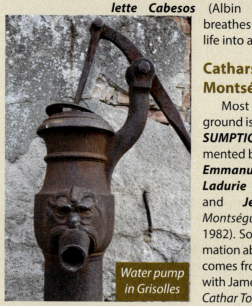

Water pump in Grisolles

Cave art

My starting point for reading about the motivation behind cave art was **Graham Hancock**'s *Supernatural*. This draws heavily on the work of **Davis Lewis-Williams** who has explored the theory that cave art must be the product of the hybrid-reality produced by shamanic trance. Hancock, however, takes this an important step further in arguing that trance and the art it produces cannot be understood in an entirely objective way. He also extends the idea to explain legends of meeting little people and claims of abduction by extraterrestials.

Christian iconography

Duchet-Suchaux G and M Pastoureau: *The Bible and the Saints*. Paris: Flammarion Iconographic Guides 1994, translated by David Radzinowicz Howell.

Livingstone Elizabeth A. (ed) *The Oxford Concise Dictionary of the Christian Church* 1977, plus a companion to the Bible.

Gods, goddesses and Black Virgins

The literature on the goddess religion and black virgins is extensive. Most books cover the phenomenon in general, not just as it applies to France. **Ean BEGG** is a good place to start.

Gothic architecture

Jean GIMPEL has the virtue of brevity. **John JAMES** is good on individual churches. I also consulted various guides to architecture.

Labyrinths

It is worth supplementing **W. H. MATTHEWS** (good, but dated) with **Adrian Fisher** and **Georg Gerster**'s *The Art of the Maze* (Weidenfeld and Nicholson, London 1990) and various maze-enthusiasts' websites.

Megaliths

The Megalithic Portal (megalithic.co.uk) is generally a good resource. There is an excellent site on Morbihan department: www.culture.gouv.fr/culture/arcnat/megalithes/en/index_en.html

Rennes-le-Château

Although some of the information and theories in *The Holy Blood and the Holy Grail* by **BAIGENT et al** have been discredited, the book still presents some interesting ideas that should be approached with a sceptical mind. **Bill PUTNAM** and **John Edwin WOOD** provide balanced analysis of the evidence. For a detailed study of the whole affair, in an appealingly visual format, see the excellent, visually-inspired publication put together **Antoine CAPTIER** et al.

Stained glass

Painton COWEN's book is the work of reference for rose windows. **A. T. MANN** has some interesting sections on Chartres. Beyond these two, there is a huge amount of analysis of medieval stained glass in both English and French.

Tarot

My principal source for this feature was Roxanne Flornoy via letarot.com which has a good English section.

Templars

Malcolm BARBER is the authority on the Templars. **John Michael Greer** is good on other secret societies. I also looked at **Alain Demurger**'s *Brève Histoire des Ordres Religieux militaires* Gavaudan (Fragile, 1997).

UFOs

Most of my information comes from an interview with the director of Geipan supplemented from ARZ (1), chapter 19.

Wheel of Fortune, Beauvais

Not much is known about the *Wheel of Fortune* window at Beauvais but there is a paper by **J. David McGee** which is full of interesting thoughts about it: scholarworks.gvsu.edu/cgi/viewcontent.cgi?article=1679&context=gvr

Dragon carved on the portal of Grisolles church

Bibliography

Arz, Claude (1). *Voyage dans la France Mysterieuse*. Paris: Le Pré aux Clercs 2011.

Arz, Claude et al (2). *A la decouverte de la France mysterieuse*. Paris: Reader's Digest, 2001.

Baigent, Michael, Richard Leigh and Henry Lincoln. *The Holy Blood and the Holy Grail*. London: Jonathan Cape, 1982.

Barber, Malcolm. *The New Knighthood*. Cambridge: Cambridge Universtiy Press, 1994.

Begg, Ean. *The Cult of the Black Virgin*. London: Arkana, revised edition 1996.

Black, Jonathan. *The Secret History of the World*. London: Quercus, 2007.

Brabbs, Derry. *The Roads to Santiago*. London: Frances Lincoln, 2008.

Captier, Antoine, Christian Doumergue and Mariano Tomatis. *Welcome to the Berenger Sauniere Museum*. Translated by Karen McDermott. Rennes-le-Château: Terre de Rhedae Association, 2012.

Charpentier, Louis. *Les Jacques et le Mystère de Compostelle*. Paris: Rober Laffont (J'Ai Lu series), 1971.

Cirlot, J.E. *A Dictionary of Symbols*. London: Routledge & Kegan Paul, 1962.

Cowen, Painton. *Rose Windows*. London: Thames & Hudson (Art and the Imagination series), 1979.

Fillipetti, H and Trotereau, J. *Symboles et pratiques rituelles dans la maison paysanne traditionelle*. Nanterre: Berger-Levrault, 1978.

Fulcanelli. *Demeures Philosphales*. Paris: Pauvert/Fayard 1976. Originally published 1930.

Fulcanelli: Master Alchemist. *Le Mystere des Cathedrales Esoteric Interpretation of the Hermetic Symbols of the Great Work*. Translated by Mary Sworder. London: Neville Spearman, 1971. Originally published 1926.

Gimpel, Jean. *The Cathedral Builders (Les Batisseurs des Cathédrales)*. Paris: Editions du Seuil, 1958.

Greer, John Michael. *The Element Encyclopedia of Secret Societies*. London: Harper Element, 2006.

Hancock, Graham. *Supernatural*. London: Arrow Books, 2006.

Huxley, Francis. *The Way of the Sacred*. London: Aldus, 1974.

James, John. *The Traveller's Key to Medieval France: A Guide to the Sacred Architecture of Medieval France*. London: Harrap Columbus, 1987.

Lawlor, Robert. *Sacred Geometry*. London: Thames & Hudson (Art and the Imagination series), 1982.

Lunquist, John M. *The Temple*. London: Thames & Hudson (Art and the Imagination series), 1993.

Mann, A T. *Sacred Architecture*. London: Element, 1993.

Matthews, W H. *Mazes and Labyrinths: Their History and Development*. London: Longmans, 1922; republished by Dover 1970.

Michell, John. *The Earth Spirit*. London: Thames & Hudson (Art and the Imagination series), 1975.

Mullins, Edwin. T*he Pilgrimage to Santiago*. Oxford: Signal Books, 2001.

Nozedar, Adele: *The Illustrated Signs and Symbols Source Book*. London: HarperCollins, 2010.

Pauwels, Louis and Jacquers Bergier. *The Morning of the Magicians*. Translated by Rollo Myers. London: Souvenir Press 2001. First published as *Le Matin des Magiciens,* Gallimard, 1960.

Pepper, Elizabeth and John Wilcox. *Magical and Mystical Sites*. London: Weidenfeld and Nicholson, 1977. Part II: chapters 17–20.

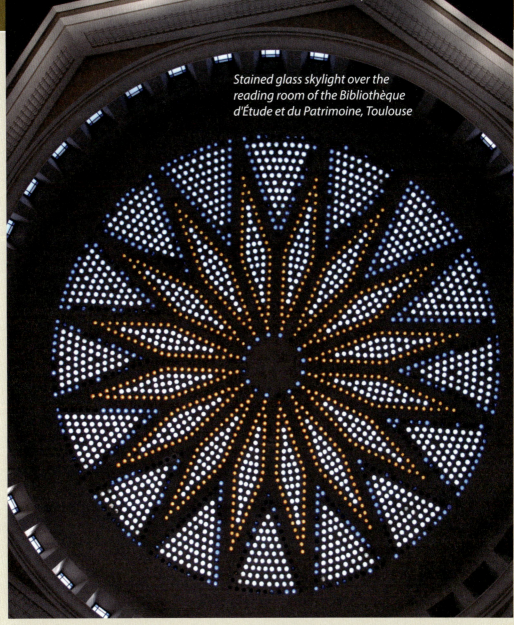

Stained glass skylight over the reading room of the Bibliothèque d'Étude et du Patrimoine, Toulouse

Purce, Jill. *The Mystic Spiral*. London: Thames & Hudson (Art and the Imagination series), 1974.

Putnam, Bill and John Edwin Wood. *The Treasure of Rennes-le-Chateau: A Mystery Solved*. Stroud: Sutton, 2003.

Robb, Graham. *The Discovery of France*. London: Picador, 2007.

Sharkey, John. *Celtic Mysteries*. London: Thames & Hudson (Art and the Imagination series), 1975.

Sumption, Jonathan. *The Albigensian Crusade*. London: Faber and Faber, 1978.

Toman, Rolf. *Romanesque*. Potsdam: H.F.Ullmann/Köneman, 2004.

Whiteaker, Stafford. *The Good Retreat Guide*. London: Hay House, 2010 (6th Edition).

Wilson, Colin with Damian Wilson. *The Encyclopedia of Unsolved Mysteries*. London: Harrap, 1987. Chapters 11, 14, 16, 19, 21, 28, 32 and 33.

Index of Places

Abbaye aux Dames 231
Abbaye de Allouville-Bellefosse 200
Abbaye de Bec-Hellouin 200
Abbaye de Bonnefont 184
Abbaye de Brantôme 69, 83
Abbaye de Chaalis 205
Abbaye de Cluny 28, 109, 130, 208
Abbaye de Fontdouce 231
Abbaye de Fontenay 208
Abbaye de Fontevraud 211, 225
Abbaye de Fontfroide 136
Abbaye de Jumièges 200
Abbaye de La Chaise-Dieu 83
Abbaye de la Trinité 200
Abbaye de Lieu-Restauré 205
Abbaye de Moissac 101, 105, 112, 130, 228
Abbaye de Montmajour 69
Abbaye de Port-Royal-des-Champs 205
Abbaye de Royaumont 205
Abbaye de Sablonceaux 231
Abbaye de Saint-Gilles-de-Gard 224
Abbaye de Sénanque 109, 219
Abbaye de Silvacane 109, 219
Abbaye de Solesmes 211
Abbaye de Thoronet 109, 219
Abbaye du Mont des Cats 53
Abbaye Royale 231
Abbaye Saint-Genis-des-Fontaines 233
Abbaye Saint-Martin-du-Canigou 52, 233
Abbaye Saint-Maur 69
Abbaye Saint-Michel-de-Cuxa 52, 233
Abbaye Saint-Roman 69
Abbaye Saint-Sauveur 225, 230
Abbaye Saint-Wandrille 114, 200
Abbaye Sainte-Croix de Quimperlé 225
Abri du Poisson 57
Aix-en-Provence 102, 172, 219, 220, 221
Albi 14, 83, 91, 118, 137, 228
Alet-les-Bains 110, 222
Alouville-Bellefosse 45
Amélie-les-Bains 233
Amiens 120, 201, 217
Angers 211, 213
Angoulême 112, 230
Arc de Triomphe 82, 92
Arcy-sur-Cure 169
Arles 36, 82, 112, 219, 220, 224
Arles-sur-Tech 233
Arras 154
Arreau 239
Ars-sur-Formans 38, 218
Arthez-de-Béarn 148, 235
Arville 156, 211
Aubeterre-sur-Dronne 68, 230, 232
Auch 36, 87, 230, 231
Aujac 232
Aulnay 35
Auray 192
Aurignac 55
Autun 110, 208, 232
Avallon 195, 208
Avignon 156, 219, 220
Avignonet-Lauragais 141
Avioth 38, 206
Avrillé 230
Axiat 111
Barnenez 74, 192
Barran 230
Basilique Notre-Dame de Sion 52
Basilique Saint-Denis 205
Basilique Saint-Just de Valcabrère 235
Basilique Saint-Pierre-aux-Nonnains 102
Basilique Saint-Quentin 201
Basilique Saint-Sernin 29, 112, 224
Basilique Saint-Victor 69
Basilique Sainte-Marie-Madeleine 39, 221
Baud 192
Baugé 212
Baux-de-Provence 69
Bayeux 120, 126
Bazas 117
Beaucaire 69
Beaune 208
Beauvais 202, 249
Bel Air 53
Belloc et Urt 131
Bénévent-l'Abbaye 43, 110
Bergheim 172
Bétharram 43, 67, 126, 237
Béziers 136, 137, 143, 222
Bibracte 208
Bieuzy 69, 192
Biollet 188
Blancafort 211
Bleurville 69
Blois 35
Bois de Brocéliande 194
Bordeaux 35, 68, 110, 154, 182
Bougon 230
Boulogne-sur-Gesse 53
Boulogne-sur-Mer 69
Bourges 35, 119, 122, 123, 164, 211
Bozouls 84, 86
Bram 136
Brantôme 69, 228
Brassempouy 96
Brest 192
Brianny 83
Brienne-le-Château 206
Broca 43
Cabaret 136
Caen 200
Cahors 35, 228, 229
Canal du Midi 43
Capestang 222
Carcassonne 43, 133, 137, 139, 222, 224
Carnac 52, 72, 73, 74, 192, 193, 196
Carpentras 219
Carvaillon 219
Castres 229
Cathédrale de la Resurrection 225
Cathedrale Saint-Jean 218
Caudebec-en-Caux 114
Caunes-Minervois 2, 69
Cave aux Sculptures 69
Cazères-sur-Garonne 235
Cellefrouin 83, 230
Cénevières 166, 169, 228
Céret 233
Cernay 172
Chailly-sur-Armançon 169
Chambon-sur-Lac 83, 225
Champagnolles 106
Chapelle de Caubin 148, 235
Chapelle de la Vierge 212
Chapelle de Saint-Michel-d'Aiguilhe 52, 216
Chapelle des Sept-Saints 193
Chapelle des Templiers (Laon) 156
Chapelle des Templiers (Metz) 156, 159, 225
Chapelle des Templiers du Dognon (Cressac-Saint-Genis) 156, 230
Chapelle du Rosaire 182, 183, 220
Charlieu 112
Charroux 225, 230
Chartres 35, 38, 43, 69, 99, 114, 115, 118, 119, 120, 122, 123, 128, 213, 214, 217
Château de Cénevières 169
Château de Chailly 169, 208
Château de Chastenay 169
Château de Comper 194
Château de Dampierre 169, 171, 173
Château de Ménilles 163, 200
Château de Terreneuve 169, 230
Château du Champ de Bataille 200

Château du Plessis-Bourré 162, 169, 211
Châteauroux 211
Châtenois 172
Chaudon 69
Chaumont 208
Chauvigny 112, 230
Cheylade 8
Chinon 115, 156
Cholet 211
Citeaux 208
Civray 230
Clairvaux 208
Clamart 205, 217
Clermont-Ferrand 52, 188, 216
Cloître des Pénitents 131, 200
Cluny 28, 109, 130, 208
Colmar 207
Colonne Médicis 203
Colonne Zodiacale 205
Concressault 172
Condom 116
Congressault 211
Conques 35, 83, 110, 228
Corme-Écluse 231
Couiza 227
Coulommiers 152, 156, 205
Coustouges 233
Cressac-Saint-Genis 156, 230
Créteil Cathedral 182
Curieux de Conques 228
Cussac 223
Dame de Saint-Sernin 76
Dampierre-sur-Boutonne 169, 230
Demoiselles de Langon 192
Dénezé-sous-Doué 69, 211
Devil's Bridge 147, 233, 235
Dhagpo Keundreul Ling 188, 216
Dijon 69, 127, 208, 209
Dolmen de La Caixa de Rotlan 233
Dolmen de la Pierre de la Fée 219
Dolmen des Combes 222
Dolmen des Fades 75, 78, 222
Dolmen of Soulobres 72
Domaine des Pierres Droites 193
Domfront 195
Domme 69
Domrémy-la-Pucelle 206
Draguigan 219
Écuillé 169, 211
Église de Barran 212
Église de l'Assomption 225
Église des Jacobins 224
Église Monolithe 231
Église Saint-Bonnet 225
Église Saint-Come-d'Olt 212
Église Saint-Denis-de-Condé 211
Église Saint-Étienne (Beauvais) 202

Église Saint-Étienne (Neuvy-Saint Sepulchre) 225
Église Saint-Jacques-et-Saint-Philippe 206
Église Saint-Jean-de-Montmartre 203
Église Saint-Merri 147, 203
Église Saint-Pallais 232
Église Saint-Pierre d'Yvetot 225
Église Saint-Pierre-aux- Nonnains 206
Église Saint-Séverin 127
Église Saint-Sulpice 203
Église Saint-Trophime 36, 112
Église Sainte-Croix 112
Église Sainte-Onenne 194
Eguisheim 207
Eiffel Tower 18
Elne 233
Étang de Montady 222, 224
Etorn Valley 192
Étretat 9, 40, 169, 200
Évreux 200
Évry 120, 188, 205, 225
Évry Cathedral 120, 182, 205, 225
Eygalières 219
Felletin 83
Fenioux 83, 230
Ferrières-sur-Sichon 216
Figeac 35
Florac 222
Foix 137, 147, 235
Font-de-Gaume 57, 228
Fontaine de Vaucluse 43
Fontaine Saint-Michel 203
Fontanges 69
Fontenay-le-Comte 169, 230
Forêt de Brotonne 200
Forêt de Chaux 45
Fosse Dionne 43
Fréjus 102, 188, 219
Gap 38, 220
Gargas 235
Gensac-sur-Garonne 147, 235
Ger 70
Germigny-des-Prés 213
Gibraltar 32, 35, 238
Glozel 21, 216
Godewaersvelde 53, 201
Gouffre d'Esparros 62
Gouffre de Padirac 62
Grande Mosquée de Paris 203
Grande Pagode 204
Grande Synagogue de la Victoire 203
Great Broken Menhir of Er Grah 74
Grenoble 102, 218
Grotte de Chauvet-Pont d'Arc 57

Grotte de Font-de-Gaume 57, 228
Grotte de Gargas 57, 59
Grotte de L'Aven Armand 62
Grotte de Labastide 62
Grotte de Lascaux 57
Grotte de Niaux 57, 58, 60, 61, 66
Grotte de Pech-Merle 57, 228
Grotte de Rouffignac 228
Grotte du Mas d'Azil 57, 235
Grotte du Sorcier 228
Grottes de Bétharram 67
Guédelon 128
Gurat 69
Haute-Isle 69
Hauterives 218
Hendaye 240
Hong Hien pagoda 219
Hôpital des Pélerins 26
Hotel Lallement 211
Ile de la Cité 35
Ile de Sein 192
Ile Feydeau 92
Jardin de l'Alchimiste 219
Jumièges 110
Kerlescan 196
Kermario 196
Kernascléden 83
Kientzheim 83
L'Hôpital-Saint-Blaise 38, 238
L'Hospitalet 229
La Cavalerie 228
La Celle-Condé 211
La Couvertoirade 156, 228
La Haye-de-Routot 45, 200
La Recevresse 206
La Rhune 52, 238
La Sainte-Baume 221
La Salette 38, 218
La Trappe 130
La Ville-Dieu-du-Temple 224
Labastide 57, 62, 64, 65
Lac de Gaube 46
Lac de Grand-Lieu 211
Lacaune 76
Lacommande 83, 238
Langon 192
Lanleff 192
Lannion 193
Laon 119, 156, 201, 225
Larmor-Baden 197
Larreule 103, 183
Lascaux 54, 57, 228, 229
Laus 38, 220
Laussel 96
Le Barroux 130
Le Bugue 228
Le Havre 182, 200
Le Mans 74, 119, 131, 211, 212
Le Ménec 196

Le Neubourg 200
Le Puy-en-Velay 35, 38, 53, 216, 246
Lentilles 206
Les Alyscamps 82
Les Eyzies 228
Les Sables-d'Olonne 230
Lescar 110, 113
Lespugue 96
Lézignan-Corbières 222
Libourne 231
Limoges 35, 38, 154
Limoux 43, 222
Lisieux 38, 200
Loches 115
Locmariaquer 74, 196
Locronan 38, 193
Loudun 172
Lourdes 15, 39, 43, 98, 236
Louviers 21, 131, 200
Lunel 224
Lyon 53, 218, 223
Mâcon 209
Maison Carrée 222
Maison d'Adam et Ève 212
Maison des Compagnons du Devoir 212
Maison des Mégalithes 196
Maison des Sorcières 172
Maison Jayet 169
Mancioux 79, 235
Mané Gwen 53
Manoir de la Salamandre 169
Marciac 37
Marmande 229
Marseille 53, 69, 176, 188, 220, 221, 223
Mas de la Brune 219
Massif du Donon 206
Maubourguet 1
Maulevier 211
Meaux 205
Melle 35
Mende Cathedral 122
Ménez Bré 53
Ménez-Hom 52
Ménilles 163, 200
Metz 102, 126, 156, 159, 183, 206, 225
Millau 69, 72, 178, 183, 228
Millau Viaduct 72, 178, 183
Minerve 136, 137, 222
Mirepoix 120, 235
Missir mosque 188
Moissac 35, 101, 105, 112, 130, 228
Mont Blanc 53
Mont des Cats 52, 201
Mont Dol 53

Mont Mézenc 223
Mont Saint-Michel 16, 39, 52, 198, 210, 246
Mont Sainte-Odile 39, 52, 206
Mont-Louis 233
Montady 222
Montaner 146
Montauban 224, 228
Montbard 208
Monteneuf 193
Montignac 228
Montmajour 69
Montmartre 10, 39, 52, 69, 82, 203
Montmédy 206
Montmirail 219
Montmorillon 230
Montoulieu 147, 235
Montparnasse 82, 203
Montpellier 224
Monts de Lacaune 229
Montsaunès 156, 235
Montségur 53, 130, 135, 137, 138, 226, 234, 248
Morlaàs 22, 36
Morlaix 192
Moulins 216
Mur païen 52
Murat-sur-Vèbre 76
Musée d'Emile Fradin 216
Musée de Cluny 19, 31, 112, 124, 203
Musée de la Sorcellerie 172, 211
Musée du Louvre 204
Musée Fenaille 76, 84, 86, 229
Musée National d'Archéologie 205
Najac 24, 241
Nancy 206
Nantes 83, 92, 195, 211
Naours 69
Narbonne 222
Neuvy-Saint-Sépulchre 211, 225
Nevers 35
Niaux 57, 58, 60, 61, 66, 235
Nice 223
Nimes 222
Niort 230
Notre-Dame d'Avioth 206
Notre-Dame de Fourvière 53, 218
Notre-Dame de Jerusalem 220
Notre-Dame de la Garde 53, 220
Notre-Dame de la Merci 225
Notre-Dame de Paris 35, 119, 126, 205
Notre-Dame de Royan 182
Notre-Dame des Graces 16
Notre-Dame-du-Haut 182
Notre-Dame-la-Grande 112
Noyon 119
Obernai 206

Octagone de Montmorillon 83, 225
Oloron-Sainte-Marie 36, 112, 238
Oppidum d'Ensérune 222
Orange 220
Orcival 39
Orléans 211, 213
Orthez 238
Ostabat 238
Ouessant 192
Pagode de Vincennes 188
Paimpol 192
Paimpont 194
Palais Idéal du Facteur Cheval 186, 218
Palais Jacques-Cœur 164, 211
Panthéon 83
Paray-le-Monial 39, 109, 169, 209
Paris 10, 26, 35, 39, 53, 69, 82, 83, 119, 122, 123, 124, 126, 127, 150, 154, 156, 164, 175, 182, 188, 202, 203, 210, 217, 245, 246
Parthenay 231
Pas de Peyrol 51
Pau 235
Payns 156
Pépieux 75, 78, 222
Père Lachaise 82, 203
Périgueux 35, 228
Perpignan 233
Petite France 207
Petite Venise 207
Peyre 69
Peyrepertuse 140, 222
Pic de Bugarach 223
Pic du Canigou 53, 233
Pierre Saint-Julien Menhir 211
Planes 225, 233
Plouarzel 192
Plouha 83
Ploumilliau 193
Plum Village 189, 229
Poitiers 35, 102, 112, 230, 231
Pons 26, 230
Pont de la Légende 238
Pont du Diable 147, 233, 235
Pont-Audemer 200
Port-la-Nouvelle 137
Portal Royal (Chartres) 114, 115
Porte Miègeville 224
Pougne-Hérisson 231
Prieuré de Serrabone 52, 112, 233
Puy-de-Dome 52
Quéribus 132, 137, 138, 222, 234
Quillan 223
Quimper 192, 193
Randol 130
Reims 119, 120
Rennes 193, 194

End Notes

Rennes-le-Château 12, 146, 213, 221, 222, 223, 226, 245, 249
Ribeauvillé 172
Richerenches 156
Rieux-Minervois 82, 112, 224, 225
Rioux 112
Riquewihr 7, 207
Rocamadour 39, 229
Rochemaure 115
Rodez 76, 84, 86, 144, 228, 229
Romegoux 232
Ronchamp 182, 209
Roquepertuse 232
Rouen 200, 206
Rouffach 172
Rouffignac 57
Royan 182, 231
Rumengol 39
Sable-sur-Sarthe 211
Sacré-Cœur 39, 53
Saint-Agnant-de-Versillat 83
Saint-Bertrand-de-Comminges 100, 112, 235
Saint-Bonnet-la-Riviere 225
Saint-Cirq-Lapopie 45
Saint-Dalmas-de-Tende 220
Saint-Denis Cathedral 118, 119
Saint-Émilion 17, 68, 231, 244
Saint-Étienne 218
Saint-Étienne-le-Laus 220
Saint-Gaudens 235
Saint-Génis-des-Fontaines 112
Saint-Germain-en-Laye 205
Saint-Gilles-du-Gard 112
Saint-Girons 235
Saint-Jean d'Alcas 228
Saint-Jean-d'Angély 35, 230, 231, 246
Saint-Jean-de-Luz 238
Saint-Jean-des-Vignes 201
Saint-Jean-du-Doigt 39
Saint-Jean-Pied-de-Port 25, 31, 33, 35, 36, 238
Saint-Lizier 235
Saint-Martin-du-Canigou 131
Saint-Martory 235
Saint-Maximin-la-Sainte-Baume 39, 220
Saint-Michel de Brasparts 53
Saint-Nectaire 216
Saint-Pierre-aux-Nonnains 102
Saint-Quentin 201
Saint-Ronan 39
Saint-Savin 12, 93
Saint-Savin-sur-Gartempe 110, 231
Saint-Sernin 29, 110, 112, 224
Saint-Sever 3
Saint-Tropez 18, 219

Saint-Trophime 36, 112
Sainte Tombe 233
Sainte-Anne-d'Auray 39
Sainte-Anne-la-Palud 39
Sainte-Baume 154
Sainte-Chapelle 122, 123, 204
Sainte-Croix-en-Jarez 218
Sainte-Eulalie-de-Cernon 156, 228
Saintes 230, 231, 232
Saintes-Maries-de-la-Mer 38, 220, 221
Saintonge 231
Salon-de-Provence 219, 220
Sanctuaires de Bétharram 237
Sarlat-la-Canéda 83
Saumur 69, 211
Sauveterre-de-Béarn 238
Selestat 172
Senlis 119
Sens 119
Serrabone 52, 112, 233
Sète 43
Sion-Vaudemont 52, 206
Soissons 119, 201
Solesmes 131
Soligny 130
Souillac 112
Source-Seine 209
Souvigny 112, 216, 217
Square du Temple 156, 164
Strasbourg 39, 119, 206, 207
Sudanese mosque 219
Table des Marchands 197
Taizé Community 209, 244
Talmont-sur-Gironde 110, 230, 231
Tarascon 126, 221
Tarascon-sur-Ariège 235
Tarnac 115
Temple de Lanleff 225
Tende 220

Termes 222
Ternois 146
Thann 172
Tonnerre 43
Toulouse 5, 29, 36, 43, 85, 89, 92, 94, 95, 109, 110, 112, 137, 138, 147, 154, 156, 223, 224, 228, 230
Tour Magdala 227
Tour Saint-Jacques 35
Tournus 209
Tours 35, 154
Trans-en-Provence 223
Tréguier 39
Tréhorenteuc 194, 195
Trizay 231
Troyes 119, 123, 156, 206
Tumulus d'er Grah 197
Tumulus de Bougon 74
Tumulus Saint-Michel 52, 74, 197
Vaison-la-Romaine 220
Valensole 223
Vallée des Merveilles 21, 220
Vals 68, 97, 235
Vannes 192, 193
Vaour 149
Vauvert 224
Vence 182, 183, 220
Vendôme 156, 211
Vernet-les-Bains 233
Versailles 18, 92
Vézelay 28, 35, 39, 69, 109, 112, 195, 208, 209, 221
Viaduc de Millau 72, 178, 183
Viala-du-Pas-de-Jaux 228
Vichy 21, 216
Vienne 218
Villa Bethany 227
Ville-Dieu-du-Temple 224
Villerouge-Termenès 137, 142, 222
Vincennes 188

If you wish to walk from Saint-Jean-Pied-de-Port to Santiago de Compostela, we recommend the following *Camino Guides.*

caminoguides.com

Acknowledgements

I am grateful to the many people have helped me make this book, directly and indirectly: Rosemary Bailey, Joël Berdy, David Bowden, Mo Duck, Marie-Paule Erades, Jane Ewart, Chantal Fihey, Marie Grellier, Lyndsey Heredero, Marion Kaplan, Richard Kelly, James McDonald (of *Cathar Country Tours*), Barry Miles, Yves Nauche, Jacqueline Robinson, Sarah Smith (of *The Connexion* newspaper, which ran several articles based on this book), Dorothy Stannard, Stafford Whiteaker, Stewart Wild, Jean-Claude Salanova, Jim and Jenny Wright, and the staff of tourist offices and monuments up and down France who have answered my innumerable questions.

I owe a special debt of gratitude to: Thierry Bogliolo (of Findhorn Press) for his faith in this project from the outset and his inestimable contribution to making it a reality; Emmanuelle and Denis Curbelié and their family for their support at a critical time; Roxanne Flornoy for helping me to understand the tarot; Claudia Naydler for her comments and advice on astrology; and Clara Villanueva for her encouragement and, above all, her critical eye.

Photography credits

The photographs in this book are by Nick Inman except those on the following pages:
54 Lascaux II UNESCO World Heritage Site © Semitour Périgord (www.semitour.com)
60 and **61** Grotte de Niaux © Sites Touristiques Ariège/SESTA - E. Demoulin.
69 and **back cover bottom** Caves aux Sculptures, Saumur © Pôle Touristique International de Saumur et sa région saumur-tourisme.com
72-73 © Office Tourisme Carnac – Todesco
152 Myrabella / CC-BY-SA-3.0 & GFDL Wikimedia Commons, via Wikimedia Commons
156 Courtesy of Commanderie d'Arville
159 Philippe Gisselbrecht/Office de Tourisme de Metz
161 Teilhard de Chardin: Teilhard P 1955 by Unknown – Archives des Jésuites de France. Licensed under CC BY-SA 3.0 via Wikimedia Commons.
161 Pir Vilayat © Zenith Institute.
162 © Château du Plessis-Bourré
164 Courtesy of Office de Tourisme de Bourges
165 © Marie Jaurand (Office de Tourisme de Bourges)
166 Courtesy of Château de Cénevières
168 Courtesy of Château de Chailly (JC Valienne) chailly.com
169 Courtesy of Office de Tourisme de Paray-le-Monial ©TourismeParay
171 and **173** Courtesy of Château de Dampierre chateau-dampierre.com
176-7 Tarot cards © The Flornoy Estate; sign: © Roxanne Flornoy
178, 219 (bottom), 220, 221 and **224** Emmanuelle and Denis Curbelié
182 Cathédrale de Créteil. Architect : Architecture-Studio. Photograph : Yves Mernier
186 Otourly (Own work) [GFDL (www.gnu.org/copyleft/fdl.html) via Wikimedia Commons]
194 Pierre André Leclercq (Own work) CC BY-SA 4.0-3.0-2.5-2.0-1.0 (creativecommons.org/licenses/by-sa/4.0-3.0-2.5-2.0-1.0), via Wikimedia Commons
195 Courtesy of Office de Tourisme du Pays de Mauron en Brocéliande valsanretour.com
196-197 © Marion Kaplan
198 trialsanderrors CC BY 2.0 (creativecommons.org/licenses/by/2.0), via Wikimedia Commons
202 Pierre Poschadel (Own work) [CC BY-SA 3.0 (creativecommons.org/licenses/by-sa/3.0), via Wikimedia Commons
213 Manfred Heyde (Own work) CC BY-SA 3.0 (creativecommons.org/licenses/by-sa/3.0), via Wikimedia Commons